A publication of the

CENTER FOR RESEARCH AND DEVELOPMENT IN HIGHER EDUCATION
University of California, Berkeley

LELAND L. MEDSKER, *Director*

Challenges to Graduate Schools

The Ph.D. Program in Ten Universities

Ann M. Heiss

Challenges to Graduate Schools

 Jossey-Bass Inc., Publishers
615 Montgomery Street • San Francisco • 1970

CHALLENGES TO GRADUATE SCHOOLS
The Ph.D. Program in Ten Universities
by Ann M. Heiss

Jossey-Bass, Inc., Publishers
615 Montgomery Street
San Francisco, California 94111

Library of Congress Catalog Card Number 73–129770

International Standard Book Number ISBN 0–87589–072–5

Manufactured in the United States of America
Composed and printed by York Composition Company, Inc.
Bound by Chas. H. Bohn & Co., Inc.

JACKET DESIGN BY WILLI BAUM, SAN FRANCISCO

FIRST EDITION

Code 7021

11/9/70 pd. 9.75

The Jossey-Bass Series
in Higher Education

General Editors

JOSEPH AXELROD

San Francisco State College and University of California

MERVIN B. FREEDMAN

San Francisco State College and Wright Institute, Berkeley

To
Ruth and T. R. McConnell

Preface

The research reported in *Challenges to Graduate Schools* is a response to a concern about the role of the university in a world in tumult. Specifically it is an attempt to learn how the university organizes itself to educate the men and women who, hopefully, will assist in the reduction of that tumult when they assume leadership roles in the challenging years ahead. Essentially, this is a report of institutional vitality and self-renewal. The need for the revitalization and reform of American primary institutions is compelling, and nowhere more so than in our graduate schools. As the teacher of teachers, researchers, professionals, artists, statesmen, and leaders in business, industry, and the military, the graduate university is in a crucial position to influence the totality of life. It is also in a strategic position to suggest priorities and to offer guidance in the problems which beset citizens. However, serious observers agree that the university must reform the style and structure of its own house and revitalize its own spirit before it can serve as an effective model or resource for other institutions.

In an atmosphere intense with debate over the mission of the university and the quality of its academic program and at a time when efforts are being made to make universities responsive to a wide variety of social, technological, political, and ecological challenges, it seemed important to examine the character of some of our most outstanding graduate institutions. On the premise that an appraisal of the strengths and weaknesses in their doctoral programs might provide insight into the educational needs of those who will inherit the future, the Center for Research and Development in Higher Education, Berkeley, approved the proposal for this study and provided the support.

Data for the study were obtained from knowledgeable persons including graduate deans, academic deans, department chairmen, members of the graduate faculty, and current doctoral students. Each group was asked to respond to questions on which they had particular expertise or background. For example, we sought the opinions of administrators and faculty members on such issues as the need for radical structural reorganization in the university; the role of the university in mission-oriented research; its role in the teaching of values; and what significant changes, expected in the major disciplines in the foreseeable future, require changes in graduate programing. We asked students to appraise their doctoral experiences in the light of their expectations or goals.

The future of graduate education is the present. In planning for that future a number of basic questions must be asked. Of fundamental importance for a meaningful discussion is the question What should the purpose and nature of graduate study in an age of accelerating change be? Specifically, what is the graduate institution and what is its value to the individual and to society? If, as many contend, the purpose of education is to develop humanism, graduate study should reflect this intent. But, if graduate institutions are viewed as corporate structures through which society achieves its goals, the program should substantiate this notion—probably at the expense of collegial warmth and humanism. Can the graduate program fulfill both goals? In too many cases, these questions are not asked, and the purpose of graduate education is unexplicated. Because institutions have not clearly articulated their goals, they have exposed themselves to pressures from every direction. In addition, their planning has not been effective because the concept of institutional purpose has not been clearly communicated to, understood by, and accepted by those who implement graduate programs. In view of the increasing acceleration in knowledge production and the demands made upon the modern university, a reappraisal of the stated purpose of graduate study and of the organization of programs to achieve that purpose is vital.

As demonstrated by the protests of contemporary student groups, there is a corollary need for definitive data on the students' goals and purposes in pursuing graduate studies. Also needed are comparative data on the extent to which students actively seek and find institutions which satisfy these goals and on the extent to which they understand their own responsibility in the achievement of their goals.

In addition, increasing pressures to convert the university into a center for learning rather than a center for teaching dictate the need for new social inventions which will involve students and faculty as partners in the educational experience. In some cases, this may require role reversals, alterations and extensions in the learning environment, options for independent study, and development of exploratory or experimental programs. Organizational forms are needed which make the college or university a place for intellectual exploration instead of just a path leading to an occupation.

The massive complexity of the compelling issues in graduate education precludes the possibility of simple solutions or unilateral resolutions by individual segments within the graduate school. Rapidly accumulating evidence shows that departments or disciplines which fail to study the impact of discoveries in other disciplines on their own and on the social order in which they develop may find themselves engulfed or bypassed by newly created fields. The alignment and realignment of some related fields of knowledge into single entities may reflect a trend away from fragmentation and toward a recognition of the need for relevance. More and more serious scholars are concerned about what they fence out by placing themselves behind their own disciplines. In the graduate school, one of the major obstacles to the removal of barriers between disciplines is the lack of a method for interdivisional planning. Where departments do not take the initiative for stimulating joint offerings, isolationism becomes the norm. When the structure of knowledge is rapidly undergoing rearrangement, some question whether the department structure may not have lost its utility altogether.

Tangential to the need for research on interdisciplinary organizational rearrangements is the need for extraorganizational schools, institutes, and centers which, through cooperative curriculum offerings or facilities, offer joint degrees or adequate resources for graduate work. Notable examples of these organizational forms are the Claremont Graduate School, the Graduate Theological Union, and the joint degree in special education offered by San Francisco State College and the University of California, Berkeley.

Another compelling issue in doctoral education—and one which involves both purpose and life style—revolves around the balance (or lack of balance) in preparing teachers and in preparing researchers. This issue looms ominously large in the literature. The lack of preparation for college teaching in most doctoral programs, the ineffectiveness of the teaching assistantship (as broadly used) for this purpose, and the poor quality of graduate instruction in general strongly suggest the need for reform in the way the teaching assistantship is planned as preparation for teaching. These charges also suggest the need for a distinctive doctoral degree for those who seek careers in college teaching. There is considerable criticism—but little published evidence—that the loss of interest in teaching as a career develops during doctoral studies because students observe that at this level awards and rewards are based on a measurable criterion labeled *scholarly productivity* and invariably interpreted as published research. If, as is frequently claimed, the publish or perish ultimatum upgrades research and stimulates an interest in it, this system is commendable. If it downgrades teaching or discourages one's interest in teaching as a career, the quality of education at all levels unequivocally diminishes.

Another issue is the requirements in the doctoral program, which provoke continual debate. A reexamination of the course unit structure, the examination and grading system, the foreign language requirements, and the dissertation as "evidence" of original research is long overdue. Many graduate students express what appears tantamount to a moral imperative in their demands that these requirements be justified as contributory to or indicative of scholarship. Corollary to this demand is the need for a review of the organization of graduate study. For instance, other than administrative convenience, is there a sound rationale for continuing to use the credits, hours, units, and grading system of the undergraduate program? Is there overstructuring at the graduate level? To what extent does this form of bookkeeping encourage underachievement among students? To what extent does the practice of piling up units of credit destroy unity in the program and encourage the part-time approach to scholarship? Instead of a series of discrete courses, should graduate study be a tailor-made program which includes seminars, independent study, independent research, observation and participation in the field, research writing, and similar activities, all on an integrated basis?

Although these criticisms, which college and university students currently make, are directed against administrators, analysis of their demands reveals that the actual target is the faculty, particularly among disaffected graduate students who complain of alienation from the community of scholars and who describe the graduate school climate as cold. Apparently many persons are drawn into doctoral study on the assumption that their relations with the faculty will be collegial, that is, scholarly and warm. The fact that collegiality is not automatically bestowed on entrance but is developmental and based on evidence of scholarly commitment seems to discourage and embitter some first-year students. How can the academic environment be improved to deserve its claim that it provides community and collegiality?

Many individuals cooperated in the search for answers to these questions. To each of them I extend a warm expression of gratitude. The list includes the presidents or chancellors of the ten universities in the sample, the graduate and academic deans, the department chairmen, the members of the graduate faculty, and the doctoral students who generously responded to our request for information.

Numerous colleagues at the Center for Research and Development in Higher Education gave counsel, encouragement, or service, often above and beyond the call of duty. Among these were the members of the advisory committee for the study, which consisted of Leland Medsker, director of the center; T. R. McConnell, its former director; Algo Henderson, former director of the Michigan University Center for Higher Education and now, happily for us, at the Berkeley center; Joseph Axelrod; and, as an external adviser, Leona Tyler, dean of the Graduate School at the University of Oregon.

Charles Gehrke and his staff deserve thanks for their assistance with the computer programing, as do Harriet Renaud, Julie Pesonen, and Norman Rae for providing editorial services and Anne Sherman for coordinating all the details involved in administering and recording the results of the Omnibus Personality Inventory data.

An effort was made to involve many graduate students in the project. Some were volunteers who sought experience on a large research project; some participated as independent-study students and received academic credit for their participation; some served as advisers; others were research assistants. The quality of the ideas and the interests expressed by these younger colleagues not only challenged me but also contributed toward a clarification of the issues which are of moment or of long-range concern to Ph.D. students.

Special notes of appreciation are due to Natalie Gumas, who contributed substantially to the design of the questionnaires, developed the code books, coordinated the data-processing, and otherwise gave expert and friendly support; to Mauri Day, who contributed valuable ideas to the design of the study and whose position paper, "The Nature of the University," formed the basis for a substantial part of Chapter Three; to Nancy Kuriloff for her essay on the teaching assistant, which contributed importantly to the study, and for her stimulating ideas regarding the need for a liberating and intellectually satisfying approach to doctoral study.

Other students and former students to whom I am indebted include Anne Davis and Frank Voci, who assisted in the development of *An Annotated Bibliography of Graduate and Professional Education;* Jerry McCarn, Arthur Angel, and Jill Morton, who conducted extensive reviews of graduate catalogs; Mark Sussman, Ray Lingel, Carol Shay, Jan Molen, and Linda Wong, who assisted with the statistical summaries and with the many other details connected with a study of this nature.

To Kathy Kunst and Margaret Seely, who performed yeoman secretarial and other services during the early stages of the project, and especially to Ruth Ann Crow, whose cheerful contribution to the preparation of the manuscript and willingness to perform the hundred and one other activities associated with the role of a researcher's secretary, go special thanks. The help of each is deeply appreciated and gratefully acknowledged.

Berkeley, California   ANN M. HEISS
August, 1970

Contents

Challenges to Graduate Schools

The Ph.D. Program in
Ten Universities

Center
of Conflict

1

The university in America is in deep trouble. Ironically, the major source of that trouble lies in its past success: as it succeeded in advancing cultural values, contributing new knowledge, and providing services to society, the university became a major contributor to the new and drastically different social dynamic which is currently evolving in this country. The character of that dynamic threatens the nature of all institutions, and especially those concerned with higher education.

The university cannot pause to study inchoate movements and at the same time keep pace with their consequences. This places it in the anomalous position of being unable to respond adequately to many of the changes which it has itself helped bring forth. Although it has often correctly diagnosed the conditions which induce ill health in other institutions, the university is sometimes unaware of a rising fever within itself. This is not altogether surprising; in a

healthy university, the absence of fever, not its presence, is a cause
of concern.

Currently the university is held accountable for many of
society's ills. Its function as a bastion of rationality is suspect and
its role in improving the quality of life is under widespread attack.
The most important criticisms currently leveled against it include
the following:

(1) By building their images, programs, and expectations
around the predominantly Western, white, middle class culture, institutions of higher education have substantially advanced the position of individuals in that group, but in so doing have alienated and
increased the social distance between whites and all other cultures.

(2) By failing to adhere conscientiously to the ideal expressed in the aphorism "Let knowledge grow from more to more
that human life may be enriched," the university has succumbed to
the blandishments of industrial and military forces whose research
interests have frequently produced ideas and inventions that are
antithetical to human life because they threaten man's environment,
evoke his aggressiveness toward others, or reduce his capacity to
participate in decisions which involve his survival or the survival
of mankind.

(3) By basing its reward system on "published research"
the university tacitly contributes to the division of its faculty into
first-class citizens or research luminaries—some of whom become intellectual gadflies spending a great deal of their time off campus—
and a second-class group which is given responsibility for instruction, administrative housekeeping, and maintaining continuity in the
academic program.

(4) By failing to develop academic programs which engage
the interests and abilities of students on ideas and activities that are
related to their needs as *persons,* the university has dehumanized
education and reduced its appeal to youth.

(5) By failing to represent in its governance all those who
are its citizens, universities project the model of autocratic rather
than democratic institutions.

Despite these indictments, those who understand the nature
of institutions of higher education generally agree that in a democracy the university is the primary institution which serves as the

conscience of society. Lippmann underscored the significance of this when he observed: "The hierarchy of priests, the dynasties of rulers, the countries, the civil servants, and the commissars have to give way—and there is left as the court of last resort when the truth is at issue the ancient and universal company of scholars."

To say that the university is in trouble is tantamount to saying that graduate education is in trouble. In addition to unprecedented changes in the character and size of its student body, the graduate school faces pressures for innovative curriculum reform, new substantive fields of study, new doctoral degrees, structural reorganization, and new teaching and research technologies. In view of the increased public need for informed intelligence to cope with the disorders in society, graduate education probably stands on the threshold of its greatest challenge. Since it alone is singularly qualified to offer the basic services needed in the education and training of professional persons and in the development of research scholars, it is probably the most strategic segment in our educational system. Yet it is, at the moment, one of its most insecure segments. Rising costs and declining support, uncertainties concerning the military draft, overcommitted staff members, student disenchantment with the life style of scholars, and a cumbersome system of degree processes all combine to make life in graduate school like life in a pressure cooker.

Throughout its history the citadel of graduate education in the United States has withstood the assault of its critics virtually intact. Almost invariably it emerged from encounters with men like James (1911) and West (1913) more rigid in its organizational structure and more conservative in its view of itself. Because the criticism came largely from within its membership, the academic community tended to regard it as the rhetoric of men who were disaffected with academic life, or they dismissed the issues as not sufficiently academic for the academic man to debate. Even Flexner's broadside exposé of the quality of education in medical schools in 1925 was seen by academicians as an indictment of the professional medical degree only; planners and supervisors of Ph.D. programs took few lessons from his report. As a result of its encapsulated existence, graduate education progressed methodically and independently, developing its own elite, formulating its own hierarchical system, socializing higher education to its own values and norms, and prescribing the rituals through which to commemorate the rite of passage for those who sought membership in its guild.

Although graduate departments have periodically tinkered with reform in their advanced programs, the Ph.D. process as a whole has remained practically impervious to substantial change since its inception in the early 1900's. Course offerings have expanded, but few systematic attempts have been made to revise the requirements or to examine the extent to which the doctoral program needs adjustment in order to prepare today's scholars for the challenges of new technologies, or to give them an understanding of the new ethos stirring in America. Tradition sits securely in the chairs of most graduate departments. Efforts to bring about fundamental changes in the Ph.D. program have usually been aborted by the specter of "lowering the standards"; graduate schools continue to find security and comfort in models imported nearly a century ago from Europe—the birthplace of formal university education. The fact that the model is no longer viable—even for Europe— makes some academicians uneasy, but few have been made uneasy enough to mount a full scale campaign for basic change. In the interest of preserving programs and requirements on which reciprocal agreements and understandings can be reached, graduate schools maintain a solidarity that is reflected in the monotonous rhetoric of their graduate catalogs, in unimaginative rituals that have lost even their symbolic meaning, and in organizational structures that narrowly educate and artificially separate scholars.

In view of current strident accusations that universities are not relevant to the needs of society; that they have failed to be instruments for constructive change; that they do not address themselves to issues which are vital to man's progress or equality; that they are elite enclaves which perpetuate their own hierarchical class and caste system; that there is a wide breach between their rhetoric and their commitments; and that their governance is often in the hands of those who wield power "over" rather than power "with" the community, the serious consideration of reform is a categorical imperative at the graduate level. Graduate schools of arts and sciences especially need to reexamine how they have fulfilled their purposes.

The rising tide of undergraduates who are qualified for admission to advanced programs has brought about a revolution in aspirations toward graduate study. Less than a decade ago approximately 33 per cent of entering college freshmen expressed an interest in education beyond the bachelor's degree. By 1963 the figure had risen to 48 per cent, and five years later Astin (1968) reported that 62 per cent of entering freshmen expressed an intent to obtain some degree beyond the bachelor's. An estimate of the order of magnitude to which graduate schools will have to accommodate may be seen in college enrollment figures and projections. These show that by 1957 the college population had reached three million (a figure it took them more than three hundred years to reach), but only ten years later that figure had doubled, to over six million. Although graduate school enrollments are somewhat less spectacular, they are nevertheless impressive. In 1968–69, some 787,000 were enrolled in graduate programs. The U. S. Office of Education (1968) expects this number to increase to 1,140,000 by 1976.

As they watch these aspirations and projections rise, those who are responsible for graduate education are faced with the fact that public and private support for higher education is declining (Hall, 1969). Universities operating on reduced budgets find it difficult to reconcile the sharp curtailment in federal fellowships and traineeships, the reduction in congressional appropriations, and the cutbacks in state assistance with the mandate to produce the trained intelligence and manpower which the country requires. They find little comfort in a report of the National Science Board (1969) which notes that while graduate education is already the most expensive form of education per student, it will in 1970 exceed the cost of all other forms of higher education combined.

It is even more difficult for planners of advanced study programs to reconcile the decrease in graduate support with the rise in the barometer showing the needs for new forms of educated and trained manpower. Brzezenski (1968) predicts that the nation will soon be caught irretrievably in a current of forces which are evolving so broadly and accelerating so rapidly that it will transform the basic structure, mores, and values of our society by the year 2000. He believes that this movement will come with such hurricane force and be compressed within such a short period of time that the shock effect of the change it provokes will be more profound and more radical than any that civilization has previously experienced. Because the United States is so far advanced in the determinants of this transformation—technology and electronics—and because the application will produce great separation, fragmentation, and differentiation among mankind, Brzezenski believes that a special obligation is imposed upon America to ease the pain of the resulting confrontation.

The first ripples of this fast-gathering current already eddy around the university. Because the creators of the "technetronic society" are found in large numbers in the university, and because it simultaneously houses the trained intelligence which can foresee the latent consequences in the shift to such a society, the university is in a pivotal position to plot the direction, to lubricate the gears, and to generally assist in the changeover. However, at the moment in history when its full attention should be centered on clarifying the ambiguities and interpreting the trends reflected in the prevailing social currents, the university is hamstrung by staggering financial inadequacies or by the rulings of those who want to divert or hold back the tides. There is a growing foreboding among faculties and administrators that university scholars may have to stand by with their hands in their pockets as those tides sweep by.

Probably at no point in the history of higher education has there been so much confusion and controversy over the role of the university as prevails today. Contributors to scholarly journals, reporters for the daily press and slick magazines, communicators in the electronic media, and the man on the street marshal facts and construct arguments which demonstrate the wide diversity of opinion that exists about its purpose and function. They also demonstrate and amplify the vast body of genuine misinformation about what a university is and what its responsibilities are.

Organizationally and administratively, in purpose and in form, whether planned or unplanned, modern institutions face radical change. Those that have been designed for continual review and renewal are in a favorable condition to face change without causing intolerable stress to their foundations. Institutions without this protective mechanism may find themselves so fragile as to lack resistance, or so rigid as to lack resiliency against the storms that will tear at their structures. Of all our institutions, those devoted to education stand most in need of systematic and periodic reinforcement. If they are designed to operate in a dynamic state, or to maintain themselves in what engineers refer to as "dither," they may avoid the deterioration caused by inertia and the undue stress required for tooling up to perform new functions or to handle crisis situations.

Because of their implicit role in the current upheavals in society, educational systems are caught in the crossfire between those who want to tear down existing institutions and those who want to preserve the status quo. In Gardner's words (1968), our institutions are beset by "too many unloving critics and too many uncritical lovers." Well-designed educational institutions generally survive both varieties of criticism and serve as models of self-renewing institutions. As such, they emerge from each renewal neither intact nor drastically transformed but with goals relevant to the needs of the age and with policies based on reason rather than on personal whimsy.

To operate as *planning* rather than as *planned* institutions, colleges and universities will have to make heavy demands on faculty time. Because time, energy, and money spent on education is time, energy, and money invested (rather than consumed), institutions must constantly evaluate whether the renewal of goals or the introduction of innovative programs justifies the expenditure. Faculty members enjoy their major power and responsibility in the role of decision makers on academic programming; thus ultimate responsibility for excellence resides essentially with them. However, it resides first in those who select the faculty, and second in those who select the students.

NATURE AND PURPOSE

In defining the nature or purpose of the university, scholars make the explicit assumption that there exists some inherently defining characteristic necessary to all institutions which call themselves universities, and that universities *as* universities manifestly serve some clear and ultimate end or ends. These are variously and broadly expressed as the dissemination of knowledge through teaching, the extension of knowledge through research, and the performance of services through consultation or similar types of activities.

However, not all students of the idea of a university accept all three ends as natural to it.

An analysis of the history of thought about the nature of the university indicates that this vastly complex institution is the product of many historical influences and many contemporary pressures. A common and pervasive belief persists in all historical references, however, that the university is an ideological institution. That is to say, the purposes of the university are bound to the ideals of its civilization, and the knowledge it promotes is valued to the degree to which it brings men closer to the realization of those ideals. However, since individuals filter ideals through different lights and different points in time, they set forth different and sometimes countervailing purposes, functions, and values for the institution. As a result of these variables, Newman's (1947) idea of a university differs substantially from Jaspers' (1959), and Perkins' (1966) concept differs radically from both.

For Newman the purpose of a university is to contribute the good and worthy man who is capable of raising the intellectual and cultural level of society. He envisions the university as a cloister of aspirants who seek timelessly valued knowledge that will enlighten their minds and develop their capacity for rectitude in thought, judgment, and action. The function of the university, then, in the Newman tradition, is to teach known truths or to disseminate knowledge necessary to the fulfillment of its purpose. This knowledge is valued intrinsically. Mastering it is its own reward.

For Jaspers, on the other hand, the purpose of the university is rationally to pursue and extend the boundaries of knowledge, and to educate scholars and professional persons who will continue their activities within the university or as experts within society. Thus the function of the university is twofold: research, and teaching for professional development and for furthering the intellectual dialogue. Jaspers sees the university as a cosmopolitan community with no fixed dimensions of knowledge, hence his concept of it represents a much more dynamic institution and one that is much more susceptible to the changing ideas and needs of society than is Newman's. For Jaspers, knowledge is valued primarily for its instrumental uses, although he does not reject its intrinsic worth.

While the ideas of Newman and Jaspers epitomize the two

basic concepts of the university, there is a third somewhat inchoate view which emerges from the writings of Perkins (1966), Galbraith (1958), and writers of various papers and speeches which circulate more or less as fugitive literature. In this concept the intrinsic value of knowledge is recognized but the instrumental value that accrues from working in partnership with public or private groups who need the service of experts is of much greater value. In this sense, the university accommodates itself to the demands of society and its knowledge is valued to the extent that it can be used to research and resolve the problems of society. The scholar as well as the professional person works directly to be of service. The university is an institution without walls. Its scholars not only have a commitment to the solution of social problems but also assume the political, public, and ethical responsibilities which follow because of their superior knowledge.

In varying proportions these three schools of thought may be found operating on any major university campus. Together they serve as the framework for many of Kerr's descriptors of the "multiversity" (1963). To some extent the image, if not the purposes, of a particular institution may be determined by the way in which the three views are distributed within the institution. They are not necessarily fixed for any particular discipline. However, in his study of the difference among academic scientists and nonscientists, C. P. Snow (1959) suggests that their cultures are basically different partly because they perceive the purposes of their institutions differently.

In an essay entitled "The University at the Service of Society" (1967), the trustees of the Carnegie Foundation for the Advancement of Teaching note that while it is natural for universities to be involved in national programs, they must find congruence between the self-destructive effects of too much preoccupation with service and the equally damaging effects of indifference to social needs. In proposing a working philosophy, the Carnegie trustees suggested that it is appropriate for the university to identify social problems, to serve as a forum or refuge for those who dissent or hold unconventional views, to manage on a temporary basis national projects for which no other agency is available, and to provide a leadership role in joint attacks on social problems. It should not, however, "bite off propositions, develop positions, or be a protagonist for causes."

In a conference entitled "On the Role of the University as Agent of Social Change," sponsored by the Center for Research and Development in Higher Education, Berkeley, and the Western Interstate Commission for Higher Education, speakers were in general agreement that universities fulfill an important responsibility when (usually through research and scholarship) they serve as critics of society. There was considerably less agreement on whether universities should advocate particular reforms or take corporate positions on issues. Citing the dangers that can accrue when a university becomes embroiled in contentious partisanship, McConnell (1968) suggests that the line at which conditions and limitations of university involvement in social reform must be drawn is implicit in its essential character and its unsurrenderable value, namely its guardianship and maintenance of intellectual freedom. "If this is lost," he warns, "our form of society will be lost."

Other authorities note that one of the most sensitive issues facing the university in its role as social critic is how it can affect the course of social change without incurring hostility or reprisal from a society content with its present course. Metzger (Hofstadter and Metzger, 1955), a historian of academic freedom, notes that while "one cannot help but be appalled by the slender thread by which it hangs," the accommodation which persists whereby our social system subsidizes universities to freely criticize and inquire into it "is one of the remarkable achievements of man."

Speaking of the failure of the HARU project, an effort by the people of Harlem and the City University of New York to make a joint attack on the basic causes of poverty, Clark (1969) sadly admitted that the project failed because the professors who devoted themselves to it perceived poverty as a social problem when in reality it was a political one. It failed in its objectives because Harlem politicians took over control. The politicians recognized that if the people themselves discovered the way out of poverty, they would eventually learn how to control their politicians. This has been the fate of innumerable social-action programs that were designed or led by politically naïve professors. Such professors reasoned that once a problem is identified and the instruments for solving it are available, a program can readily be designed to resolve it. They were rudely awakened when, as implementers of the design, they found themselves caught in a crossfire between rival social agencies or contending political entities.

Over the past three decades, during which they conducted a large share of state or federally sponsored research, university professors have had rich opportunities not only to gather new knowledge in their fields but also to learn the political realities of research consequences. Because these realities have often been greatly disillusioning, some professors now refuse to do federal or state research. Others do it and write pallid reports. Some others try to change the system from within. A growing group of young professors is becoming activist in the reform of socially related political structures, including the university's.

Although the university and the state are ostensibly partners in their efforts to improve man's knowledge of himself, an uneasy equilibrium always exists between them. Universities are powerful in the sense that the knowledge which they produce has power, but ultimately control lies not with the producer but with the user of knowledge. It is precisely for this reason that universities are chary of direct alliances with governmental projects or programs that can be used to political advantage.

In his Godkin Lectures on "The Uses of the University," Kerr (1963) notes that the land grant movement, which was a response to an egalitarian and populist trend in the 1870's, created a new social force in world history. In a later paper he suggests that present-day realities point to the need for an urban grant university which would provide services appropriate to and needed by cities, just as the land grant schools service rural areas. Kerr warns that if such a service is made available to those who run or build cities, it must be given in the clear understanding that the application of knowledge, *not* partisan urban politics, is its goal. The mechanism for establishing an urban grant university is already available and many of the services such an institution could provide are already in operation somewhere in the university. The urban grant university would give unity and organization to such an effort.

It is demonstrably evident that the nature and extent of the relationships between the university and external agencies have markedly altered the character and style of life in America. These relationships have also changed the institutional style of our major universities. Primed by the Land Grant Act of 1882, a system of communication conduits was initiated between land grant institutions and external agricultural groups. The conduit permitted ideas and inventions generated at the university to be funneled quickly through the system. En route they were picked up by those who found them useful. By the same token, the system provided the university with challenges, resources, and information useful for its purposes. This was the first formalized communication system of the hundreds now operating between universities and external institutions. Today the conduits are highly sophisticated, highly complex, and in a few cases highly controversial.

Although knowledge is the interest which members in the communication system have in common, money is generally the cement which holds the system together. It enables the university to expand its effective scope and in certain ways to improve its quality. On the principle that those in the system who profit from new information are willing to pay for it, elaborate procedures have been developed whereby an external agency or agencies may underwrite a study in which the university attempts to discover the missing knowledge. If it finds it, the university places that knowledge in the public domain.

On the Maeterlinck theory that "the rising tide lifts all the boats," universities have allowed their external interrelationships to grow more or less unchecked. However, as with most proverbs that apply to administration, one can usually find a contradictory one. Some critics offer one to the effect that "big boats swamp little boats." They fear that in its preoccupation with the interests of its external associates the university may deplete resources that properly belong to its on-campus responsibilities, particularly teaching. Referring to these interrelationships, leaders of various protest factions accuse the university of becoming involved with "interlocking directorates" and becoming morally callous "in allowing educational imbalances and inequities to develop." By tying some of the university's relationships to problems in the social order the implication is made that the university is responsible for society's failures.

Almost every serious student of higher education believes

that there is a compelling need for the university to undertake an intensive examination of its external commitments. Some suggest that that same type of self-examination should be made by those who profit by the commitment. These observers suggest that if the quality of the university's instructional effort is poor because innumerable outside demands have been made on its resources and expertise, then business and industry, the government and its politicians, the mass communications media and social organizations of every conceivable description are implicated in the indictment. These observers contend that business and industry are implicated because in addition to their practice of "buying" consultant services and cultivating university connections for prestige, they frequently make unconscionable forays into the university's personnel ranks by offering salaries or fringe benefits no university can match. The government is implicated because by "contracting" for research it often puts pressure on the faculty members' instructional responsibilities at inopportune times or to an unwarranted degree. The military is implicated in a number of ways, not the least of which is the insecurity its draft regulations create for the student and for university admissions officers, budget directors, and academic planners. Some politicians are implicated because they use the university as a private forum, others because they circumscribe its support and curtail its ability to meet increased demands, still others because they involve the university in public controversy against which it has neither the time nor the talent to defend itself. With regard to the involvement of the mass media, some responsible observers believe that by slanting their coverage of educational news in favor of sensational and negative reporting these agencies are directly responsible for much of the current lack of trust in higher education. Local or specialized groups are implicated more by omission than commission; some make heavy demands on the institution for speakers and other special services, but the majority of these social organizations fail to keep informed of the university's problems, to serve as an understanding polity, or to defend it against those who would take away its autonomy.

In addition to those mutually benefiting relationships which serve to speed the processes of producing and using knowledge, all universities are characterized by their extended involvement in the activities of society. This includes, on a more or less formal basis, associations with agencies of the state or local government such as schools, health centers, field stations, or courts and with many informal but socially concerned organizations such as service clubs or fraternal orders. Faculties are associated with a long list of professional organizations in which many hold office or membership. They also serve as consultants or advisers for many agencies.

Students in large numbers, through course work or volunteer activities, are in contact with a wide spectrum of social needs and issues. Their voluntary contributions to the work of the Peace Corps, Vista, tutorial programs, civil rights, poverty programs, youth recreation, hospital auxiliaries, juvenile courts, and political campaigns have not only promoted our general social betterment but also expanded and informed their own social awareness. Participation in R.O.T.C. and in military service made others conscious of a different kind of social responsibility. Few have not experienced it vicariously.

With the awakening of social consciousness many students have also developed an awakening of social conscience. In applying the tools of inquiry and analysis to the examination of their values, some found that these were often in conflict with their own experiences or observations. As they examined how educational institutions practiced the values they taught and how other institutions honored the ideals they claimed to live by, students began to question institutional morality, and by inference the morality of those responsible for their programs and policies. This brought them full circle to that institution which presumably serves as the conscience of society—the university. In its impotence to respond on the basis of moral positions the university disappointed and alienated many with whom it had had rapport and gave others (both on the right and the left) a new stick with which to flog it.

Historically, the university was conceived of as an extension of the church, or as a similarly privileged institution. As such, it was given the right to provide sanctuary and the right to define and criticize public morality. In the American tradition, vestiges of sanctuary may be found in the right provided in the concept of academic freedom. However, the separation of church and state induced the secularization of knowledge and inhibited public universities from interpreting knowledge in terms of moral standards. The concept of the university as an ethically neutral podium (or as a completely open forum) helped to promote the notion that the role of the individual professor is to intellectualize knowledge rather than to relate it to any particular value system. Some define this withholding action as fence-straddling or as a contradiction of the university's role as social critic. Others serially denounce the university for having (or not having) culture-free objectives and goals, or for upholding (or not upholding) established values and traditions. More recently, in calling for a reaffirmation of its corporate morality, some graduate students have asked: What value freedom can the university claim when it accepts federally supported research which reinforces the values of the existing political structure?

LEGITIMATION OF AUTHORITY

There is probably no greater imperative facing the university today than the need to legitimize its authority. Although it is common for universities to live in a continual state of conflict, the character, dimension, and force of recent confrontations have been so powerful as to tax the capacity of the minds and the resiliency of the backs of those responsible for guarding its autonomy. Requests for a role in governance come from groups at every level within the university, but are by no means limited by its boundaries. The struggle is as old as the institutions themselves. The major difference today is that diverse new contestants have entered the arena. Some have come without gloves on. Their maneuvers for power are open rather than subtle. Their language is plain and simple though often rhetorically contrived. Some have hunted down administrators and held them at bay until a promise to accept their demands could be extracted, only to find that the official acceptance was not honored by the academic community at large. Others use legitimate means to request legitimate and reasonable ends but suffer frustrations because they receive no hearing or no feedback on their requests.

It is becoming patently clear that unless their goals are defined and accepted as being not incompatible with the goals of those in its polity, institutions of higher education will continue to tilt at windmills in their attempts to establish their legitimacy. The offices of their legal staffs will increasingly be involved in interpreting the ever-growing and entangling body of legalisms which now bind university behavior. With varying degrees of sincerity, intensity, and rationality other university constituents demonstrate their need for a clearer understanding of the university's function. These persons voice their concerns or piques from hundreds of podiums, from the esoteric heights of The Center for the Study of Democratic Institutions to the local television station, whose newscaster obtains most of his information about the function of a university from the "action" pictures caught by a mobile television unit—now almost a permanent fixture on the university campus.

The strain of contrived crises and continual political pressures has begun to take a heavy toll on university personnel. The flight from administration has become as critical as the "flight from teaching." Many capable and sensitive individuals who lovingly elected the academic life are finding it less and less rewarding. Some have become dispirited as they see the soul of the university profaned by campus agitators and by politicians who, ignoring its great resources of reason and educated intelligence, force reason to submit to passion and generate the image of the university as a hotbed of radicalism. Some universities learned to their sorrow and dismay that a hundred or more years of unprecedented devotion to the preservation, transmission, and production of knowledge and of service to the nation could apparently be quickly overshadowed by the rhetoric of such unlikely university protagonists as the Students for a Democratic Society. They were even more dismayed to find that those who should have moved in to help heal the breach and assist in the necessary response instead aggravated the problems by holding the university responsible for its inability to defend itself against physical assault, to respond effectively against raw power, or to take reprisals.

Because of the mounting attacks and counterattacks that universities are experiencing, some observers are of the opinion that the university will soon be a euphemism for a place from which the truly scholarly have fled. Many have already done so. Others are poised for flight. Some remain on the fringe of great campuses where they can keep in touch with colleagues and students. If the irrational attacks and constraints on the university are removed, many of them may return, bringing some of the student dropouts with them.

The acceleration of change during the past two decades has made necessary a sober reassessment of our entire cultural system. As an essential component of that system—and one of its prime movers—the university as university is in special need of such an evaluation. In view of the multiplicity of new roles it has been asked to perform, it is increasingly imperative that the university examine the growth and the parings it has experienced around its edges to learn whether these have induced serious mutations at its core. It is also imperative that the university examine the means through which it hopes to ensure its continuity, namely its Ph.D. programs. If the university fails to submit itself to this assessment its health may be lost in the performance of tasks incompatible with its nature, and doctoral candidates will then be deprived of the kind and quality of education their futures will demand.

Barzun's often testy remarks on the American university persistently sound the imperative that the university not only must know what its purpose is but also must continually redefine and clarify that purpose lest it drift into the notion that it is "a national force—primed by federal funds and sustained by the delusions of self-adulation." He predicts (1968) that unless the university takes an honest look at itself "parts will begin to drop off, as the autonomous professor has begun to do, or it will go into spells of paralysis, as the student riots have shown to be possible. Apathy and secession will take care of the rest until a stump of something once alive is left to vegetate on the endowment or annual tax subsidy."

On a more hopeful note, Barzun agrees with Gardner that universities are capable of self-reform; they have changed in the past and can do so in the present crisis. Because all are beset by internal friction and belabored by external pressures, Barzun strongly recommends that "if the university is to save itself by making the changes that it is already eager to make, it must not act singly but in groups" (1968). Concerted action, he says, is particularly important when the changes affect the Ph.D. program, because "no great university can afford to modify it, lest rumor call the change a dilution and the value of the degree go down" (1968). And Gardner warns: "We are witnessing changes so profound and far-reaching that the mind cannot grasp all the implications. With respect to most events . . . we are not just passive observers but are helping to produce change. That is the story of dynamism not deterioration. . . . Unless we foster versatile, innovative, and self-renewing men and women, all the ingenious social arrangements in the world will not help us" (1963).

It was in an attempt to study university dynamism and the process universities use to "foster versatile, innovative, and self-renewing men and women" that this study was undertaken. It began with a search for institutional excellence.

Assessment
of Institutions

2

Weinberg (1968) suggests that a major problem in assessing university quality has its origins in the essential differences between the university's view of excellence and society's view of it. He notes that universities are, by nature, discipline-oriented, and their idea of excellence is whatever deepens understanding of or insight into the problems generated or resolved within the various disciplines. In this context, with respect to productivity, the specialist is king in the academic community. On the other hand, society attributes excellence to whatever works; its standards are pragmatic and its kings are the nonscientists or synthesizers.

When universities find that their standards are in conflict with society's expectations, they traditionally defend their positions on the premise that universities are, to all intents and purposes, self-authenticating institutions. In perceiving themselves as institutions that are purposively responsible for motivating society to transcend its values, universities generally reject as invalid all external efforts to evaluate them. Because of this stance current debates over the quality of graduate education focus on the charge that excellence has often served as a euphemism for exclusiveness. Some critics claim that by rigidly upholding outworn traditions, requirements which have become ritualistic, norms which measure much that is irrelevant, and values that are no longer valued, the university denies its role as a liberator of ideas and as an institution in pursuit of truth.

In a statement on excellence in education, the American Council on Education (1960) noted that quality is the result of a composite of elements including the teacher, the learner, the curriculum, and the educational environment. According to the authors of the ACE statement, the impetus provided by the collection of fine minds and by well-designed and well-organized physical facilities, the esthetic appreciation to be drawn from good literature, conversation, lectures, and various art forms, and the timeliness and timelessness of the instruments of knowledge will, when properly combined, provide an ethos and an environment conducive to intellectual quality.

Unfortunately, most universities document their claim to quality in quantitative terms. That is, they cite as indices of greatness the number of Ph.D.'s they produce, the number of fellowships and grants they receive, and the number of publications, citations, or awards achieved by their faculties. Over 240 institutions in the United States currently purport to offer doctoral study. Contributing to the perplexities involved in trying to equate their programs is the great diversity that exists in their character and standards. Although qualitative estimates may be inferred from the data which show that fifty of the 240 institutions award 90 per cent of the Ph.D.'s that are earned yearly, Cartter's (1966) study showed that there are broad variations in quality even among these productive universities. The fact that many of the remaining 190 institutions award only one or two degrees per year (and that some award none) also offers clues to the qualitative variability among graduate programs. The unevenness of doctoral programs can probably be seen most strikingly when one examines the quality and size of the graduate faculty in any given institution. It may also be ascertained from an examination of the library resources and physical facilities which the institution offers.

Practically every major study of graduate education has concerned itself, at least indirectly, with the question of academic excellence. However, only four nationwide attempts have been made to assess graduate institutions directly on that variable. These studies based their findings on surveys in which the opinions of "qualified judges" were elicited and then classified to form a ranking order of quality in graduate departments. The use of qualified judges as reliable data sources was supported by Eells (1962), who in his 1957 study of leading graduate schools found that "most doctoral candidates tend to select superior institutions: superior institutions tend to attract the most doctoral candidates. Therefore, quality of graduate schools may be judged either by qualified judges or from the number of graduate students who secure the doctorate at them."

The first of the four studies was conducted by Hughes (1934), who in 1924 sent a questionnaire to a selected group of distinguished national scholars in which they were asked to evaluate the quality of graduate instruction in thirty-eight of the sixty-five universities then offering the Ph.D. Hughes replicated his study ten years later for the American Council on Education. In that study he classified graduate departments on the basis of their adequacy and their distinctiveness. In a 1957 study Keniston (1959) asked department chairmen to rate the relative positions of twenty-five major universities with respect to the quality of their graduate programs. More recently Cartter (1966) replicated and expanded the Hughes and Keniston surveys in a study initiated by the American Council on Education and supported conjointly by the National Science Foundation, the National Institutes of Health, and the U.S. Office of Education. Cartter's survey included the assessment of twenty-nine departments in 106 graduate institutions by 900 department chairmen, 1,700 distinguished senior scholars, and 1,400 carefully selected junior scholars. Respondents in the Cartter study were asked to indicate which among six given terms ("distinguished," "strong," "good," "adequate," "marginal," or "not sufficient to provide acceptable doctoral training") in their judgment best described the quality of the graduate faculty in their field in each of the institutions in the sample. They were also asked to rate the effectiveness of the doctoral program in their field in each of the institutions by indicating which of the terms—"extremely attractive," "acceptable," or "not attractive"—best described the competence and accessibility of the faculty, the curricula, the educational and research resources, and the quality of their graduate students. Using numerical ratings for each of the descriptive terms, Cartter drew up tables of the leading departments by rated quality of the graduate faculty, and of leading departments by rated effectiveness of their graduate programs.

In an effort to discover the issues and problems which confront graduate institutions as they attempt to achieve and maintain excellence in their doctoral programs, the first step in this investigation was to undertake a fairly exhaustive review of the literature. The review culminated in the publication of *An Annotated Bibliography on Graduate and Professional Education* by the Center for Research and Development in Higher Education (Heiss, Davis, and Voci, 1966). This search revealed that most of the literature on graduate education falls into the general category of criticism. Much of it is polemical, some is speculative, little of it is supported by hard data. Topically, it reflects a concern about the increasing numbers of students, since numbers create a strain on existing educational resources and facilities and increases in enrollment affect the Ph.D. supply-demand ratio. That literature which pertains directly to the student reflects unrest and impatience with the socialization of becoming a scholar. The literature also expresses concern about the decreasing sources and amounts of financial support for graduate study, the length of time required to complete degrees, the rigidity of doctoral requirements, the narrowness of specialization, the imbalance between education for research and education for teaching, the stress the program imposes on some students, the quality of the finished product, and, more recently, the effects of the military draft on graduate study.

In general, the published research on doctoral education appears to be useful. Even though most of it has been conducted on specific issues within specific institutions, the problems (and the requirements and programs) in doctoral education are so basically alike that what is said about a few institutions is relevant for most.

One might also suggest that when models like Berkeley (Heiss, 1964), Harvard (Elder, 1958), Columbia (Barzun, 1958), and Minnesota (Alciatore and Eckert, 1968) confront themselves publicly on the effectiveness of their graduate programs lesser institutions hasten to take notes. A few studies made recommendations for improving graduate education and some of these have been implemented. However, there are no published records to indicate that reform in graduate education has been widespread nor have any subsequent evaluations been made on which to judge the success or failure of the reforms that have been introduced. Because universities monitor one another so diligently, Barzun (1968) suggests that unless they act in unison no major reforms in graduate education will occur. In his judgment, no major institution would deviate alone from the accepted pattern of doctoral requirements lest it be accused of diluting standards. Carmichael's (1961) recommendation that new degree forms should be developed found a response when Yale introduced the degree of Master of Philosophy and, more recently, Dunham's (1969) endorsement of a Doctor of Arts degree is receiving favorable reception in several graduate institutions.

In reading the research on graduate education, it is important to distinguish between those studies which substantiate their findings with data obtained from Ph.D. recipients and those which report on data obtained from individuals who are still in the degree process. This is particularly true if one is concerned about current trends. For example, Berelson's (1960) nationwide study of graduate education and Alciatore and Eckert's (1968) study of Minnesota Ph.D. recipients gives a much more positive picture of satisfaction with graduate education than does Elder's (1958) criticism of the Graduate School at Harvard and Radcliffe, Barzun's (1958) examination of graduate programs at Columbia, or this writer's survey in which Berkeley doctoral students appraised their programs (Heiss, 1964).

Undoubtedly a major reason for the differences in the findings is the fact that Berelson's data and the Alciatore-Eckert data were obtained from Ph.D. recipients—that is, the successful candidates—whereas, the other three studies relied heavily on data from respondents who still had hurdles to clear. The latter probably included an appreciable number who for one reason or another did not complete the program. The differences may be also due to the fact that Berelson's respondents were reporting retroactively on experiences which in some cases were ten or more years in the past, whereas the data from current students graphically illustrate their "here and now" impressions. For this reason, student studies often capture the excitement—and sometimes the stress and despair—which some students experience as they pursue the Ph.D. By pinpointing the pressure points they may provide documentation about areas of possible reform or the need for a reevaluation of the program.

In a national survey of attrition among doctoral students, Tucker (1964) found that approximately a third of those who register in doctoral programs eventually drop out. Although he believes that they do so because they lack a commitment to a specific area of specialization, or are not motivated toward completing the requirements, or went as far in their doctoral program as was consistent with their levels of ability, his data indicate that many give up the quest for the degree because of institutional restraints that appear irrelevant, or faculty insensitivity to graduate students, or because the department failed to stimulate an interest in the intellectual life. Tucker's (1964) work also provides valuable insights into the types of sociological and psychological problems which caused the dropouts to lose interest in completing their degree requirements. In reporting that academic failure accounts for only a small percentage of the dropout rate, he offers twelve portraits of selected respondents which dramatically demonstrate that a wide range of factors determined their decision to withdraw.

The fact that Tucker found dropouts to be more critical of their graduate programs than were their peers who persisted and received the degree may suggest that success modified one's desire to criticize or that the uncritical are more apt to reap the rewards. In either event Tucker's data point to the need for more research on the relationship between one's attitudes (or intellectual disposition) and ones growth and development in the scholarly life. Although his data show that prestigious universities have lower rates of attrition than schools lower in status, he found that 30 per cent of his respondents had dropped out of institutions that Keniston had ranked as "leading graduate schools."

Several researchers have attempted to study the process of socialization which graduate students experience as they move along in their doctoral programs. Gottleib (1960) found that students tend to take on the characteristics of their mentors, especially when they receive some personal assurance of acceptance. Assurance may take the form of an offer of an assistantship or of an award or a recommendation for a teaching appointment within the department. It may merely take the form of friendliness. Carper and Becker (1957) found that graduate students face three basic sets of group expectations as they attempt to identify with their chosen field: the generalized cultural expectations current in the society; the specific expectations of their families; and the expectations of the occupational group. These researchers found that the ideologies of the occupational group were influential in keeping the graduate in the field despite the tensions produced when family expectations were incompatible with their choices. The ideologies apparently provided the student with the rationale and support he needed to identify as a member of the group.

Davis and his associates (1964) conducted a nationwide survey of the financial support of arts and science graduate students which confirmed what most institutional studies had found, namely that the major obstacle to persistence in graduate study and the greatest single source of stress is the problem of finance. Outstanding universities are characterized by their ability to provide some subsidy for most of their doctoral candidates. With respect to organization and administration, a recent study by Parsons and Platt (1968) of the American academic system suggests that outstanding universities are characterized by a structure of governance in which the traditions of de facto collegiality are maintained in the making of decisions and the conventions and norms of academic freedom and tenure are valued.

In an effort to discover the standards upon which institutions of higher education were judged, Hatch (1964) examined the literature and materials on file in the Clearing House of Studies in Higher Education and found the following factors listed as indices of outstanding institutional quality: The institution is disposed to make a distinction between the acquisition and the examination of knowledge; it provides adequate learning resources, jealously guards academic freedom, rewards good teaching, administers its counseling program for institutionwide impact, and performs its institutional research on important matters. The program is characterized by its flexibility, permissiveness, openness to experimentation, uniqueness, provision for independent study, and high but attainable goals. The course work challenges the students to develop their own initiative, develops their critical faculties, recommends extensive reading, requires a large block of out-of-class study time and offers little instruction labeled as "remedial."

Bissel (1968) cites four characteristics which he considers to be earmarks of quality in a university. The institution is a stronghold of scholarship in the pure theoretical subjects that lie at the basis of any expansion of knowledge; for example, chemistry, physics, biology, philosophy, literature, political science, economics, and history occupy a special place in a great university because all divisions of it must regularly return to them. The great university has graduate and undergraduate divisions that are both strong. The great university maintains a balance between its long-range goals and its short-range obligations, or between its obligation to pure scholarship and its obligation to the society of which it is a part.

The research reported here represents an attempt to study the components of excellence in graduate education as described in the Hatch and Bissel inventories. The most important questions asked were these: What do members of the graduate faculty perceive as the role of the university in the modern world? How are top ranked graduate institutions organized to achieve excellence; how do they maintain excellence? How are graduate institutions organized to achieve needed change? Who are the "change agents" in graduate institutions? How do faculty members appraise the viability of their academic departments? How do doctoral students appraise the quality of their academic programs? What are the trends in doctoral education as perceived by deans and department chairmen?

Because of its comprehensiveness and currency, and because its reliance upon the "testimony of expert witnesses" meets the test of reliability for subjective surveys, the Cartter rankings were used as the base from which the sample for this study was drawn. Although the sample was basically selected so as to be representative of ten graduate institutions that ranked high on a scale of effectiveness, it was also selected so as to exclude denominational schools and technical institutes and to include the variables of geography, size, and type of control; thus it does not purport to represent "the" top ten institutions in the Cartter report. Since his report documented the fact that regardless of their rank on a scale of overall excellence, qualitative differences can be found *within* as well as *between* graduate institutions, it was thought that a diverse sample would permit an examination of the causes of unevenness in academic quality. In general, the universities selected for study may accurately be described as among the most prestigious graduate institutions in the United States. The sample includes the University of California at Berkeley, Columbia, Cornell, Illinois, Johns Hopkins, Michigan, North Carolina, Northwestern, Stanford, and Wisconsin. Each of these institutions is a member of the elite Association of American Universities, whose membership is limited to "those institutions of the North American continent the quality of whose graduate work in certain fields is high and whose additional claims for inclusion are strong either because of the general standing of their program . . . or because of the high standing of one or more of their professional schools" (1965).

The departments selected for study are three from each of the four broad academic divisions—humanities, social sciences, biological sciences, and physical sciences. They are the departments of biochemistry, chemistry, economics, English, French, history, mathematics, philosophy, physics, physiology, psychology, and sociology. They were chosen in the belief that their subjects lie at the base of knowledge in practically all other fields of graduate study.

Drawing upon the issues and problems defined in the literature, the second step involved the development of interview schedules for graduate deans and deans of the Colleges of Arts and Sciences and another schedule for department chairmen. Essentially the schedules were designed to elicit data on the organization for graduate education, the role of deans and department chairmen, the process through which curriculum is reviewed, the machinery

through which interrelationships are implemented, and the anticipated changes in the academic preparation of scholars who will
graduate within the next five years. In the fall of 1967 the writer
held interviews on each campus with the graduate deans, the deans
of the colleges of arts and sciences, and the department chairmen
in the twelve departments included in the sample. Approximately
twenty additional people (who were invited to the interview by the
department chairmen) also contributed information for the study.
Usually the latter were graduate advisers or directors of graduate
studies. In a few cases a former department chairman participated
in the interview because the current chairman was too new to be
thoroughly oriented to the department. Interviews were conducted
in the interviewee's office and lasted from ninety minutes to three
hours. In all, 160 people were interviewed or involved in interviews.

A third aspect of the study included the development and
administration of a faculty questionnaire and a student questionnaire. The faculty questionnaire was designed to evoke information
on the role of the university in the modern world, and to learn the
respondent's views on certain contemporary issues in university education and his ideas on the nature and quality of the department's
academic offerings and environment. Efforts were made to secure
the names and addresses of the members of the graduate faculty
and the doctoral students in each of the twelve departments through
a request to the department chairman. Although most of the lists
were accurate and therefore useful, some were disappointingly inadequate because they were outdated or included a wide variety of
persons who did not meet the criteria for graduate faculty or doctoral student. An attempt was made to recheck faculty lists against
the college catalog, but this also proved unreliable because of outdated information or schedule changes that had occurred between
the spring catalog printing and our request in the fall. A number of
questionnaires were returned unanswered because the addressee was
no longer a member of the department, was on a travel leave and
could not be reached by mail, or was deceased. In all, 2308 questionnaires were mailed and 1610, or 69 per cent, were returned
completed. Of these, 112 arrived too late to be included in the computer runs although their ideas are included in the analysis of the
open-ended statements. Fifty-one questionnaires were unusable be-

cause the institutional or departmental code numbers had been removed by the respondent.

The student questionnaire was formulated to gain a student's appraisal of his academic program and to obtain data on the extent to which he had developed intellectually in the course of his graduate work. The process of obtaining an accurate list of doctoral students was also complicated because some departments do not have separate listings for M.A.'s and Ph.D.'s, others have lists that include many dropouts, and still others have no lists at all. In one case, after several attempts, the quest for such a list had to be abandoned because of mailing deadlines. For this reason the responses of students in sociology represent nine institutions instead of ten. Unevenness in department size and student populations required sampling on the basis of complete lists for small schools and departments and on randomly selected samples from large schools and departments. Errors in sampling were probably introduced because of the unreliability of the departmental lists and the great mobility of students. A total of 4806 questionnaires was mailed and 3487, or 72 per cent, were returned in usable form. Of these, 319 arrived late; computer-run data were not obtained on these, although an analysis of the responses to all open-ended questions was made and incorporated in the report. Forty-one completed questionnaires were not useable because the respondent had removed the institution code number.

For more than a decade scholars at the Center for Research and Development in Higher Education have been interested in studying the intellectual dispositions of college students and in measuring the changes that occur in their attitudes and interests during the college years. The results of studies by Heist (1968), Mock and Yonge (1969), and McConnell and Heist (1962) indicate that certain personalities are more responsive to change than certain others. They also show that certain institutional variables have a greater impact on student attitudes than do some academic factors. Tucker's (1964) study of attrition among doctoral students suggests that persistence and success in the degree process appear to be associated with personality characteristics that are related to a persistent interest in the intellectual life. Sanford (1962), Newcomb (1967), Freedman (1963), Trent (1967), Keniston (1959), and others confirm these findings for undergraduate students but there are no studies that give comparable data for graduate students.

One of the purposes of this research was to collect data which would permit the Center to study developmental changes in graduate students during the period of their post-doctoral careers. To this end, the Omnibus Attitude Inventory, a self-administering instrument designed by researchers at the Berkeley Center, was mailed to approximately 1400 doctoral students who expressed an interest in participating in this particular aspect of the study. Students who received the Inventory were advised that we would like to have them take it first as currently enrolled graduate students and to retake it three years later when, presumably, most of them would have completed or nearly completed their Ph.D. programs. At that time, if funds are available, an effort will be made to measure changes that occur in their profiles of interests and to learn which, if any, might be attributable to their graduate experiences. In return for his cooperation each student received a profile of his own scores with an explanation of the various scales. He also received a table of the mean scores of the students in his field and in each of the fields represented in the study. Included in this packet was a post-card on which the student was asked to sign his name and the name and address of a person who would know where he might be contacted three years hence when phase two of the study is scheduled.

In addition to data from the interviews, from questionnaires, and from the Attitude Inventory, basic information on graduate offerings and requirements was obtained from catalogs and from other available written materials which were requested of deans and department chairmen at the time of the interview. These included student or faculty handbooks, brochures, mimeographed materials which supplemented the catalog, and various forms for application, petition, special waivers, or for certifying admission to candidacy.

Data from the faculty and student questionnaires were analyzed so as to show comparative profiles of the responses of private and public university respondents and to show comparative data for the various disciplines. Interview data were analyzed on the basis of departmental representation and on the basis of differences in the responses of deans and department chairmen. Profiles of the group mean scores were obtained for the fourteen scales on the

Omnibus Personality Inventory, as were comparative group mean scores for the various disciplines. Statistical summaries of the questionnaire and of the Omnibus Personality scores achieved by students in various disciplines are contained in a separate publication available through E.R.I.C., the Educational Research Information Center.

Faculty Opinions

3

In an atmosphere intense with debate over the mission of the university, and at a time when efforts are being made to transform and regenerate our academic institutions, it seemed appropriate to examine the perceptions which faculty members have of their role and the role of the university in the contemporary world. Because they are the prime preservers, disseminators, and contributors of the knowledge valued by universities, it was assumed that they would have a clear conception of its nature and purpose. In a study of graduate education it seemed particularly appropriate to learn on what basis the faculty makes decisions, assigns priorities, and models its academic style.

To this end, an attempt was made to develop an adequate set of alternative statements for describing the nature of the university to which the graduate faculty in the ten institutions in the sample were then asked to respond. The statements were derived from the literature discussed in Chapter One, which purported to define the idea of a university. From this literature three basic positions which seem to be logically independent were culled. Because they appeared to be significant for both historical and contemporary writers, it was thought that they would be meaningful if used in the general context of a faculty questionnaire. Thus an attempt was made to distill the essence of each of these positions and to state each in normative terms. It was hoped that in stating their position on the statements faculty members would clarify, for the purposes of this study and for themselves, the ideals toward which universities should strive.

The first position is derived from the writings of Newman, Hutchins, Veblen, Barzun, Wilson, Mill, and to some extent Arrowsmith. It holds that knowledge is valued intrinsically and that the purpose of the university is to preserve, disseminate, and promote insights into knowledge to ensure educated citizens who will carry the life of rational inquiry into their respective communities. In the opinion of those who hold this position, the university should be detached from society because the knowledge central to its purpose transcends the relative goals of any particular society.

The second position was culled from ideas expressed by Bacon, Huxley, Flexner, Jaspers, Ortega de Gasset, Ashby, Kerr, and Heyns. These authors contend that knowledge has both cosmopolitan and eclectic value and purposes. That is to say, knowledge is an end in itself but also has instrumental value. Although the university is detached, it has a well-developed social conscience. Thus while the search for knowledge is the guiding force, scholars in the university also help to clarify what the real needs and problems of society are and suggest ways of improving it. This position also extends the instrumental uses of the university into practical form by assigning to the university the task of educating and training professionals. When graduated, these individuals will go out into society and apply to the solution of its problems the knowledge and analytical skills learned in the university.

The third position is drawn from the writings of Perkins, Taylor, Goodman, parts of Galbraith, and various friends of the New Left. These observers hold that knowledge has both intrinsic and instrumental value but that its primary worth comes from the latter. In this view, the university is an institution without walls. The scholar is committed to the investigation of social problems as they relate to his field of competence or vice versa. His emphasis is on service, and he works directly with public or private groups in the society who need expert assistance. The essence of this approach is that the scholar and the intellectual community should realize and assume the political, ethical, and public responsibilities which follow from their educated intelligence or superior knowledge. The university is not a detached critic or society's bad conscience; it is a partner in the affairs of the world. Hence the instrumental value of knowledge is relative to the current trends or policies determined by particular groups within society.

The writer acknowledges that it would be possible to combine isolated aspects of these three positions and create new alternatives. Nevertheless with respect to the present state of our knowledge, these three positions are basic to any discussion on the nature and purpose of the university. They are either implicitly or explicitly assumed, accepted, or negated by those who assess the university as a purposive institution, and so it seemed appropriate to use them as the basis for the assessment attempted in this part of this study. In order to allow provision for new viewpoints however, respondents were invited to write their own statements if they were unable to accept any of the positions given.

Here is the statement to which the graduate faculties in twelve disciplines in the ten institutions were asked to respond:

From an analysis of the history of thought about the nature of the university, three positions seem to emerge. We have attempted to cull the essence of these positions in the following statements. Will you please indicate which statement comes closest *to your own view of the university?* If you cannot accept any of these positions, please submit your own.

(1) Knowledge is its own reward. The advancement, preservation, and dissemination of knowledge are valued ends in themselves. Although the university is detached from society, its activities lead to gradual social improvement.

(2) Knowledge has both intrinsic and instrumental values. Hence, the goals of the university ought to be twofold: to seek knowledge, basic to the concerns of mankind; and

to provide education in intellectual analysis for those who
will bring about social improvement.

(3) Knowledge has intrinsic value, but its primary value
is derived from its instrumental uses. The university ought
to be directly involved in defining and serving social needs.

The position which comes closest to my own view is
(1) ———, (2) ———, (3) ———.

(4) My own position differs from all three and is as follows:

Among the 1374 faculty members who checked the statement which came closest to their own view of the university, approximately 14 per cent selected position (1), which holds that the
university should be detached from society and interested primarily
in the intrinsic value of knowledge. Some 81 per cent selected position (2), which assigns a dual role to the university—the dissemination and promotion of knowledge, and the education of individuals who will go into society and use that knowledge to bring about
improvements in the social order. Slightly less than 5 per cent
aligned themselves with position (3), in which the university is
perceived as primarily concerned with the instrumental value of
knowledge and directly involved in defining and serving social needs.
A total of ninety-five respondents submitted their own statements
and ninety-four left this item blank in their response to the questionnaire.

There were only slight differences in the percentage of faculty respondents in privately controlled universities (16.2 per cent)
and in publicly controlled universities (12.6 per cent) who accepted
the detached university role described by Newman. And only slightly
fewer respondents in private universities (2.6 per cent) than in
public universities (5.8 per cent) subscribed to the view that the
university should be directly involved in defining and serving social
needs.

It is of interest to note that in one private institution which
was the site of an explosive student-community protest shortly after
these responses were registered, not one faculty member gave unqualified acceptance of the role of the university as a direct agent in
the solution of social problems. Also noted was the fact that the
public university whose respondents subscribed in largest numbers

to the role of the university as a socially involved organization has had no widely publicized student-faculty protest incidents. In a third (public) institution which has been in the eye of practically every student-community hurricane, the responses of the faculty on the three positions deviate only slightly from the averages obtained in other institutions.

When departmental responses were analyzed separately it was found that more of the faculties in French, English, and history than in other fields were inclined to accept position (1); 20 per cent did so. And more respondents in economics and sociology were inclined to reject the withdrawn posture which this position implies. Although respondents in all fields voted heavily in favor of position (2), which prescribes a dual function for the university, there appeared to be more unanimity of agreement among psychologists, sociologists, biochemists, and chemists than among faculty members in other fields. Conversely, respondents in economics are less cohesive in their perception of the university's role than are respondents in other areas; 10 per cent of the former accepted position (1), 77 per cent subscribed to position (2), and 13 per cent endorsed position (3).

Respondents in the department of French unanimously rejected the notion of the university as definer or server of social needs, as did 99 per cent of the chemists and 98 per cent of the philosophers. Supporters of this activist position were more frequently found in economics (13 per cent) and in sociology (10 per cent). Among the 189 who did not check one of the three positions, ninety-five wrote their own statements, two said that their view represented a composite of positions (1) and (2), and three said that their position included elements of (2) and (3). The remainder did not respond to this item in the questionnaire.

Among the ninety-five faculty respondents who composed their own position statements on the role of the university, approximately one-third indicated that they found it counterproductive to define such an institution without incorporating the substance of all three of the given viewpoints. Admitting their inability to divorce the 'ideal" from the "real" role of the university or to distinguish between the "real world" and the "university world," these respondents cited the widespread diversification in contemporary life and education as evidence to support their contention that universities should, simultaneously, assume multiple roles and support a faculty that is representative of each and all viewpoints. According to those who composed their own statements, a de facto approach to definition acknowledges the growing pragmatism and consequent pluralism in the modern university. They argue that because the university places high value on openness, precise definitions do not come easily and some polarization is inevitable. For example, in those few remaining enclaves where knowledge is valued for its own sake, the charge is often made that in catering to new demands the university becomes a veritable service station. Conversely, those who subscribe to the theory that the university should manifest a social consciousness claim that the detached university is anachronistic. For some of the latter, if the "times are out of joint" it is largely because the university is out of step. Others see no teleological relationship between the two.

Half of the twenty faculty members in the humanities who contributed their own position statements were reluctant to accept unequivocally the concept of "social improvement" as an expressed goal for the university. Rather, they subscribed to the idea that when a university endeavors to instill an understanding of the meaning of the past it also serves as a critic of what is, and as an advocate of what might be. Faculty members in departments of English tended to emphasize the fact that as an institution of western culture the major contribution of the university is to encourage a style of life which puts a high value on knowledge, truth, creativity, and sensitivity. They consider these values conducive to all social development. When it draws society into meaningful contact with a humanist tradition, respondents in the humanities believe that the university plays its most constructive and positive social role. However, most of the commentators stressed the improvement of self or of the individual as a prior condition to social improvement or to public virtue. Thus, they believed that the primary emphasis in the university should be on individual development.

Some philosophy professors were less sanguine about the effectiveness of the university in liberating man from "racism or mindless anticommunism" or in engaging him in crusades to "free the world." Others saw the university as serving a socially pragmatic function somewhat in the tradition of a grand-scale WPA project. According to one commentator, "the university provides an occupation, with reasonable working conditions and fringe benefits, for individuals with varying talents and multifarious interests. It provides research and vocational benefits to the state and business community. . . . Finally, it relieves the unemployment problem and allows a 'déclassé' atmosphere for middle class students."

Less cynically perhaps, several respondents defined the role of the university in Utopian terms rather than in terms which mirrored present reality. Some defined its main purpose as contributing to happiness whereas others believe that the university's reason for existence is its promotion of intellectual and spiritual understanding among faculty and students as they are related to the whole world.

The burden of the objections voiced by the social scientists who could not give unqualified acceptance to any of the positions offered in the questionnaire tended to center on the fact that the statements "lacked static." According to the economists, historians, and sociologists who composed their own position statements, the nature of the university resides in the composite capacity of its faculty and students to become better teachers *of themselves*.

Although they acknowledge its intrinsic value, social scientists as a group tend to place primary value and dependence upon the instrumental value of knowledge. Some suggested that the best means for seeing that such values arise is to let individuals pursue their particular interests and to let universities preserve, advance, and disseminate knowledge as if knowledge were a pure virtue in itself. In this context the university serves as a haven removed from the pressures of society in which innovation and daring can be pursued in the interests of the needs of that society. Thus, as he analyzes ideas and examines the evidence on which humanistic values are predicated, the individual is enabled to judge whether to accept, reject, or attempt to improve current situational arrangements in society. To the sociologists who spelled out their positions, ideas and action are "the stuff of universities." While they contended that the university should be responsive to those who seek a more just and humane society through direct action, they stated that it should be detached from other groups or organizations in society—especially from governmental, political, and business entities.

Economists in the sample had some difficulties in accepting the concept of "social improvement" in qualitative or abstract terms. In the opinion of one commentator, "academia's minority status (number-wise) necessitates that it work within the context of society's needs without seeking to define them." Another who found the concept of "social improvement" too broad suggested, "The function of the university is to teach its students what they (or their families) want to learn." Some historians implied that however long the time lag or impractical the demonstration, the latent instrumental uses of intrinsic knowledge justify its emphasis by the university. Observing that they find no theoretical distinction between the value of these two forms—since, in their judgment, all knowledge is double-edged, its own reward or punishment, instrumental for good or ill—most historians tended to see the primary role of the university as a developer of critical intelligence and of moral concern for human welfare. Thus, according to these respondents, by merely teaching students how to think, the university fulfills a service to the individual and to society.

The twenty-six chemists, mathematicians, and physicists who contributed their own statements about the role of the university were in general agreement that universities are legitimated principally by their intellectual or ideational activity. Thus, for the scientist, the paramount role of the university is "to provide the scholar with the means by which he can satisfy his curiosity or his desire to know." Intrinsic knowledge is enough. However, about half of the writers agreed, inferentially, that while the scientist per se does not ordinarily intellectualize about the social consequences of his research, this is a defensible matter for study by other segments of the university. For example, approximately one-third of the writers implied that it was up to the social scientists "to prove their relevance by explicitly dealing with social problems and by interacting with communities in which such problems exist." Most of the remainder did not comment specifically on the role of the physical scientist but instead negated the social sciences as too immature in their development or understanding of social organization to be able to contribute workable solutions.

In the opinion of one mathematician, "the social sciences are just one step beyond mythology. Their ideologies are substitutes for the religion of earlier eras. If we tie the university to them it would be like returning to the Middle Ages or worse." Another stated, "We don't understand the human brain as an organism; . . . we know even less about social organisms." Still others were apprehensive that in responding to social issues the university might lose its essential nature or destroy its role as an institution devoted to learning. One respondent hypothesized that given the current social pressures, "it might become necessary to abandon universities to ineluctable forces which crowd them with mediocre students who need a trade school rather than a university. In this event, serious scholars will move to more selective institutions like the Institute of Advanced Studies or le College de France."

Judging by the tenor of their statements, most natural scientists perceive themselves in a singular role in the university, that of intellectualizing about nature, but they tolerate a dual role for all others who intellectualize about their respective disciplines and modify or apply the knowledge that science has produced. Some dismiss or exculpate the "pure scientist" from responsibility or involvement in the social consequences of his work by describing him as too socially or politically naïve to be responsible. The following quotes are illustrative of this viewpoint.

> The true scientist has a curiosity about nature and designs experiments on the basis of controlled quantitative methods to find answers. When he has established these facts he tries to generalize and extend them. . . . He then imparts them to others, students or fellow scientists . . . and these developments become common knowledge.

> Among those who learn the new facts are more practical-minded men, engineers, inventors, or whatever you wish to call them, who apply these discoveries to practical ends— to prevent disease, cure the ill, facilitate transportation, agriculture, etc. The results of such advances alter our social structure and our economic life; . . . they produce a healthier, happier people. They also produce lethal weapons, crowded urban conditions, industrial revolutions. The scientist is *not* to blame. All nature appears by chance to produce evil with the good.

> Because a scientist is proficient in experimental or theoretical work—especially if he is a good scientist—he is generally

not competent in matters of politics and economics. He, with few exceptions, reads no history. There have been few broadly trained scientists—generally the scientist is too narrow, too idealistic, and too naïve to add to or be responsible for social or economic reform. He had best stick to his science and teaching, in which he is competent.

Respondents in the physical sciences perceive the university variously as a site where knowledge is explored, a forum for the open discussion of ideas, an institution for maintaining the intelligentsia, detached from but not insensitive to society and its problems, independent of politics, and not subservient to the government. Using personal attributes as descriptive they depict the university as a custodian, teacher, and discoverer. Its evocative function is to broaden the base of intellectual analysis of the world around man, but it is not necessarily a purposive instrument of social change.

None of the physical scientists who wrote their own statements associated themselves with the view that the university should be directly involved in defining or serving social needs. Rather they tended to favor a "fall-out" concept; they believe that the dynamics created by the scholars' quest for knowledge and the students' drive for self-fulfillment would, if facilitated by freedom of interaction, balance the intrinsic and instrumental qualities of knowledge and stimulate responses appropriate to the intellectual and social climate. In this somewhat romanticized view, the physical science respondents believed that a multidisciplinary synthesis would occur and a "naturally" balanced institution would develop.

In contrast to the physical scientists, the twenty-one biological scientists who formulated their own position statements on the nature of the university tended to view that institution as basically responsive to social needs but also open to pluralism. None in this group of respondents saw the university as singularly detached from society, although as psychologists, physiologists, and biochemists they tended to couch their definitions in terms that were applicable to human rather than social needs. For example, a biochemist wrote, "The university ought to be *substantially* concerned with learning how to teach men to love one another and with disseminating such knowledge to society at large." Another said, "I would have accepted position (3) had you substituted *human* for social." Still another said, "The overriding problems of our society are human, not technological. . . . While not neglecting technology and its supporting sciences, the university will have its greatest relevance if it is mainly concerned with human questions."

In general, most of the biological scientists wrote definitions which connote the idea of a university as a "total environment" which "breeds intellectual gadflies who are aware of the cultural and technical histories of the ideas or issues they criticize," allows scholars to pursue their studies without "worrying about instrumental pay-offs," and also operates, in part, as a "social service station." Although none of the biological scientists subscribed to a noninvolvement role for the university, some inserted a warning about relating the faculty indiscriminately to social action. One commented, "Faculty members in my field (psychology) tend to combine high intelligence with emotional immaturity; . . . they should not direct programs of social action." And one physiologist made a general disclaimer of responsibility by stating, "I don't know anything about 'right.' All I know is what happens. I also don't know whether change is improvement. All flows, nothing remains."

Demonstrably, at least for the faculties represented in this study, the university in the modern world is a many splendored thing.

UNIVERSITY AS SOCIAL RESOURCE AND SOCIAL CRITIC

The history of American higher education is filled with cases in which universities were in conflict with the culture in which they existed. However, with only a few exceptions, these encounters were locally contained and made little impact on the system as a whole. Prior to 1940, university professors were primarily concerned with transmitting, preserving, and reflecting on known knowledge and were rarely in a position to affect public policy. With the advent of World War II, the federal government called upon universities for the educated talent needed in the interests of national defense. Scholars were asked to put aside their own research interests to devote themselves to the research needs of the nation for new science and technologies. The locus of the professor's primary effort was moved from the classroom to the research laboratory or to some external purpose. The life style of the professor—particularly in the sciences—began to undergo dramatic changes.

By the end of the war, it had become obvious that leadership in scientific advancement was imperative if America was to survive. Faced with the need for new pools of knowledge and the rapid conversion of that knowledge into useful services, government leaders were reluctant to see university researchers return to their former detached stance. New impetus was given to both fundamental and applied research in areas of overriding need such as food, health, and public welfare as new programs were developed to promote research to alleviate those needs. It soon became apparent that federally supported university research was here to stay. Convinced that "human want is obsolete," more and more university professors became interested in developing the knowledge and technology to render it so.

The intellectual ferment generated by the vast subsidies that began to pour into universities was unparalleled in educational history. Virtually overnight research became a giant on the campus and the quiet pace of instruction and scholarship gave way to the immediacy of the many new research goals. The intimate atmosphere of the campus was lost as major campuses went into the research "business." The Russian preemption of leadership in outer space aroused a national sense of urgency to keep ahead or to excel. Technological developments in mass communication provided the media through which this interest was sustained and promoted. The scientific competence of a people became a symbol of its political effectiveness. The race for intellectual superiority was on. The multiversity began to take form. The august Educational Policy Committee of the University of California (1960) could declare, "The notion of absolute freedom in research is an academic myth; the direction of research is always influenced by the social and scientific climate of a period, even though such influences may be unperceived by the individual investigator." As university research became a commodity sought after by the federal government—and later by business and industry—the professor and his graduate students became political and economic entities both on and off campus. And as financial support of university research by the federal government became firmly established as a stable item in the operation of American universities, the nature, instructional capacity, administrative machinery, and internal relationships of higher education were drastically changed. The seeds of the present distrust of the university were planted as the university faculties divided into separate cultures and subcultures.

Many responsible persons who are interested in protecting the autonomous character of educational institutions have voiced concern over the inherent dangers that are present when a university must depend upon external funding for one of its primary functions. Of all the problems initiated by external support none threatens to have more serious consequences than those associated with the nature, direction, and control of the university's research program. Because the strategy of some federal funding agencies was to attempt to deal directly with the researcher, universities were sometimes caught in the position of being facilitators of sponsored research rather than decision makers on their own research activities. Criticism of university involvement in sponsored research has recently mounted. In a few cases it has become openly hostile.

Some who argue against federally funded university research believe that when the government does something for a university it does something to a university—that is, it uses it or manipulates it to serve political purposes or upsets the instructional-research balance or enhances the work of one field at the expense of others. Others believe that when the government does something for the university it does something against the university—that is, it takes away its autonomy or its freedom to direct itself. These groups confront another group which believes that when the government does something for the university it does indeed do something for it—it stimulates scholarship, expands resources, supports graduate study, or enables new frontiers of knowledge to be explored.

It is natural and important that the argument on this issue should be debated within the university, where it is particularly germane. Informed persons observe that if it is not raised there, as an ontological question, the university may one day find that its reason for existence—the search for truth—will have been lost and instead of functioning as an independent fourth branch of the government it will have become merely its right or left arm.

Internal and external tensions surrounding this issue have

recently increased. Some public officials have openly rebuked professors who have questioned the strings which federal agencies attach to their research subventions. For example, in an informal discussion, a science adviser to former President Johnson's Science Committee chastised the academic-scientific community for "insisting upon its purity and refusing to communicate with the public to justify its actions." He noted that while "the public sees the university as an institution which consumes one-fourth of the nation's disposable income," the academic-scientific community prefers to believe that "its virtues are so self-evident that a right-minded society must necessarily support it—on the university's terms." A question underlying this debate is whether universities should be involved at all in so-called mission-oriented research. Because it touches areas of interest to this study, the question was pursued as an aspect of the investigation. It has deep relevance to graduate students who have recently brought the debate out in the open.

The historical antecedents of present-day emphasis on mission-oriented research are found in the Morrill Act of 1872, which legitimated government supported institutes for research on university campuses. With the introduction of land-grant universities, mission-oriented research was initiated and conducted in experiment stations that were expressly organized to produce knowledge of direct benefit to agriculture. Other disciplines began to serve their particular clientele in field service centers, clinics, or research bureaus. Because the concept of mission-oriented research has overtones of outside direction or of "buying a researcher" to whom a specific project is then assigned, many scholars feel that individual freedom and creativity are sacrificed when research involves a contract rather than an outright grant. On another dimension, some scholars lack interest in mission-oriented research because it often focuses on the application of knowledge rather than on basic discovery. Added to this is the charge that the "product" obtained too often serves the interests of particular economic groups rather than those of the general public. The recent controversy over DDT offers a prime example.

In times of national emergency, universities usually expand their policies or call upon reserve policies to legitimate their participation in research that has questionable educational gains. For example, during World War II institutions justified their involvement in the Manhattan Project and other war-related activities on the premise that these were undertakings pursued in the interest of national defense. Since the cessation of that war, the troubles of the Cold War and the realities of the Korean and Vietnamese wars have kept the university researcher, if not as ease with his conscience, at least reasonably convinced that his research is vital to national security. Recently, however, a growing revulsion against war as an instrument for the resolution of conflict and a pervasive malaise about wars of intervention in particular have made university researchers less willing to participate in federally funded projects. Some claim that by accepting federal funding for research in the physical sciences—which has produced knowledge that has been used in the instrumentation and implementation of war—universities are implicated in the perpetuation of war. Rather than using its wide resources of reason and trained intelligence to improve the quality of life and thought and to proportionately support disciplines which are committed to understanding and reconciling differences among men, the critics charge that the effectiveness and the essential mission of the university have been violated.

The intensity of the discussion about mission-oriented research may be seen in the wide range of opinion that obtains among members of Congress, university officers, and university researchers. Some contend that the university bites the hand that feeds it when it disdains mission research. Others accuse it of an essential disloyalty. Students in increasing numbers contend that universities abrogate their own mission when they become involved in the missions of the Defense Department or in such operations as the ill-fated Camelot Project, which aroused international controversy when it was learned that its goal was to study the potential for internal conflict in Chile and other nations. Recent disclosures of other kinds of alleged international probing, such as the Central Intelligence Agency's financing of National Student Association delegates to the International Youth Conferences, and various other CIA-supported activities under university aegis, rocked the academic community and made it chary of those bearing gifts.

The element of foreign policy intrigue which was raised by these disclosures not only harmed particular institutions but also introduced a distrust among the international community of scholars. Likewise, such associations expose the university to the suspicion that to all intents and purposes it acts in these cases as a front for the government. Two institutions, George Washington University and American University, recently announced their withdrawal from federally sponsored research and the curtailment of research centers because, as Fritschler of American University observed, "the notion that research closely identified with a military mission should not be done on campus is an idea whose time has come."

Turbulence created on the domestic front by various forms of social and political protest often motivates the federal government to send out emergency distress signals to universities in an effort to tap their resources of trained intelligence and information. Faculty respondents in this study observed that inducements are currently being offered to educational institutions to have their social science and humanities departments undertake activities that will create order in society, restore confidence in the government, and reduce or remove the causes of discontent among the alienated, depressed, disaffiliated, and disadvantaged groups in the country. Even though this activity does not wear the stigmata of war-related research, or of meddling in the affairs of other nations, not all faculty members are in agreement that research of this nature properly belongs in the university. Some are concerned that by becoming counselors to government agencies or to politicians, humanists and social scientists "will be exploited for their articulateness and become little more than make-up men tidying up some public figure's image or program for public action."

When the graduate faculty members in the ten institutions in the sample were asked whether they agreed or disagreed with the idea that in periods of great social change universities should give high priority to research that might contribute to the orderly process of social change, 19 per cent agreed and the remainder disagreed. Yet when the same respondents were asked whether universities as institutions should assume a larger, more important role than they currently do in setting the goals and programs in society, 54 per cent said that they should and 46 per cent replied that they should not.

The inference that universities should produce ideas rather

than implement them, as implied by these statistics, was supported in the free commentary which the faculty appended to their responses. Most of those who added comments to qualify their position were in favor of a balanced emphasis in the research effort, but they were unwilling to accept the proposition that priority should be given to mission-oriented research. Some argued that "missions of the moment are often trivial" whereas it is imperative that educational institutions maintain a long-range perspective. Others were concerned lest the policy be used to institutionalize response to temporary trends.

A basic objection of those who qualified their disagreement was the negative effect such a priority might have on the right of the researcher to decide for himself where his research effort should be directed. While some agreed that research support cannot be entirely random and private, they were reluctant to see universities give mission research priority lest it deprive the scholar of his detachment or "coerce some into research areas in which they have little real interest." Some commentators complained that the traditional freedom which allows the scholar to approach research abstractly, without a prior commitment "to solve a problem," is being attenuated by the length of the strings attached to research funding. Those who interpreted mission-oriented research as implying a subordination of pure research have sounded repeated warnings that a vacuum occurs in a culture which fails to contribute continually to its pool of basic knowledge. Administrators in institutions which have few problems in attracting support for applied research said that they have often encountered great difficulty in obtaining the necessary financial assistance for scholars whose research cannot be justified as a response to some immediate problem or predictable end.

Recently, increased attention has been devoted to considering the locus of responsibility for the consequences of research. To some extent this interest may be a result of the vast increases in and greater visibility of the research effort, but to a much greater extent it can probably be attributed to the nature and direction that research has assumed during the past two or three decades. Over that period research in the physical and biological sciences has generated a dialogue that has intensified and become more heated among scholars and has captured the interests of the public at large. The substance of that dialogue resonates with practical, philosophical, and moral overtones. Students and other concerned persons have, with increasing stridency, challenged the preoccupation of the university—ostensibly a human institution—with research that does not advance the quality of men's lives. They argue that the utilization of educational resources is reprehensible when those resources are used to develop knowledge that makes man a target rather than a cause.

The public's interest in establishing responsibility for the consequences of research was dramatically revealed in a series of television documentaries aired by Public Broadcast Laboratories (PBL) and in several national and international conferences aired by Intertel and by National Educational Television. In the PBL program one of the few points on which participating scholars from medicine, law, political science, philosophy, and theology could agree was the fact that an essential ingredient in all research is *trust in the researcher.* This involves not only his competence in his substantive field but also his willingness to assume reasonable responsibility for the consequences of his research discoveries.

The heat of the current controversy over the ethics of university research, or university-related research, has motivated some institutions to reexamine their policies and practices. In particular, their critics challenge the use of educational resources (which, presumably, are intended for man's betterment) toward ends that have negative and often destructive consequences for mankind. Thus, they have openly questioned the legitimacy of the university's involvement in the design and development of environments that cut off green spaces or impair man's access to housing, transportation, work opportunities, or clean supplies of air and water. Several major universities hosted student-organized programs in which these issues were debated. Others were targets of organized protests against their alleged insensitivity to the consequences of their own expansion plans on the community in which they operate.

Concomitant with the increased attention given to these issues, a growing crescendo of voices rises from inside and outside research centers concerning the morality of drug use, organ transplants, and other actions which put life-and-death decisions into the hands of the researcher. The case in which the designer of an artificial heart played a role in the decision to use such a device on a human patient elicited a charge of improper ethical practice from several medical groups. As new discoveries occur in genetics and biochemistry more and more researchers will be asked to justify their work on moral or ethical grounds. And, as fundamental discoveries enable man to penetrate farther into the universe, the tendency not merely to raise questions but also to try to answer them will involve researchers more and more in their consequences.

In an attempt to learn whether university professors believe that the researcher is implicated in the consequences of his discoveries, an item on this point was included in the research questionnaire. Respondents were asked whether they agreed or disagreed with the following statement: "Knowledge has consequences. Therefore, the university scholar has a responsibility to take a position on the consequences of his discoveries." Some 75 per cent of the respondents agreed with this position and 25 per cent disagreed. Proportionately, more respondents in philosophy, English, biochemistry, and sociology agreed with the proposition (82 per cent) and more economists, chemists, physicists, and mathematicians rejected it (32 per cent). Among those who qualified their rejection of this proposition were several who said that they agreed with it in principle but felt that it could not be implemented in any practical way. Among commentators who expressed a qualified agreement were those who thought that the researcher should take a position only when asked to do so or when the nature of his findings required a formal statement. When faculty members were asked whether they thought students in their departments were concerned about the consequences of research, 58 per cent replied that they were, 21 per cent thought they were not, and the remainder said they were unable to evaluate the students' concerns on this issue.

When faculty members were asked whether the university as an institution should assume a larger, more important role than it currently does in helping society define its goals and set its programs, 54 per cent agreed and 46 per cent disagreed. Only a few respondents qualified their response to this item, but among those who did the feeling was strong that this issue should be decided by the consumer rather than by the producer. While they agreed in general that professors might serve as advisers or consultants in the area of their expertise, they were reluctant to commit the total institution to this task lest it appear as though the university were telling society how to live and what to value. Some were reluctant to give academicians a larger social role because "they already have too much influence." Others believed that an improvident social system might develop as readily under academicians as under politicians. While they were willing to allow competent and sensitive scholars to play an important role, some withheld agreement because they considered many academicians "arrogant and irresponsive to the needs of other segments of society."

Essentially, commentators who believed that the university should play a larger role in society did so on the premise that the university should put its resources at the disposal of those who formulate public policy. Some noted that the most flourishing institutions were those in which scholarship and research were related to the burning questions of the day. Others saw the university as an organization which takes its form and substance from the society in which it lives and must therefore be willing to return the fruits of its work to society. Dissenters on this item in the questionnaire tended to believe that the university's role is that of social critic. As such, its primary contribution is to analyze and criticize the programs and goals which society proposes. Commentators on this issue reasoned that if the university were involved in setting those goals it would thereby disqualify itself as a social critic.

In all, 55 per cent of the faculty respondents from the public universities and 48 per cent of those in the private universities voted in favor of a larger social role for the university than it currently assumes. More respondents in physiology, philosophy, French, psychology, and biochemistry accepted this role for the university (63 per cent) and more chemists, mathematicians, and economists rejected it (43 per cent). In view of student criticism of the lack of relevance in their instructional programs these data are important.

The question of whether colleges and universities should teach values is one of the most provocative issues in higher education. Since it goes to the heart of the democratic process (which supports diversity in opinions and the right to protest), the question virtually forces institutions of higher education into a neutral corner.

On the assumption that it can retain its autonomy only by being detached, the university generally prefers to define its role as critical analyst rather than as advocate. This stance is not clearly understood by the general public nor always appreciated even by academicians. It is becoming increasingly difficult to maintain as various polities pressure the university to protect—or protest—establishment values.

The drive to have values taught always elicits the query: whose values? Recently this dilemma has been greatly exacerbated by the character of student protests in which traditional values on such matters as patriotism, loyalty to one's country, and respect for authority have been challenged as mechanisms for control rather than ideals to be valued. The protestors' demands for reexamination of the evidence on which these values are legitimated and the revolutionary nature of their rhetoric—and sometimes of their behavior —have stimulated a rash of state and federal bills which, if passed, would legislate both values and morality. Such action implies that certain values are universally held and legislatable. The role of the university as the one remaining institution that is free to examine society's conventions or values would be appreciably weakened by the passage of such bills. Essentially they would bind the university and destroy its unique character as an institution which pursues truth no matter how the result of that pursuit might upset prevailing values.

Historically, scholars themselves have engaged in continual debate over whether the university should remain neutral with respect to the teaching of values. The debate becomes heated in critical transition periods. Currently proponents and opponents find fuel for their debate in the diverse and divergent opinions and attitudes now prevalent with respect to student unrest, social injustices, the crisis in religions, and the Vietnam issue. These and many other traditions which have their roots in value systems are presently under fire. Some critics blame the educational system for feeding the conflict. Some charge that the system has failed to protect or promote established values. Others accuse it of protecting the wrong values or of introducing revolutionary ones. On these issues the university is invariably a vulnerable target.

When graduate faculty members in the institutions in this

study were asked whether in their judgment a university should re-main neutral with regard to the teaching of values, 58 per cent re-sponded that it should not and 41 per cent thought that it should. Approximately 1 per cent did not answer the question directly, but some of these (along with other respondents) contributed support-ing or qualifying statements.

Faculty members in philosophy, biochemistry, psychology, physics, and English were more frequently inclined to believe that it was not incumbent upon the university to remain neutral with regard to value questions (66 per cent), whereas economists and sociologists more frequently than other groups believed that it should. When their supporting or qualifying statements were ana-lyzed, it was found that those who rejected the notion of value-free teaching generally supported their position on the argument that universities are by nature valuing institutions, and as such they can-not be neutral with respect to the civilizing values of men. Others accepted the premise that universities should be concerned about values but rejected the idea that the institution (and by inference its faculty) should take positions on them. On the premise that the university has no ideological function, the latter insist that the teach-ing of values can lead to obscurantism and indoctrination or can force the university to accommodate its teaching to the dominant social or political thought. Some noted that intellectual history is replete with examples of cases in which such interdictions were im-posed. On the other hand, exponents of the idea that the university is a valuing institution argued that the essential goals on which university roles are predicated are worthy of universal promotion. They listed these goals variously as the search for truth and justice, a belief in the universality of knowledge, a deep-rooted commitment to freedom, a concern for the relevance or the eventual worth and applicability of scholarship, a basic belief in human worth, and a respect for the dignity of all mankind.

On the theory that such values touch all men intimately, proponents of value teaching discounted the possibility that the uni-versity can—or should—disassociate itself from advocacy. Equally serious opponents were firm in their contention that regardless of the nature of the issue, universities should examine and report their findings with detachment. Sounding the caveat that the academic freedom of the student must be protected, some scholars conceded that a distinction can be justified between corporate privilege and individual privilege. In this context they contend that while the institution is bound to preserve and protect its detachment, individual professors have the right to indicate their own position on issues in the area of their competence.

The battle lines appear to be drawn around the fact that the concepts of truth, justice, freedom, human worth, and relevance have a moral quality and thus imply an ethical "oughtness." Since oughtness is relative and can easily mask self-interests, most respondents thought that universities should provide a pluralistic and balanced approach to controversial issues and leave the student free to decide which approach he can reasonably accept.

Some respondents implied that the university must sometimes purposely create internal tensions in the hope that new insights and relationships will emerge. If the resulting tensions are perceived by some participants as antagonistic to the local culture, the university must absorb the tension as part of the risk involved in the process of examining society. Others believe that while some conflict must be anticipated when the university questions the way society views certain values, the institution can only be harmed—or in error—when it purposely induces antagonisms. The intensity of faculty feeling on this issue was shown in the frequency with which individuals cited local examples of induced conflict. Their major point was that these confrontations often left wounds that were more damaging to the factions involved than was the condition or issue which elicited the original action.

Administration of
Graduate Education

4

The institutions chosen for this study represent a diversity of organizational patterns for administering graduate education. Four of the ten universities organize their graduate offerings in graduate schools; two have graduate divisions, one operates as a graduate college, another is organized around graduate fields, one is structurally organized around three graduate faculties, and another operates as a continuum of the undergraduate organization and has no separate administration for graduate education.

In seven institutions a graduate dean administers graduate education. Of the three others, one is administered by a provost, one by a dean of graduate faculties, and another by an academic dean of arts and sciences. Appointments to these positions are made by the chief campus officer to whom the graduate office is responsible. Usually the graduate dean relates directly to a vice-president, provost, or dean of academic affairs and in a few cases to an officer in charge of research. The graduate dean and his counterpart serve indefinite terms at the pleasure of the chief campus officer.

A graduate council, a council of academic deans, or a committee of the academic senate serves as the policy-making body for graduate study. Usually this group reviews all new programs and degrees, although broad-based planning rests with the departments where the academic expertise resides. Graduate deans are usually ex-officio members of the council. As such, they help to set policy but their primary role is administrative. In the case of one institution which has geographically separated campuses, graduate education is coordinated by a council which includes graduate deans and faculty representatives from each campus. In another case, the graduate dean administers graduate programs that are offered on three separate campuses. In addition to overseeing the graduate program, graduate deans or their counterparts are usually responsible for administering fellowships, scholarships, and traineeships, and other forms of student aid or other matters of general interest to graduates.

Graduate deans usually relate to departments through graduate advisers who serve as their deputies and act as liaison men with graduate students. Deans may also relate directly with students through graduate student organizations, advisory committees, graduate clubs, teaching assistant unions, or on an individual basis through appointments. They relate formally to the faculty through its academic senate or its committees on graduate degrees and somewhat less formally through the graduate advising system. Those deans who are included in the line through which research proposals flow for approval may have closer ties with academicians than do deans who are not consulted about faculty research activities.

Nichols (1965) describes the role of the graduate dean as ambiguous. Its ambiguity derives partly from the fact that his office reflects every facet of the diversity found in American education and partly because recent attempts to "federalize" American higher education lead inevitably to the graduate division. As the producer of "doctors, lawyers, and Indian chiefs" for every social need, the graduate dean is "charged with leading the leaders among academic

men, and with using his capacity for leadership to contribute to
the development and maturation of more academic men" (Whaley,
1965). The awesome nature of this task, and its potential for cen-
tralizing control in a czar, has led major universities to refrain
from investing this office with power. Any influence the dean has
must emanate from his reputation as a scholar or from his particular
charisma. The effective graduate dean must, of necessity, be a superior human being. The President of the American Council on
Education noted that of the 245 graduate deans in the United States
the balance of power to bring about change (or maintain the status
quo) rests in the hands of just over forty. These are generally found
in major universities.

There were no discernible patterns in the duties and responsibilities of the deans interviewed in this study. On a purely subjective evaluation they appeared to be personable men who saw
themselves as overseers of academic excellence. However, most of
them were quick to admit that their powers were limited to their
ability to stimulate the faculty or to push it toward reform. Usually
their innovative role is played from the sidelines, where, in the
words of one dean, "I might beat the drums and the bush to get
interest, cash, space, or whatever else is needed to get innovation
or reform underway." As initiators of change, graduate deans described themselves as innovators by persuasion rather than by administrative power. Only one dean, who receives an independent
allocation of funds for developmental purposes, said that he could
provide seed money to encourage new ideas for graduate education.
Others said that they often "work on the academic deans to induce
them to provide the faculty or the money needed to implement new
ideas."

Seven graduate deans said that they had no budgetary control and no voice in the appointment and promotion of the graduate
faculty other than a perfunctory or courtesy role. Three others held
budgetary control because graduate education was organized as an
arm of the administration and as deans they held an office in it.
In all but three cases deans played a role in the selection and appointment of teaching and research assistants, trainee fellows, or
post-doctoral fellows. Because funds for these purposes are allocated

or withheld by the graduate office, the dean can control and direct their distribution. This is a bone of contention on which some faculty members chew vigorously.

When graduate deans were asked to comment on the problems associated with their roles, three said that their positions were weak because they had no role in development and no authority with respect to the operation of research. In the words of one, "Research is the heart of the Ph.D. program, yet as dean I have no role to play in it." Another dean complained that the graduate office should play a major role in planning where the university should place its emphasis but that he was not a member of the university planning committee.

Keeping up with the work involved in processing anywhere from 3500 to more than 10,000 graduate students occupies a major portion of the graduate dean's time. Currently his major concern centers on what one dean described as "the terrifying nightmare of financing graduate education." Deans in the private institutions were particularly troubled because they realized that their institution could price itself out of the competition for good students if it had to resort to increasing tuition. Academic deans in public institutions reported that they had already taken steps to accommodate to reduced budgets by not filling some vacancies, curtailing new programs, and becoming more selective in admissions. Deans were concerned not only about where and how to get the money to support graduate students but also about how to allocate that which was available and how to avoid supporting those whom one dean called "capitalists' students." Some thought that recent Congressional rulings and new draft laws would increase this problem and place a heavy and costly administrative burden on the university.

Graduate deans registered deep concern about the university's inability to provide supervised teaching experience for those who plan to join college faculties. Several deans felt that this was the greatest single problem in the doctoral program. They expressed the belief that many teaching assistants are antagonistic to the institution because they get little or no help in this area. Another dean believed that the doctoral program fails to convey the message to the student that if he wants to solve the problems of this technological age he must develop himself in a systematic way and not expect to jump stages. He noted that a credibility gap appears to exist between what the faculty say about careers in the particular discipline and what students see them do. He suggested that students need better information on how one moves sequentially into a career. According to this dean some students expect instant recognition when they acquire the Ph.D. If they fail to get it, they strike out at the university or the establishment as having been negligent in its placement role.

Deans were particularly distressed at the low morale and high attrition rate among graduate students. Some said that they often acted in a mediating role in attempts to find help for students who panic in the face of their problems. Some do this by urging departments to make their environments less impersonal and more stimulating. One dean reported that he spends "a considerable amount of time trying to keep good students cool, urging departments to avoid placing them under undue stress, and keeping up morale on both sides." Still another dean said that he constantly urged department chairmen to make clear to the students what their requirements entail, and tried to impress upon the faculty the fact that the doctoral student is their major responsibility.

As a general rule in the institutions studied, the faculty members in each discipline are organized around a chairman, head, or executive committee. These persons hold office generally, but not exclusively, by virtue of their selection by the faculty. Candidates for these roles are usually screened by a "search committee." If the faculty approves the committee's choice, the recommendation is transmitted to the academic dean. If the dean approves the name of the appointee, it is transmitted through the appropriate channels. In some institutions the departmental constitution provides that the faculty may elect its own executive committee, and in other cases the elected chairman selects the members himself. In one institution, executive committee members are automatically eligible for membership by reason of their roles as directors of subdivisions within the department. In most cases executive committees make as well as administer policy. In other cases the committee makes policy and the chairman administers it.

In one institution statutory regulations give faculty members the right to decide whether their departments will be administered by a chairman or by a head. The distinction lies in the fact that the head exercises executive discretion on many matters whereas the chairman is supposed to submit all issues for faculty consideration. In actual practice, the working style of those who were interviewed in this institution appeared to represent a combination of these roles. That is, heads often perform as chairmen, chairmen sometimes act as heads. Because the appointment of a head reduces the amount of time the faculty must devote to administrative details, strong departments usually select heads. If the faculty can persuade a well-respected colleague to assume this role, the probability is he may become a career administrator.

With rare exceptions, department chairmen operate through standing or ad hoc faculty committees which make formal reports or recommendations to the chairman. These formal reports or recommendations are important because they become matters of record. On the other hand, most of the chairmen who were interviewed for this study said that they obtained their best insights into departmental matters and their best ideas for their resolution through informal channels. These included face-to-face encounters in conferences, phone calls to knowledgeable staff members, memos, discussions over coffee in the faculty lounge, or a personal request for advice. In these less formal meetings department chairmen said that they found it possible to personalize and verbalize their own needs to sympathetic staff members, to gauge the intensity of the faculty's concern on sensitive issues, or to learn how the votes on a specific question were distributed.

There were wide differences among the chairmen with respect to the frequency with which they called faculty meetings. Some called the faculty to order weekly. Others said that they called one or two meetings a year. Still others hold semimonthly business luncheons and several reported that they held an occasional all-day session or department retreat. The latter sessions were called principally for purposes of information sharing or exchange. Some of these were held in a meeting place off campus or in the home of the chairman.

Commonly, among the institutions in this study, an appointment to a department chairmanship involves a five-year commitment, although in some cases appointments are limited to three years. Even though the constitutions of most departments specify a limited termination period for those who hold this office, 10 per cent of the chairmen who were interviewed described their appointments as permanent. According to one, "tenure in the chairmanship" develops as the result of faculty satisfaction with the incumbent—or by faculty default. For example, in one institution the chemistry department had had only four chairmen in this century, yet the faculty participates yearly in a pro forma vote on this office. In another case the call for a vote was never made and the incumbent was accepted because he made few demands on the faculty's time for committee work.

About 25 per cent of the departments in the sample are administered on a rotating chairmanship in which members serve their turn. In these cases the term is generally from one to three years, and appointments are renewable for another term (or for some predetermined period) if the incumbent and department members are agreeable. Several of those interviewed described themselves as "acting chairmen" serving in the absence of the regular man or in the interim between the naming of a permanent replacement. Rotating chairmen, acting chairmen, and some three- or five-year appointees explicitly stated that they view themselves in a "holding" rather than a leadership role. Many said that they were anxiously anticipating the expiration of their term or the "fulfillment of their duty to the department." Only a few seemed to find the department chairmanship a rewarding role. Many said that the work was inclined to bog one down in unstimulating administrative or dull routine matters. Many spoke nostalgically of getting back to teaching or research.

The administrative styles of department chairmen and their role perceptions deserve study. Among the chairmen interviewed in this sample, wide differences in style were evident. Some said that they sought to give form, substance, and direction to their departments; others described themselves as "office managers," "department secretaries," or "messengers" for the faculty. Some said that they held legislative as well as executive authority and used both; others said that while they held authority they would not act on most matters without faculty consultation. Still others felt that their role was to carry out the wishes or decisions of the faculty "even though I did not agree with them." A few said that if they found themselves in opposition to a major recommendation of the faculty they would express their opposition and submit their resignation at the same time.

Many chairmen said that they immersed themselves in most administrative details but many others delegated details to administrative adjuncts. Some continue to teach in order to keep abreast of their field and in informal contact with the faculty; others devote full time to the chairmanship. A few of the latter said that they remained aloof from informal contacts with the faculty in an effort to retain their independence. In large departments the chairman is usually aided by an associate or assistant chairman whom he appoints or by a nonacademic administrative assistant who assumes responsibility for the business details of the department. Departments which have large research grants and contracts may also have a separate administrative assistant who coordinates and manages these complex transactions.

With respect to departmental administration, academic deans tended to prefer the five-year appointment for chairman. They believed that this brought a fresh approach to the leadership of the department and enabled a chairman to institute his ideas yet encouraged a periodic review of the department's direction. In two cases, deans preferred a three-year appointment with an option for reappointment for a second term. Other deans felt that the shorter term left little opportunity for innovative planning and usually resulted in the chairman acting as a tentative manager of departmental operations.

The committee structure on most college campuses is complex, diverse, and wide-ranging. It can consume a staggering portion of the faculty members' time and energies. It is so interlocking in some institutions that periodic stalemates occur because of the difficulty in scheduling meetings. Those who have studied the university committee system sometimes describe it as a feeble effort "to give the aura of democracy to what is basically a federation, or at best a representative democracy tempered by an oligarchy" (Clark, 1967). Although they expressed faith in the principle of advise and consent, deans and department chairmen said that they found the committee system cumbersome. Some described the committee as a device for escaping responsibility. Said one chairman, "If you set up a committee, you can steer yourself off a cliff and blame someone else as the driver." Others view the appointment of a committee as a delaying tactic. All were uneasy about the proliferation of committees and of the inroads which committee matters make on the faculty members' time and energy. The problem is acute in small departments in which the faculty usually act as a committee of the whole. This organization requires that all members must keep abreast of departmental issues and with all those affairs that affect the department's standing in the total institution.

Technically, standing and ad hoc committees act in advisory capacity, but most chairmen said that in practice they ask for full faculty discussion of committee reports before they make decisions. Beyond this point administrative behavior seems to vary. Some chairmen rarely ask for a faculty vote on committee recommendations, either because they want to retain discretionary influence or, in cases where faculty opinion is divided, because they do not want to force lines to harden. Other chairmen ask for a faculty ballot on all academic matters but act independently on all other departmental affairs.

Clark (1967) notes that as career logic channels the energy and insight of the faculty inside departmental walls, the members tend to withdraw their energies and their interests from the problems of the total institution and to develop a trained incapacity to see its problems or to consider them to be serious. Others (Kerr 1963, Millett 1968, Jencks and Riesman 1968) have observed that as university faculty authority shifts from protecting the rights of the whole to protecting the rights of particular segments or individuals, the latter often take on the characteristics of academic empires or entrepreneurs. In these roles some units or some individual professors devote a large share of their energy and time to gathering funds, space, and other resources on the strength of their own reputation or independently of the university. Those interviewed implied that such weakening in the collective power of the faculty strains internal relations and makes campus-wide decisions difficult to achieve. At the department level it leads to tentative or pragmatic

rather than to firm academic planning, encourages political gerry-
mandering among special-interest groups, and leaves the graduate
student insecure and plagued with uncertainty.

According to some department chairmen the academic entrepreneur is a mixed blessing in the department. If it is heavily
supplied with them, the chairman may be hard pressed to staff the
teaching program. Often he must resolve his dilemma by dropping
sections of classes, increasing class size, or appointing two inexperi-
enced instructors for the price of the entrepreneur who is off win-
ning funds and influencing agency people. Some observers see the
rise of the entrepreneur as a causative factor in the growing impersonality on the large campuses.

Several of the institutions studied have recently made attempts to reformulate the administrative decision-making process
so as to involve faculty members and students more directly in governance. Deans and department chairmen occasionally voiced their
concern about the commitment and qualifications of those who participated. One person interviewed reported that after a period during which the institution was overloaded with administrators—
which gave the faculty the idea that they had no responsibility—
his institution had attempted to correct this impression by getting
the faculty participating and involved. The result, in his judgment,
was "an administrative blunderbuss." He noted:

> We need to return to the idea that there are people with re-
> sponsibility for change. We must define this responsibility
> and reward the one who assumes it. . . . He can't take
> pride in his job if he has no leadership to exercise. . . . If
> he is a referee when things go wrong and is responsible for
> things he can't control he is a fool to stay with the job. . . .
> If a man qualifies as an administrator, he should have re-
> sponsibility for making decisions without having to consult,
> refer and communicate with everyone down the line.

The case for the full-time administrator was supported in many of
the comments made by those interviewed in this study. Although
most of the incumbent chairmen disclaimed interest in administration as a career, they stressed the importance of the office and saw
the need for individuals who could commit themselves fully to administrative leadership.

The departmentalization of knowledge, and the internal hierarchical system of the university which is based on rank, degrees, and awards, are important determinants of the style of life into which the faculty and the Ph.D. candidate—as a future college or university teacher—are shaped. Because departments generally enjoy wide autonomy in setting up and regulating their academic requirements, they are not only strong administrative units but important social units as well. With only minor exceptions, interdisciplinary or interdepartmental interaction has been rarely encouraged on the university campus, even between those units whose lineage can be traced to a common source. Most faculty and Ph.D. students are tightly locked into programs confined to their own discipline.

Those who defend the department as a viable organizational form tend to base their arguments on matters of administrative convenience rather than on logical disciplinary centralities. Basically, the department serves as a device for covering all the bases that must be touched by those in control of budgets, personnel appointments, promotions, scheduling, and space allocation. In practice, the department often serves as a watershed to prevent leakage of students or resources into contiguous areas or to otherwise protect the interests of its members. It is basically a social device. As a social entity it provides a shelter or a home for those who hold interests in common. In this sense, it serves as the single most powerful obstacle to the development of the integrative process—or to an all-encompassing community—which, presumably, is the ultimate goal of scholarship. As a modern counterpart to the guild, the department works basically for the interest and security of its members. This leads to alignment and communication with members of the discipline who are located elsewhere. As professionalization grows greater segregation and exclusiveness result. Some of those interviewed suggested that collective bargaining or unionization may be the next step taken "to close the circle for the guilds."

For the most part, each graduate department acts as a separate enclave which exercises an effort toward keeping its members "academically pure." Under this rubric many departments not only discourage their own students from taking work "outside" but also bar "outsiders" (non-majors) from their courses lest they "weaken the level of the discussion or upset the standards." Implicitly or explicitly the student soon learns that interest in an outside field may jeopardize his standing as a serious scholar in his own field. By reducing the orbit of the student's academic contacts, the department restricts his models to the immediate faculty and socializes him to its norms and values.

As the purveyor of fellowships, assistantships, research funds, and other awards, the department evokes the deep loyalty of the student and heightens its charismatic role. Later in his career the professional association replaces the department. It displays its particular charisma by making him visible among his colleagues. If it elects him to its leadership, his interest in outside affairs, in teaching, and in students may have to be set aside or given less of his time, energy, and attention.

Departmentalization as an organizational model for promoting scholarship has been severely criticized in the literature on higher education. Many critics suggest that until departmental walls are removed or at least made semipermeable, wide-scale systematic reform will be impossible, and the students' pleas for a recognition of the interconnections of knowledge will go unheeded. Various critics have described the extent to which some departments contribute to the fragmenting of the university's effort to preserve a sense of community. By acting as autonomous power blocks, organically related but operationally elite (or by adding appendages in the form of research institutes, groups, or centers), Kerr (1963) notes that some departments remove themselves from direct institutional surveillance and set the stage for the rise of the multiversity.

In this same vein, Lichtman (1967) observed that many departments operate under a kind of "mutual security agreement that assures each the safety of his own domain." The net result of this behavior is a kind of feudalistic system where obstacles (or inducements) are produced at certain points to prevent egress. Still others believe that departmentalization has created a phenomenon described as "the ethnocentrism of disciplines," in which "in-group" partisanship or "tribalisms" become destructive of the spontaneous integrative socializing characteristic of a community of scholars (Campbell, 1969). On some campuses, except in crisis situations, faculties rarely act collectively in terms of their responsibility to the institution as a whole. A measure of the extent to which departments are subdivided and of the degree to which community exists within them was obtained from faculty responses to the question: How would you describe the research relationships of the faculty in your department?

Forty-four per cent of the respondents said that their departments included one group of faculty members who worked together as a team plus various other individuals who preferred to work alone. Twenty-six per cent described their department as made up mainly of individual scholars each of whom worked independently. Twenty-two per cent reported that their faculty comprised several research groups and eight per cent said that all members of their departments worked as a single unit on a broad research project. Although many of the faculty members reported that they do not work on group research per se, 89 per cent of the respondents said that the research of the department was either "closely" or "somewhat" related. The remaining 11 per cent described the research activity of individuals in their departments as unrelated. Implied in these data are the kinds of experiences available to students and the kinds of "models of men at work" they perceive.

Some of those interviewed observed a direct correlation between increases in departmentalization and decreases in community on their campuses and even within departments. In some cases, departments are subdivided into aggregates of groups each of which is interested in a particular segment of the central specialty and has little interaction with other segments. In the words of the chairman of the department of sociology in one institution: "Everything has become grist for the sociologists' mill, including the mill. We now have five sub-specialties in the department . . . each group goes its own way. . . . I've asked each coordinator to tell me what there is about his sub-specialty that does not fit into the general concept of sociology. . . . The lines of communication between department members are being more and more attenuated." One academic dean noted that some departments under his jurisdiction rarely got within communication distance of other departments. He found within the same department "enclaves whose interests are marked off in centuries, decades, specific movements, events, or persons." In his judgment departmentalization "allows some men to spend their lives immersed in thirteenth-century literature or in the writings of Shakespeare viewed from the technician's bench, thus they fail to learn for themselves what message these works have in our time." It seems clear from the data that some men also fail to convince a socially concerned student generation that the work of their discipline is relevant to society. Because they fail to get involved in dialogue or in the interaction that takes place outside of their own departmental walls, these professors lack the distance of the analyst and often fail to apply a liberal approach to learning per se.

Only 46 per cent of the graduate faculty respondents thought that the department was the best organizational form for their own scholarly development and for the development of their doctoral students. The remainder believe that some variant of the intergroup organizational structure is more conducive to scholarship or more functional for teaching and research in their field. Figures 1 and 2 show the types of their preferred organization patterns and the pattern on which the various disciplines are currently operating. While a majority of the respondents preferred forms which provided a more extensive and effective scope for interdisciplinary relationships than is feasible under the departmental pattern, 78 per cent of the respondents reported that their academic activities were organized around a single department. This does not necessarily mean that interdisciplinary relationships were nonexistent, but it does mean that administratively relations with other fields were awkward, cumbersome, and costly and that the faculty tended to avoid official relationships.

Little in the education of most college and university teachers has prepared them for an interdisciplinary (or a social action) role. Instead, their intense identification with their own discipline renders most scholars uncomfortable and inept outside of its protective confines. If his preoccupation with a special area of interest did not exist before the scholar's formal admission into the academy, everything inside it, from its idioms to its ideologies, constrains him to acquire it.

Arrowsmith (1966), Jencks and Riesman (1968), Barzun (1968), and others have commented on the need for men who can jump across departmental lines, men who will not toe the line, individuals who are as large as life, irrepressible, perhaps troublesome,

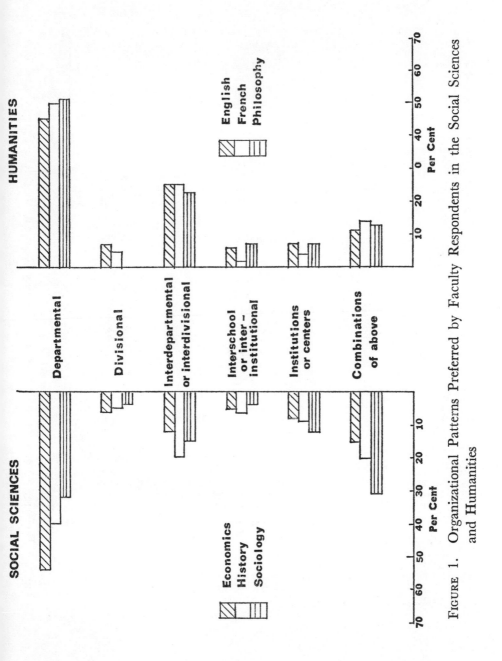

FIGURE 1. Organizational Patterns Preferred by Faculty Respondents in the Social Sciences and Humanities

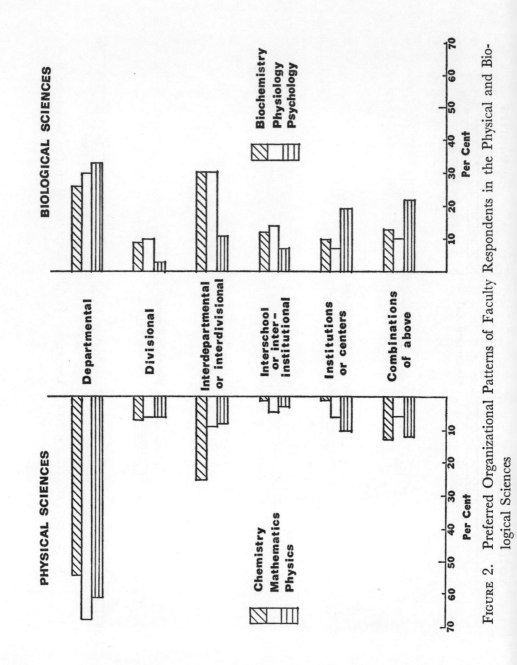

FIGURE 2. Preferred Organizational Patterns of Faculty Respondents in the Physical and Biological Sciences

but exemplary. In the judgment of one of these observers, if there are not enough interdisciplinary individuals to be found in the university itself they must be imported into it in every conceivable way. Deans and department chairmen in this study reported that this is done through the appointment of visiting professors, scholars-in-residence, or lecturers. Some institutions appoint professors-at-large, whose skills lie at the interface of several disciplines or whose interests bridge the gap between related fields. Unfortunately, these short-run solutions do not adequately address the central problem, which is how to create mechanisms by which scholars in related fields can relate to each other with a minimum of administrative encumbrance.

Progress in planning interdisciplinary graduate programs is greatly inhibited by the organization of disciplines around the departmental structure. The administrative and personnel complications are considerable when, through a joint appointment, a professor attempts to straddle departmental boundaries. Even though they find value in the interdisciplinary approach, department chairmen reported that the idiosyncrasies in the ranking and promotion system often make it professionally unwise for a professor to accept an appointment as a member of an interdisciplinary group. This is particularly true for the young professor who has not yet achieved tenure. His problems arise because the part-time nature of his appointment may cut him off from voting or from certain privileges and rights reserved for full-time members, such as participation on important decision-making committees. Lacking these contacts he often fails to gain a sense of identification in either department. This is crucial in terms of his chances for promotion, especially if he is known only peripherally to those who are asked to review his cause. One department chairman may find him acceptable for promotion but his other chairman may not know him well enough to endorse his advancement. If there is any unevenness in the quantity or quality of his jointly sponsored efforts, or differences in the criteria used by the departments in determining promotion, he may be caught in an impasse. In some cases, the expectations of one department in which the instructor holds an appointment conflict with the expectations of the other. Although department chairmen said that they generally negotiated informally to resolve these problems, the uncertainty and strain of the process often drive the interdisciplinary person back to one "home."

Department chairmen reported that unfortunately promotion committees often suspect that the man who accepts a joint appointment is not quite up to the quality of the full-time faculty. In other cases he is looked upon as a generalist who lacks the scholarly depth of the specialist. In still other cases resentment occurs because those who hold joint appointments are, as a rule, excused from administrative duties. This puts an added burden on the regular department members. Sometimes the man who holds a joint appointment is physically separated from his primary discipline or he may be housed in two places. This arrangement tends to attenuate communication, weaken the identification process, and present scheduling problems.

In several of the institutions in our sample, only tenured professors are given joint appointments. In one case, the administrative policy of the institution specifies that all joint appointments must be arranged in uneven apportionments of the instructor's time; the department which holds the greatest share of his time becomes responsible for negotiating his advancement, granting him voting privileges, and providing him with a primary home. Often, in order to circumvent administrative involvement, the joint appointment is regarded as a "courtesy appointment." Such assignments require little or no formal rearrangements, although in some cases the participant is given a title which designates or identifies him as a member of a "field" program. One of the institutions in the sample operates with a general budget for all instructional purposes, which allows interdisciplinary associations to be made simply on the basis of faculty interest and student need.

The history of formal interdisciplinary programs reveals that they have had short life spans. Several department chairmen in the sample described interesting and innovative programs which had wide popular appeal at their inception but fell apart within a short time. Causes for their demise usually included the lack of a continuous administrative authority, the heavy demands imposed on those who hold responsibility in two areas, the lack of identification with a "place," and the administrative red tape involved. Department chairmen reported that "interdisciplinary persons" were difficult to

find and that those who did accept appointments often found themselves "overworked and overlooked."

In spite of these problems interdisciplinary programming has
been on the increase in all institutions in the study. One university
is currently reviewing a proposal to establish a division of interdisciplinary studies which would provide the administrative mechanism for processing and expediting new courses and programs. In
the same institution a pilot Ph.D. program in Mathematics-Science
and Education has operated successfully for three years. The expectation is that on the basis of experiences gained in developing this
program, the interdisciplinary division plan will be approved. If it
is, it will reduce the administrative paraphernalia and provide ease
of operation for new programs that have natural affinities.

Interestingly enough, 60 per cent of the faculty respondents
foresee an increase in interdisiciplinary offerings in the next decade,
35 per cent expect the present level of activity to be maintained,
and only 4 per cent expect interest in these relationships to decline.
Evidently they do not expect that the introduction of interdisciplinary offerings will dilute or appreciably diminish the emphasis
on specialization. In fact, corollary with interdisciplinary increases
53 per cent of the faculty respondents envision an increase in specialization in the immediate future, 43 per cent expect the emphasis
on specialization to remain at present levels, and only 4 per cent
foresee a decrease in this emphasis.

Appreciable numbers of doctoral students in each of the
twelve disciplines reported favorably on their interdisciplinary experiences, as shown in Table 1. As indicated by these data, the program in physiology appears to have exposed students to interdisciplinary relationships more frequently than they were in other fields.
The interdependent nature of the subject matter in physiology and
the special environment needed for its research has apparently fostered an alliance between the academic department and the medical
school. In those institutions in which theoretical and clinical studies
are geographically separated, department chairmen reported that
the student who is interested in pure research often finds that he
relates only tangentially with his discipline. This creates some problems of identification and articulation but generally broadens the
student's background. The recent development of centers and other

Table 1

DEGREE TO WHICH STUDENTS IN VARIOUS DISCIPLINES FOUND
INTERDISCIPLINARY RELATIONS MEANINGFUL
(in percentages)

Discipline	Very Meaningful	Moderately Meaningful	Rarely Meaningful	No basis for judging
Biochemistry	31.6	42.0	17.1	9.3
Chemistry	24.6	34.4	22.0	18.9
Economics	22.6	30.2	25.0	22.2
English	25.5	27.9	21.4	25.2
French	30.2	33.6	12.1	24.2
History	33.4	31.7	17.2	17.7
Mathematics	18.3	21.3	29.9	30.6
Philosophy	34.9	22.9	20.8	21.4
Physics	20.2	28.0	28.0	23.9
Physiology	53.8	34.0	6.6	5.7
Psychology	26.4	31.3	23.9	18.4
Sociology	39.1	30.0	14.2	16.6

institutions outside of the department may indicate the need for a mechanism which will allow freer interdisciplinary interaction. Some see the growth in the number of such independent interdisciplinary organizations as the beginning of alternate forms of university education (Sanford, 1969). The Oregon Graduate Center (Benedict, 1965) is one example of this move.

Changing
the Program

5

One fact emerges clearly from an analysis of the interviews with department chairmen. Each man (there were no women among the 120 persons interviewed) believes that the organizational relationships and form of his department is changing at an accelerated pace. Because it was not possible to establish a baseline from which the momentum began in each case, it is difficult to evaluate the extent or degree of that change or movement. It is apparent, however, that the dynamics of change as reported by department chairmen are not consonant across fields. Some departments are changing in terms of increased enrollments, others are cutting (or dropping) back; some are moving in the direction of greater specialization, others toward generalization; some are leaning toward closer affiliation with science and technology, others are curtailing their association with these methodologies; some departments are moving, if gingerly, toward greater involvement with social or mission-oriented research, a few others are drawing further inward toward discipline-oriented activities; some departments are attempting to define their purpose and limit their boundaries, others are sprawling in all directions and ignoring any responsibility for stating purposive goals.

A broad impression derived from the interviews and from institutional data on recent changes is that the general movement in departments is toward increasing interdisciplinary or multidisciplinary affiliations. If this is an accurate assessment, it is but faintly adumbrated in the organizational structure. Its real dimensions are discernible in the informal faculty interrelationships and encounters, in the increases in team research, in the growth of interdisciplinary seminars, colloquiums, and research forums, and in the introduction of new interdisciplinary journals and information retrieval systems. These may be a portent of an organizational revolution in the university. It would appear from the data in this study that unless the reformers find leaders who can give a sense of purpose and direction to their reorganization, such a revolution would be fatal to the university as we know it. At the moment the movement is amorphous, lacking in leaders, and sporadic.

One obstacle to organization along logically related (and affective) areas rather than along administratively simplified units, is the penchant of scholars for not exploring the interfaces of their disciplines. For example, many observers argue that the physical and social sciences might, with mutual benefit, collaborate on problems that have interrelating variables. But they almost invariably reach a stand-off, because the social scientists literally say to the physical scientists: "Tell us what you plan to do and we'll analyze the change it produces." To which the physical scientist replies: "Tell us what changes you want and we'll produce the technology to effect them." Department chairmen, who might play the role of mediators or guides, claim that they are kept so busy protecting the interests of "the" department that they have no time to encourage collaboration. Small departments fear that to do so would be tantamount to the lamb sitting down with the lion. Since the instinct for survival is strong in most departments, there is reluctance to enter relationships which would submerge a department's identity, undercut its individuality, or threaten its autonomy.

Graduate faculties have generally leaned toward academic

conservatism. When changes are proposed in graduate programs or policies, a faculty is prone to construe them as attacks on the academic life style. Because that style is cherished and carefully cultivated during graduate school and thereafter, attempts to change it often meet with the full weight of guild disapproval. In view of this tradition it is instructive to find that 40 per cent of the graduate faculty members who responded to the questionnaire for this study registered the belief that radical reorganization is needed in the structure of the university if that institution is to respond to the radical changes currently occurring in technology and in society. Since the structure of the university has a strong influence on the life styles and social patterns of the faculty, it seems logical to assume that a significant number of faculty members are ready to accept alterations in their conventional roles and associations.

Faculty comment in the questionnaire on the need for structural reform was mixed, but it tended to lean toward a preference for rapid evolutionary change rather than revolutionary change. While many respondents advocated substantial reforms in some parts of the university's structure, they expressed general satisfaction with its essential form. The areas that were frequently mentioned as being critically in need of change included the curriculum, the governance of students, the humanization of the institution, and the number and character of the students who are admitted. The responses of those who favored radical change were as follows (in percentages) :

Biochemistry	47.5	Mathematics	38.5
Chemistry	30.8	Philosophy	31.8
Economics	31.9	Physics	31.0
English	40.9	Physiology	37.5
French	48.1	Psychology	48.1
History	37.3	Sociology	52.4

In statements that were added to this item in the questionnaire some faculty members seemed to express a fear of "what technology is doing to us" and a distrust of those who bear gifts. Their frequent references to the "cannibalistic tendencies" of the military-industrial complex and to the "lure of corporate capital" were generally coupled with the observation that submission to these pressures threat-

ens institutional integrity and induces serious organizational imbalances in the academic emphasis. Arguing for a more humane
approach to learning, respondents suggested that while technology
may affect the way research is conducted it should not dictate the
way questions are posed, conclusions are confirmed, or evidence is
weighed.

Commenting on the need for a more humanistic approach
to university organization, some respondents suggested that the
modern university has become the successor to the church and is
now the primary institution for the preservation of purely reflective
thought, for encouraging responsible behavior, and for helping those
who need assistance. As such, these respondents argued that with
respect to technology, universities should concentrate their efforts
and reserve their resources for those aspects of science and technology that are conducive to improvements in the human condition.
Some commentators would organize technology in separate institutes or tie technology to specific disciplines. Others believed that
computer technology and communication media should be organized as a separate unit servicing all fields which might profit from
their use.

A review of the curriculum and policies of the ten institutions to ascertain whether the faculty's professed interest in change
has been converted into action revealed that three of the institutions
had made some recent changes in their authority structure in an
attempt to realign relationships and broaden the governance base,
and several others had activated wide-scale review of needed curriculum reform. While some of these resulted in modification of the
Ph.D. requirements, little that might be classified as radically different or innovative had occurred. One possible exception was the proposal by three of the universities to offer the Doctor of Arts in some
fields. It is too early to speculate on whether the recommendations
of the various study committees—at Stanford (1969), Columbia
(1969), and the University of California, Berkeley (1966)—will be
accepted and eventually implemented by the faculty. Speaking of
these recommendations, deans observed that ideas hatched in committees often fail to receive warmth or nurturance from those who
fear being inconvenienced, dislocated, or challenged by the recommended change. They observed that it is difficult to initiate reform

because—as with any system that is essentially self-authenticating—an attack on the system may seem to attack the roles and the competence of those who operate it. For this reason, deans and department chairmen reported that the most cogent force for reform arises externally, and that the most promising device for introducing reform is to bring in a "change agent" from the outside. This is especially true if a new program is to be started. An alternative would be to induce a highly respected scholar within the department to devote himself to curriculum matters on a full-time basis for a limited period.

These data probably reflect the fact that the socialization of the graduate school and the high specificity of the education and training it provides gives the university faculty little experience in instructional planning or administrative responsibility. It also provides little understanding of or appreciation for the unifying aspects of the university's total program.

The federal and foundation funds that have poured into university research during the past three decades have broadened the scope, increased the pace, and compounded the complexity of scholarship. Most notably this has altered the relationships of many campus researchers by promoting team or group research and by sparking the need for a long chain of supporting services. In some institutions the coordination of services gives the research effort the characteristics of a massive bureaucratic operation. The auxiliary staff, including research assistants, clerical help, editors, and consultants may outnumber the professional research staff by ratios as high as ten to one. The contribution of the para-professionals who assist in university research has had an important impact on the faculty researcher's productivity and work habits. There are signs that some of these assistants may eventually assume full status as principal investigators or directors of their own projects. The work and career styles of this group of university personnel appear to emulate the working style of the faculty researcher. Conversely some faculty have acquired the ideologies of the nonacademic research staff.

A service increasingly indispensable to research is that supplied by the computer. Although computers are used most frequently in the quantitative fields, 16 per cent of the faculty members in this study reported that their particular research interest lends itself to their usage. Some respondents acknowledged that, lacking knowledge or understanding of computer application, they preferred to leave this methodology to young professors or to graduate students. Still others admitted that they had an antipathy to technology and deliberately avoided research problems which require automated equipment.

Simon's (1966) observation that computer technology might be the means of disassembling and reassembling academic fences has particular relevance for graduate education. The widespread use of the computer has revolutionized the types of problems which faculty and students investigate together and has given them new tools and techniques for data processing and analysis. Practically all students are now advised to acquire some knowledge or skill in this research tool. Ninety-two per cent of the faculty respondents in biochemistry and sociology expect that training in computer usage will become a required part of the graduate student's background. Eighty-two per cent of the respondents in all fields expect to see an increase in the need for this training, 16 per cent believe that the need will remain constant, and less than one per cent expect that current demands for computer training will decrease.

Some critics of university education argue that a preoccupation with scientism and the availability of computerized research tools have seduced graduate schools into overemphasizing quantitative research methodologies or into minimizing or ignoring education in qualitative methods. They charge that this imbalance has not only inhibited attempts to develop creative approaches to knowledge but has also led to a loss of humanism in the university and in society. Some indict the Ph.D. program for these failures and point to the need for academic programs that will respect the pluralism—and in some cases the ambiguity—in the approaches required in less scientifically based disciplines or in nonquantifiable fields.

In a study of the various research methods employed in doctoral dissertations, Knoell (1966) found that some students used sophisticated computer methods on very small samples or on problems that would lend themselves better to other approaches. She noted that in some cases the student's choice of a research problem appeared to be dictated by the means available rather than by the goals of the research. Some of those interviewed also observed that the misuse of computerized methods can seriously narrow the scope of the scholarly ideas dealt with, and thus hinder the subsequent development of Ph.D. students.

When members of the graduate faculties in the ten universities in the sample were asked whether, in their judgment, the doctoral program in their departments reinforced a trend toward quantitative rather than creative research approaches, 32 per cent thought that it did, 49 per cent thought that it did not, and the remainder were undecided. Economists, physiologists, biochemists, and physicists agreed with the proposition more frequently (41 per cent) while mathematicians, philosophers, sociologists, and psychologists rejected it more frequently (58 per cent) than respondents in other disciplines.

In a corollary item, graduate faculties were asked whether the doctoral program in their departments "stressed scientism at the expense of humanism." Thirty-two per cent of the respondents agreed that it did, 54 per cent said that it did not, and the remainder were undecided. Economists, chemists, and physiologists agreed more frequently with the inference (42 per cent) and respondents in French, history, philosophy, English, and psychology rejected it more frequently (65 per cent) than did those in other fields. Obviously this issue involves a large number of variables besides research methodology. However, because the research emphasis in a graduate department generally reflects the interests, skills, aspirations, and values of the department—which are in turn reflected in its academic program—it is of interest to note the deep concern voiced by those who commented on this issue. That concern was shared across all disciplines. While they acknowledged that science and technology serve important functions, commentators decried what they perceived as an overemphasis on tools and techniques and the conversion of universities into "technical institutes" or "knowledge factories." Many appeared troubled about what one referred to as the "log-jam in new knowledge" and others were critical of the practice of collecting massive quantities of data without pausing to study their relationships, evaluate their relevance, or secure a compass heading. While they expressed admiration for the educational potential of the new technologies, faculty members often noted with regret that this potential was being spent in the interest of goals they could not accept. Judging by the fears expressed in some of the comments there is a distrust of cybernetics and of computerized systems—or, more specifically, an implied mistrust of those who use and develop such systems. To a large extent the mistrust appears to arise from the arcane aura of power which science and technology generate. Their connotation as the "hard sciences"—which originally described their instrumentation—simultaneously communicates the impression that the acquisition of knowledge in these fields requires a high level of intellectual effort and a disciplined methodology. Some humanists in the sample see this as a "masquerade" in which the hard sciences not only pose as respectable university disciplines but successfully intimidate disciples in the non-sciences to accept their methods. A few respondents worried about "communication control by technicians" and about the power held by those "who merely know how to push buttons." The contentious issues in this argument appear to be surfacing on some campuses as computer science centers petition to become formal departments or academic fields of study. In the meantime, the nature of university research makes their services practically indispensable to the graduate faculty and to graduate students.

When graduate deans and department chairmen were questioned on this issue during the interviews, they conceded that the decades ahead will make increasing demands for new kinds of trained intelligence, one of which will surely be for experts in computer technology. However, they questioned whether the university can or should provide the education and training required in this and other new technical service areas. Some expressed the fear that as pressures arise the university may find itself in the position of producing "technicians with Ph.D.'s rather than creative and imaginative scholars."

Universities have been among the first institutions to experience the impact of the revolutions that are occurring in communication. Through electronic systems and satellites orbiting in fixed positions in space, the means through which scholars communicate with each other have been appreciably expanded and considerably altered. It is now possible for the essence of a researcher's findings to be flashed around the world and made available to other researchers or users almost before the ink is dry on his written report. Shared computer services, closed circuit television, and automated library facilities reduce the tedium of research and allow more time for analysis. McLuhan's thesis that linear communication will become less important than visual communication is already being documented, and Gouldner's contention that scholars are cosmopolitan in their orientation rather than local is for all intents and purposes substantiated. According to deans and department chairmen in this study, the notion of the solitary scholar laboring to develop bibliographies in his field is rapidly being supplanted by information retrieval systems which tell him in an instant all that has been written on his topic. The impact of this on Ph.D. programming is virtually revolutionary. An interesting result of the new media of communication is the greater solidarity among national and international scholars and their increased willingness to share the day-by-day progress of their research and thinking.

Some future-oriented scholars suggest that the impending increase in automation dictates a need for universal higher education, because it offers the simplest and most obvious way to fill the vacuum left by the elimination of the necessity for a full-time commitment to work. Many believe that an age is fast approaching in which higher education will be planned on a continuum instead of in definite time intervals or stages (Fuller 1964, Kerr 1963). In this event, the regular college or university program would probably merge with segments that are now separately planned as adult, extension, or continuing education. To some extent the precedent has already been set. A large proportion of the college population now alternates periods of work or travel. This often extends their formal education over a decade or more of their adult life.

When deans and department chairmen were asked to speculate on the potential use of teaching technologies on the education of Ph.D.'s, they implied that if universal higher education becomes a reality, the new devices for information processing and retrieval could catalyze the action and provide the means through which an integrated systems approach to knowledge could be realized. Administrators in some fields reported that the initial process of systematization has begun. In literature, for example, concordances have been completed on great bodies of writing, in the biological sciences digital computers give immediate feedback on laboratory experiments and store the data for future use; in education, ERIC, the computerized Education Retrieval Information Center of USOE, has immeasurably reduced the time and effort scholars formerly exerted keeping abreast of their field by making information on new research more immediately accessible to those who need to apply its findings. Some respondents foresee the possibility that the computer and other information science systems may be the means of bringing the disciplines into closer relationships and of "reversing the progressive isolation of ideas from ideas and of man from man." To this end, some centers which house the new technologies are referred to as communication units.

The issue that involves teacher utilization, and thus stimulates wide interest and concern, is the possibility that the new information technologies and the use of machines to program instruction will reduce the need for teachers or diminish their status. Developers of the new technology hold out no such utopian expectations. Neither do those interviewed in this study. Rather they view the machines basically as instrumental responses to the problem which all teachers face—individual differences among students. They point out that as experts in a substantive field, teachers will always be needed to transmit the styles of thinking and develop the attitudes of mind which the factual programmed material elicits. However, they agree that in terms of its effects on teachers, the programming of instruction will undoubtedly require instructors to reorganize their working habits and to apply their talents differently than they now do. They suggest that the probabilities are high that teachers will have more, rather than less, work to do. The advantage will be that it will be work of a more creative and stimulating nature. Even if teaching machines come into general use by the turn of the century, there are no data which signify that the demand for teachers will be modified in any significant numbers. At least for the present, the cost of educating a teacher is far less than the cost of producing the machines needed to replace him—and the net results of using the machines appear at the moment to be far less promising. Graduate deans expressed the belief that this situation will change when a significant number of trained personnel become available. In the meantime, all the universities in this sample are engaged in basic research on this new methodology, but very few are teaching Ph.D. students how to apply it in their future teaching careers. Graduate faculties in almost all fields now advise their students to take additional math and some work in computer science. In commenting on these recommendations, some chairmen suggested that experience in this area should be accompanied by a study of the consequences as well as the limitations of automation. They warn that while machines may relieve teachers of dreary routine exercises or didactic teaching, and so free them for more important teaching duties, if the technology is not properly understood the consequences for the learner can result in a stifling of original thinking. For example, if the programmed material is not planned creatively to stimulate and develop the skills of inquiry, interpretation, and application, there is danger that only rote learning will develop and that rewards will be given only for agreement with the programmer.

As the art of teaching becomes more technological some respondents foresee the development in this country of such institutions as the University of the Air, which will be introduced in England in the fall of 1970, or of a nationwide network of computer-assisted instruction which might be connected to data banks, information retrieval systems, or learning media laboratories. Others predict the development of powerful educational syndicates for whom "curriculum development will become big business" and the implications for educational lobbying will accelerate. Almost all respondents believe that no major increase will be made in the use of teaching machines within the next decade or two. In the meantime, each of the institutions is researching the basic questions in this field.

When graduate deans were asked to indicate the essential factors which contributed to the excellence of their institutions, their responses fell generally into three or four categories. The major category was the ability of the institution to attract and to hold able scholars. Practically every person interviewed noted that the institution had a long tradition of putting the acquisition of a distinguished faculty ahead of all other resources. In the words of one dean, "everything else is facilitative."

Academic deans described their faculties as committed scholars most of whom were interested in both teaching and research.

The presence of influential persons who gave luster to the institution made it possible for the institution to attract others. Deans frequently cited the work of early department chairmen or of faculty members as having given vision to the academic program. The ability to bring a few outstanding men to each new department provided the impetus for recognition and enabled the institution to win public and private support. With a good staff and a strong program the institution was able to attract another component of excellence—good students.

In terms of personal characteristics the faculty were described by graduate deans as a group of intellectually stimulating individuals who, by and large, exhibited respect and trust for one another. Deans frequently cited examples of world-renowned scholars who had enough interest in the total institution to attend every general faculty meeting or were willing to assume special tasks for the good of the university. Some implied that this characteristic was more typical of the older than of some of the younger scholars who were less inclined to have strong institutional loyalties. Although they ascribed this difference to the fact that the young men were preoccupied with the need to produce research, whereas the senior scholar had fewer pressures, there was an almost universal concern about the fact that many young men did not manifest an interest in university-wide affairs. Some ascribed this to the restrictive criteria for membership in the faculty senate or its equivalent body.

One dean noted that it had become increasingly more difficult to find academic career men because the salaries and other inducements offered by business, industry, or the government were too attractive for the young men to resist. Deans also commented on the fact that it took more powerful incentives than the university had to offer to retain men who were becoming recognized as scholars and were therefore being sought out by other academic institutions. In the words of one dean, "In the XY department every man over forty has his bags packed."

Graduate deans attributed the excellence of the graduate program to the fact that the institution provided an atmosphere in which intellectual inquiry could be pursued with maximum freedom and independence by faculty and students alike, academic freedom was respected, and scholarship was given high priority. Other factors which were described by graduate deans as conducive to the development of excellence included an administration which encouraged diversity of opinion and interest, exercised strong leadership, believed in the value of a mature academic system, and provided the money and other resources necessary for the development of a strong university. Many graduate deans praised the contributions of past and present administrators whose vision and hard work had helped the institution to become distinctive. They noted that by being tolerant of the idiosyncrasies of productive persons, these administrators had facilitated the growth of scholarship. In general, deans and department chairmen thought that a major factor in the achievement and maintenance of quality was the careful preservation of a system in which ideas were allowed to flow without meeting deeply entrenched interests, the rules of conduct and policies were reasonable, and the "idea of change" did not need to be defended.

In addition to the high quality of these faculty and students, department chairmen attributed the excellence of their institutions to the comprehensiveness of the university library, the strength of the undergraduate program (particularly in the basic disciplines on which the graduate programs were developed), the department's mature approach to the graduate requirements, and its willingness to review and if necessary abandon programs or courses that could not attract good faculty members and good students.

Deans in smaller institutions felt that their success was due in appreciable measure to the fact that their more intimate environment enhanced the students' socialization and identification with the institution. On the other hand, deans in large institutions believed that the comprehensiveness of their offerings enabled them to attract those who had broad interests or those who wished to be in contact with a variety of sub-specialties within their disciplines.

Deans and department chairmen often praised the support of private benefactors, people in the state, and state legislatures as important determinants of the university's greatness. They cited the willingness of taxpayers, even those in less than affluent circumstances, to invest in their educational institutions as a strong incentive to its growth. The pride and trust shown by the state evoked a responsive effort on the part of the university to measure up to that trust. In several cases members of state legislatures were named as men of vision or men who had supported the institution in times of crisis or attack. There was a pervasive thread of concern throughout the open-ended commentaries on the faculty questionnaires which reflected an uneasiness about the ability of universities to maintain their excellence or to withstand some of the current attacks made on them. One scientist noted:

> I see grave danger to scientific knowledge and advancement as a consequence of the current wave of politicized motives anad efforts in society. Political motives when applied to science generate controversy. I have researched on controversy in science and the science of controversy. I am prepared to say that all controversies I have examined in the sciences were contrived for some political end result: this is why the controversy came to exist. In each instance no controversy exists within the scientific evidence. If scientists fail to enforce professional ethics and adherence to the scientific method, some important segments of scientific knowledge will sink into a quagmire of dark controversy.

Another faculty member in a state-supported institution observed:

> Intellectuals value knowledge for its own sake as do children, but most other people do not—or else the practical value of knowledge is much more important to them. Since the money here comes from all of the citizens, the political aspects of this state-supported university must strike a compromise between what the politicians and taxpayers generally expect of it (usually a first-rate trade school) and what students and faculty would like it to be. The problem is exacerbated presently in science by the huge sums of money necessary. Moreover there are fads (or priorities assigned) in academic disciplines, as in women's clothes. A century ago the humanities were revered above all else, two decades ago it was physics, now biology and biochemistry, but I see signs that these two are already waning. It may be that we will learn that scientific knowledge will not save us anymore than theological erudition—"the fault lies in ourselves." The two most pressing problems now confronting us (over population and nuclear war) both appear superficially to be scientific in nature, but I think it is now pretty

clear that the solution to both is political not technical, although technical advances can have minor effects.

Institutional size has often been cited as a factor in achieving quality in doctoral education. Administrators in this study said that the concept of "critical mass" is an important consideration in planning the ideal size of the faculty, the student body, the library, and the endowment or available financial resources needed for graduate programming. To some extent departmental size or the ratio of faculty members to students is probably a more important factor in graduate programming than is institutional size. Based on lists obtained from department secretaries some departments in this study enrolled more than five hundred graduate students while other departments in the same institutions listed less than ten. The ratio of faculty to students ranged from one to two to one to twenty. No accurate figures were readily available, but an "average" number of candidates (students working on their dissertations) per faculty member was, according to department chairmen, "somewhere in the neighborhood of four to six." Much larger ratios were obtained when the number of students per adviser was examined; there was also considerably more unevenness in these data.

Cartter investigated the question of critical mass as related to departmental size and found that even among the three smallest departments which ranked in the top twenty-five in his sample, the English departments average twenty-five faculty members, 106 graduate students, and nine Ph.D. awards per year; the three smallest departments of Classics averaged seven faculty members, fourteen students, and one Ph.D. award yearly; and the three smallest physics departments averaged twenty-seven faculty members, 126 students, and thirteen Ph.D.'s annually. The public institutions in this sample reported that some major problems had occurred as a result of recent increases in the numbers of doctoral students without concomitant increases in faculty. The main concern of the smaller institutions was that it is difficult to attract faculty members into a department in which there are a limited number of colleagues with whom to interact.

Shortly before his death, Robert Oppenheimer expressed his

concern about the ability of the university to maintain quality in the face of the shortage of competent scholars and the tremendous costs of the instrumentation required in some areas of graduate research. He was inclined to believe that in planning for future growth each university should strive for excellence in a limited number of areas rather than try to be competent in all areas or scatter its resources in areas that are already well covered by other universities or by other institutions.

Graduate deans and those who are responsible for planning advanced programs expressed concern about the rapid growth in the number of institutions that are competing for the same pool of faculty and student talent and the same sources of financial support. Of the 750 institutions which currently offer graduate work, practically all expect to expand substantially in the immediate future. Hall (1969) notes that present growth trends pose serious questions concerning the need to improve the quality of doctoral education and maintain the excellence of existing institutions.

The current press for what has been called the "instant university"—which aims for comprehensiveness at the end of a ten-year plan—poses serious questions for those who are interested in preserving the quality and integrity of higher education. The deans and department chairmen in the prestigious universities in this sample were frank to admit that the competition for good students and for competent faculty has become increasingly critical. They also note that their sources of support have decreased appreciably in recent years. In view of these cumulative problems it seems prudent not to increase the number of graduate institutions above the 750 now in operation and to suggest that some of these should curtail their involvement at the Ph.D. level. The most serious consequence of uncontrolled expansion in graduate education may be the "instant collapse" of existing institutions or segments of them. Riesman (1958) has observed:

> The quality of a school changes faster than its clientele recognizes; and colleges that have developed a novel or more demanding program cannot get the students to match it, while other institutions that have decayed cannot keep students away who should no longer go there. Colleges can change inside their shells with hardly anyone noticing and

the results can be tragic, not only for misled students, but for imaginative faculty and administrators who may not live long enough to be rewarded by the appearance of good students attracted by the change.

An example of how "instant collapse" can occur almost overnight was graphically demonstrated during the course of this study when the chairman of one of the departments in the sample accepted an appointment in another university which was trying to build a new program in his field. When he accepted the new appointment, the chairman was able to induce three of his former faculty colleagues and twenty-five graduate students to join him in his new post. One can only conjecture about the effect that this exodus has had on the institution which experienced it.

Admission and
Orientation
to Graduate Study

6

Until recently the literature on criteria for admission to graduate study reflected a strong insistence upon an objective evaluation of the applicants' credentials in order to protect "academic standards." The fact that those standards were often not clearly defined or articulated tended to make admissions committees more and more dependent upon quantitative evidence in deciding who should be admitted to graduate study. Thus, grade-point averages, class rank, and scores on the Graduate Record Examination or the Miller Analogy Test were accepted as the best indicators of probable academic success. For the most part these are still used as preliminary screening devices, but research on the influence of such factors as early culture and motivation, personality, interests, and physical vitality has demonstrated that quantitative measures sometimes obscure other important elements of intellectual promise.

Currently, in addition to objective assessments, admissions officers in the institutions in this sample attempt to obtain a profile of the applicant's outside interests, activities, and achievements through an autobiographical statement or essay in which the student expresses his career goals. Wherever possible, a personal interview is requested before a final decision is made. If this cannot be made on campus it may be made locally by a designate of the university. The belief is that in these meetings the interviewer can "tease out" information which the application forms do not reveal. Since the interviewer knows the character of the institution to which the student applies, he is inclined to judge the person interviewed on the basis of how well he matches the institution.

Usually the final selection of those who are to be admitted is based on a rank ordering of all the estimates of quality that can be obtained from or about the applicants. Understandably, perhaps, the end product toward which the estimates focus usually constitutes a composite of those qualities and standards of excellence which consciously or unconsciously faculty members perceive in themselves or admire in their colleagues. Thus, until very recently, doctoral students looked like junior versions of their faculty models and were largely WASP in their ethnic origins. Recent efforts to make higher education accessible to larger numbers of students from various minority cultures has begun to change this profile. In response to pressures, admissions officers and departments are now involved in trying to reform the "screening and gatekeeping function of the university" so as to ensure equality as well as quality. Department chairmen and faculty members reported that they are not only aware of the need to recruit minority students but are becoming increasingly sensitive to the special culture and character which minority students and staff members contribute to the university environment.

Not excluding academic qualifications, sex is probably the most discriminatory factor applied in the decision whether to admit an applicant to graduate school. It is almost a foregone conclusion that among American institutions women have greater difficulty being admitted to doctoral study and, if admitted, will have greater difficulty being accepted than will men. Department chairmen and faculty members frankly state that their main reason for ruling against women is "the probability that they will marry." Some continue to use this possibility as the rationale for withholding fellowships, awards, placement, and other recognitions from women who are allowed to register for graduate work. Among graduate men, marriage is generally seen by the admissions committee as a plus factor. But the same committee almost automatically rules out the possibility that marriage and scholarship can be compatible accomplishments in the female. In some departments the signals are quite clear: no women need apply.

The long-range aspects of operating an admission policy on this assumption are reflected in the data which show that among high school graduates, more females are eligible to enter college but more males actually do so (44 per cent to 56 per cent). Because the attrition rate during college is greater among females than among males, each succeeding educational level includes fewer women. Thus, while 44 per cent of the college entrants in 1965 were women —and approximately 50 per cent of these received the degree—at the doctoral level only 11 per cent of the degree recipients were women.

This apparent loss of interest in advanced study may be related to the reports that in addition to experiencing greater stress and receiving less encouragement than males during their degree programs, women are not awarded the placement opportunities that are available to men once the degree has been earned. In her study of academic women, Bernard (1964) found that only 7 per cent of the faculties in the better universities were women. Most of these were concentrated in the traditional "women's fields" such as education, nursing, home economics, and physical education. Scott (1970) found that of the approximately 1500 persons who hold professional academic rank at Berkeley only sixty-one are women, and Seigel (1968) reported that of 1043 faculty appointees at Stanford only forty-nine are women. Comparable data may be shown for other universities. These data also show that most of the women faculty members are appointed at the assistant professor rank and that they tend to remain at the lower ranks longer than their male colleagues.

In the interviews for this study several department chairmen volunteered the information that women are purposely screened out as Ph.D. prospects and as faculty members. For example, the chairman of a department of biochemistry mentioned that the men on his faculty had a pact in which they agreed "not even to look at applications from women." It should be noted that in this same department women with Masters degrees are employed to do the major laboratory work. In another interview the chairman of a psychology department worried about "what would happen to the department next year" as a result of admitting seven female students in a class of twenty-five. The imponderable effect of the military draft on male students had impelled the department to cover the available slots. In order to ensure the availability of research assistants the faculty had changed their "females need not apply" signals to "help wanted—temporarily." According to questionnaire commentators, the departments represented in this study orient the career socialization of men around research and of women around teaching, usually at the undergraduate level. If women do evince an interest in research they are generally led to expect that it will be as an "assistant" or as a "collaborator."

The nuances in the discontent among women in graduate schools deserve a more careful analysis than is possible in this report. However, it should be noted for the record that a study of student protest movements reveals that women are participating in numbers disproportionate to their representation on campus (Heist, 1965). There are indicators in the data in this study that while many women respond on an emotional level to the students' press for social justice or for educational reform, they also rapidly translate their experience to the conscious, personal level. In the words of one respondent who commented on the Third World Movement on her campus: "As I listened to their stories of rejection and discrimination . . . and of being acculturated to expect a lesser role or to work beneath their intellectual interests, I realized that I had been there too—in fact, that is where *I am* as a woman." The "in-tuning" of women with the thrust of those who seek identification as "person" is possibly a portent of more change to come. Borrowing from the methods of the Third World groups, educated women are currently organizing in a wide variety of ways to erase their designation and assignment to second-class status (Chronicle of Higher Education, 1970), especially in the academic and political sphere.

In response to a request for information on whether or not any special admissions policies were used on behalf of minority graduate students, seven deans reported that their institutions recognized that many of the common indexes of quality, such as the Graduate Record Examination, do not apply directly to students from diverse cultures, hence they now depend largely upon letters from professors who know the applicant's intellectual promise and can attest to his potential. In some cases quantitative estimates are disregarded and "the individual characteristics of the graduate students in question . . . are taken into account." Other than this, the only change in policy is the provision of special help through an academic adviser or an individual department member during the student's first year.

Since the academic department is in the best position to evaluate an applicant's qualifications, final discretionary power usually resides there. Thus, departments have the right to admit whom they will, and the concomitant responsibility to orient and advise those who are admitted. At the same time, according to the director of an admissions office, "departments have the obligation not to admit those whose prospects for success are low." The wide discretionary power which departments hold was pointed out in the response of one graduate dean who wrote: "The university is making a major effort to increase the number of graduate students from minority groups. However, graduate students are admitted by eighty different fields of study and we probably have eighty different policies."

Departments and graduate councils appear reluctant to pronounce a general special-admission policy for minority students. Fearing that to do so might imply that minority students have less intellectual capacity than their peers in the majority culture, institutions prefer to hold to their basic criteria of admission—especially at the graduate level. The institutions in this sample reported that they have had no unusual problem in attracting those who meet or exceed the basic standards. In general, the universities in this study report that with regard to his expected performance no compromises are made once the student is on the campus, although some students may be advised "to take a reduced load during their initial registration."

The bulk of the effort made by the ten institutions with respect to minority students is directed toward recruiting promising students and securing financial means to assist them. The extent and character of recruitment varies but it includes: letters and visits to black colleges by the admissions office staff or by faculty members; visits to the campus by prospective students who are carefully briefed on the admissions procedures; paying transportation and other expenses incurred when the department requests an interview with the applicant; and correspondence with the student's undergraduate school. Some institutions elicit the aid of minoriy students who are already on campus to help in the recruitment of their ethnic peers. One graduate dean noted: "Black graduate students made a valuable and constructive contribution . . . through their efforts we have been able to increase the number of applications from qualified students."

Each of the graduate deans reported that although the sums were not large they had been able to earmark certain funds for special minority student purposes. It seems evident, judging by their memorandums and statements to the faculty, that each of the graduate deans endorses the admission of increasing numbers of minority students and offers the services of his office to that end. At the same time they make it clear that the final effort and responsibility rest with the individual departments by whom the educational contract is made and primarily administered.

To assure that talented and deserving individuals are not automatically ruled out by deficiencies that can be corrected or waived, all but two of the private and one of the public institutions in the sample specify circumstances under which "special admission" may be approved. These admissions are variously designated as "provisional" or "probationary." Admission to full standing is contingent upon the student's ability to remove the conditions under which he was admitted, or upon his academic performance during his first term, or on both. In principle, students who lack adequate preparation for the particular graduate field to which they apply may receive tentative approval with the proviso that they enroll (or audit) upper-division undergraduate courses which can provide the missing background. In fact, however, the institutions in this study receive such an avalanche of fully qualified applications each year that they rarely utilize the special admissions rubric. It should be noted here that its availability is strategically important in enabling institutions to admit those who have exceptional talent in a special area such as artists, composers, or writers who may lack one or more of the required prerequisites.

According to information listed in their catalogs or distributed in other written forms, seven of the institutions in the study have university-wide admission requirements as well as specific departmental requirements. The former are stated in broad terms— for example, "the applicant must show evidence of satisfactory academic work" or "present an undergraduate record of distinction"; however, departmental requirements are usually expressed in specifics. These tend to include a minimally acceptable grade-point average (which in many cases is higher than the graduate school requirement), a satisfactory record of achievement in certain prerequisite courses or fields, breadth requirements, and, in some departments, a background in one or more foreign languages. Some departments require that the doctoral applicant must first obtain a Masters degree—preferably from another institution. Others prefer that the student enter directly out of his baccalaureate program and bypass the Masters.

Two of the institutions in the sample require that a certification of good health be included in the application forms. While only one institution definitely states that it has a university-wide policy of accepting no applicants over age thirty-five, other institutions leave this decision to the discretion of the various departments. In most cases, it is an important determinant of whether or not the applicant is accepted. Because of quotas and limitation on enrollment, it is becoming increasingly difficult for older applicants to obtain admission to the institutions and departments included in this study. In some cases, those over a certain age are barred from receiving scholarships.

When members of the graduate faculty were asked whether the admission policies of their departments should be changed, 76 per cent responded that present policies were satisfactory and should be retained, 21 per cent thought that they should be modified, and less than 1 per cent thought that the requirements should be tightened or dropped. Chemists, physicists, and mathematicians were proportionately more satisfied and respondents in English, sociology, and psychology least satisfied with this requirement compared with respondents in other fields. Those who commented on this issue were inclined to favor the admission of students who show a strong liberal arts background rather than a required major in the area of their graduate interest. This was particularly noticeable among social science respondents and in the humanities. Some of the latter wanted preference given to applicants who demonstrate high competence in communication skills whereas respondents in the sciences thought that student applicants in their areas should show a strong background in quantitative skills and analysis.

The personality or social skills of graduate students were seen by some respondents as important points to be considered in the selection process, although most of the commentators admitted that they would not know how to measure these assets in a becoming scholar. Said one commentator, "Einstein would have muffed a personality test had it been required for his admission to the university." Another observed, "while I long wistfully for graduate students who are polished, I must admit that many brilliant scholars (in mathematics) are hard to get along with. This does not diminish their productivity, and indeed it may enhance it."

Several of the universities in the sample admit only those who can devote themselves to full-time study. In the words of one department chairman: "We are dropping our practice of admitting streetcar students. If we do make an exception, the off-campus applicants' employment must be defined as productive employment in research or in teaching, here or elsewhere . . . We simply must find some way to make it possible for good students to devote full time to study for three or four years rather than make them drag out the degree program for a dozen. All Fellows should defend their use of time."

When faculty members were asked to speculate on the direction in which admission requirements would change in their departments within the foreseeable future, 35 per cent said that they expect requirements to be raised, 58 per cent expect them to remain constant as now required, and 6 per cent believed they will be lowered. More respondents in economics (62 per cent), sociology (48 per cent), mathematics (47 per cent), and psychology (42 per cent) anticipate an increase in their admission requirements compared with other fields, and more in philosophy and English (12 per cent) expect to see admission requirements lowered in the future. Physics, chemistry, and French, according to 79 per cent of the respondents, will remain fairly constant with respect to their admission requirements.

Twenty per cent of the faculty respondents expect that increased emphasis will be placed on the liberal arts background of Ph.D. candidates, whereas 17 per cent believe that this emphasis will decrease in importance as a prerequisite. The remainder (63 per cent) expect background requirements for admission to remain fairly constant. There appears to be considerable division or ambivalence within some departments over whether liberal arts requirements will be increased or decreased. For example, while 20 per cent of the biochemists and historians expect that doctoral students will need a stronger or broader liberal arts base in the future, almost the same number (19 per cent) expect that this base will be lowered. The departments in which more professors anticipate increases in this background include English, sociology, and psychology, in which 25 per cent of the respondents expect upward trends; the departments in which approximately the same number expect decreases include economics, physics, and physiology. The department whose respondents expect least change in either direction is mathematics.

Fifty-five per cent of the faculty respondents expect that the supply of well-qualified applicants in their fields will increase over the next five years, 32 per cent expect the supply to remain constant, and approximately 11 per cent anticipate a decline in their numbers in the immediate future. It was clear from the comments of department chairmen that the institutions in this sample are in keen competition with each other for both graduate students and faculty. Because they draw from the same pools of talent each institution tries avidly to skim off the cream. Some institutions woo graduate students with the same enticements they use to attract a prominent faculty member. This includes what one department chairman described as the "red carpet treatment." In at least one institution students are invited to spend several days on campus at university expense. During the visit they meet with individual faculty members, are shown the research facilities that will be at their disposal, and are assured of adequate support throughout their academic program. In some institutions, in addition to his stipend as a research assistant, a top applicant is promised additional emoluments in the form of support for his research, office space and supplies, clerical and secretarial assistance, editorial and printing services for his dissertation, travel funds to and from professional conferences, and special consultative help as he requires it. A less well-qualified student, or one who applies without the backing of a highly ranked undergraduate institution or a well-known professor may receive few, if any, of these inducements on application. However, he may earn them within a short period if he is ambitious or "fits in" with the research needs of a faculty member. If he does not, he is probably on his own.

One or two institutions follow the practice of admitting at the first-year level more students than they can accommodate at advanced levels. This is done in order to take up the slack caused by later attrition. Trimming is done in stages: at the end of the first year, when on the basis of his performance the student may be advised to withdraw, or at the end of the second year, when he may be awarded a terminal Masters degree.

Some department chairmen frankly admitted during the interviews that it would be impossible to reduce first-year admissions because budgetary stringencies make it necessary for them to staff undergraduate sections with graduate students. Others noted that low-paid assistants are needed to work on faculty research projects. Graduate students offer an intelligent source of these personnel. In many cases, the nuances in this practice are communicated directly or indirectly to graduate students. When the practice is overt, it tends to create stress, increase competition, and to encourage an unhealthy atmosphere in which "good ideas" are saved to impress those in power rather than openly shared with one's peers. Survival through gamesmanship becomes an all-consuming goal—the means to which are not always based on integrity.

Currently, graduate schools are being forced to review their admissions policies and to revise their enrollment quotas. The modern university's dependence upon federal support for its research operation has placed it in a very vulnerable position now that such support is being drastically reduced. Having been encouraged to tool up for research which various federal agencies supported, some institutions now find themselves cut off from that support and unable to meet their commitments to graduate students. Additional cuts in federal research contracts have, at least for the moment, considerably reduced the demand for research personnel. As a result larger numbers of new Ph.D.'s are turning to undergraduate teaching.

Realistic estimates of the need for Ph.D.'s are always difficult to obtain. Cartter's 1966 prediction that the supply would keep well ahead of the demand is not supported by the 1968 report *The Education Professions*, prepared by the U.S. Commission of Education. With respect to their placement, the Director of Fellowships for the Office of Scientific Personnel of the National Research Council observes: "To assume that all of the highly specialized research-based Ph.D.'s our first-rate graduate schools are capable of producing in the future can be placed in prestigious universities is . . . highly untenable and illogical" (Hall, 1969).

Because the turnover in college and university faculties is often subject to unpredictable events in society, it is difficult to take more than an educated guess about future needs. There are also many factors which militate against accuracy in predicating future supplies. One critical factor is the attrition rate among the faculty and among Ph.D. students. Normally for prestigious institutions the number of faculty members who give up teaching each year fluctuates between 2 and 3 per cent. A compensating factor is that approximately the same number move into the university each year from nonacademic positions.

The attrition rate among graduates who drop out of the Ph.D. program each year is estimated at 30 per cent for top-ranked universities and as high as 50 per cent for other institutions. (These do not necessarily represent losses to higher education since many who hold the A.B.D. [all but the dissertation] secure teaching appointments.) The military draft has also created some attrition, both among those who were already enrolled in graduate programs and among potential enrollers. At the present writing it is impossible to predict the effects of these losses because of the instability in manpower needs.

Seventy-five per cent of the faculty respondents in the institutions studied foresee an increase in the market for Ph.D. holders in their fields within the immediate future, 19 per cent expect that the need will remain constant, and only 5 per cent expect the demand to decrease. Higher increases were expected by respondents in economics, sociology, French, and psychology and the largest decreases are expected by professors in philosophy and physics. Cartter's (1970) observations are much more pessimistic.

The high value which Americans place on higher education is reflected in the opinion of leaders in business and industry who look upon education as a new "growth industry" and one that is destined to provide the dynamics for the nation's future economy. Leaders in these fields see no danger of a glut in Ph.D.'s, for they assume that if this country does not need them other parts of the world do. Graduate school deans and department chairmen agree that the world needs highly educated and committed persons, but they are less sanguine about their ability to admit them under present financial constraints in which national priorities appear to be skewed.

Orientation to the intricacies of the Ph.D. process is a crucial factor in the direction and efficiency of the student's progress. One aspect of doctoral study on which no institution or discipline in this study escaped severe criticism was the manner in which students are oriented to their degree programs. Judging by the nature of their comments on this issue, a considerable aura of mystique envelops the Ph.D. process. Some respondents inferred that beginners are kept in the dark by design. Others suggested that orientation to doctoral study is vague because advisers themselves do not know the requirements nor the rationale on which they are affirmed. Students often said that they would have made different or more economical decisions had their orientation been thorough. Lacking the essential information, some found that they had failed to gain early in their programs the basic skills and techniques that would enable them to move into advanced work in normal order. Some indicated that their programs had been extended a year or more because of the inadequacies in their orientation. Others cited examples to show that their fellow students were a better source of information than faculty advisers, and often provided information on such essentials as the available facilities and resources, fee or course waivers, sources of financial aid, outstanding courses, and other experiences which could enrich their programs. In some institutions advanced students were deliberately used as advisers in such matters, in the belief that as users of these services students were in a better position to evaluate them for new students.

Students often reported that they had received no briefing on the nature of, or rationale behind, the various types of examinations they faced. As a result, many said that they approached exams apprehensively and clumsily. Enterprising students eventually learn to "psych out" professors, to sound out students who have already taken exams from them, or to cultivate department secretaries who can, if they will, orient the student about examination requirements or forms. If it were possible to calculate the waste in spirit, time, and money resulting from the inadequacies of orientation to the Ph.D. program, the amounts would undoubtedly be staggering. Even after granting that students cannot be excused for not asking the questions to which they need answers, there remain many aspects of the Ph.D. process that are so shrouded in tradition or so steeped in specificity that they cannot be anticipated by any first-year graduate student.

The following quotes taken at random from student questionnaires highlight some of the problems:

> The department made no attempt to orient incoming students except for a brief speech by the adviser who quite frankly told us he expected to see only a quarter of us there the following year. He held this attitude consistently during the year— Fortunately, the graduate student club fills in the gaps.

> We were informed that the Ph.D. program in English is a compulsory three-year plan *only after* arriving here in September long after many of us had turned down fine offers at other major graduate schools.

> No advance orientation was given to me at all. I wrote in for "The Graduate Students' Guide," a handbook which

should be received before entering graduate school. None were available until long after registration. The department had a short two-hour orientation for us which was nice except it was held two weeks before classes started and those of us from outside the state ended up twiddling our thumbs for two weeks. Housing was a mess to find—they won't tell you until September 1 whether you have a room.

There is a great discrepancy between statements in the catalog and the actual experience. With a little ingenuity one can avoid certain requirements. . . . Graduate schools and their departments do not function according to written descriptions . . . the student who realizes that and looks at his department as the behaviorist looks at Congress will be more successful. . . . The best thing for the beginning student is to establish rapport with several older grad students who know the ropes and can give the informal information that is otherwise unavailable.

My adviser hasn't any idea of the graduate program requirements. When I asked how to proceed for the Ph.D. he said I was now on "the uncharted sea" and no more. He announced to me that he was happy to find so many students taking a particular course—he didn't even know that it was required for all. . . . After two years of every sort of disillusionment, frustration, and disappointment I've settled down to accepting the department as it is and trying to work as much as possible on my own.

Table 2 represents the doctoral students' appraisal of the quality of the orientation and advising they received in their particular department.

The catalog of the graduate school is the primary means of informing prospective and matriculating graduate students of the special character of the university, the special emphasis in its academic programs, and its particular resources and requirements for graduate study. By virtue of the student's dependence upon this document as a basis for deciding whether to invest in graduate study— and to choose one institution rather than another—the clarity and accuracy of its information are of major importance.

An inspection of those statements in the catalogs which purport to explain the purpose of graduate education reveals that all of the universities in the sample agree that the goal of the Ph.D.

Table 2

STUDENT APPRAISAL OF ORIENTATION AND ADVISING PROCESSES,
BY DISCIPLINES
(in percentages, N = 3161)

	Adequate	Inadequate	Not Offered	Not Sought
Orientation:				
to the university	26	20	22	32
to the department	48	29	10	13
Advice on:				
planning courses	63	28	3	6
formal requirements	75	21	1	3
strategy of doctoral study	44	30	13	13
obtaining financial aid	73	12	3	11
persisting toward goals	49	19	13	19

program is to train research scholars. Beyond a straightforward expression of that goal, the rhetoric of purpose becomes vague and confused through oblique references to "increasing knowledge," "developing scholar-teachers," "preparing teacher-scholars" or "augmenting man's knowledge of himself and the world." In only one case did a catalog statement advise the student that the achievement of his goals would depend to a large extent on his own ability to be independent. In four cases the statement of purpose was too brief to be inclusive. Three schools did not include specific statements of purpose and the remaining two schools offered statements that were either idealistic or irrelevant.

In general, graduate school catalogs provide insufficient information on aspects of higher education with which the applicant has had no previous experience. These include residence requirements; thesis requirements; the function, selection, and policies of research committees; oral examinations; the selection of a sponsor; and the policies and procedures for admission to candidacy. Reference to these activities are made in general statements which suggest that the student check with the graduate adviser in his field. Obviously, this is not always practical for those who are a distance from the campus when decisions are being made.

Catalog information on the structure or organization of graduate education is scanty. The extent to which the graduate division is decentralized is rarely explained, and the autonomy which departments exercise in establishing their own additional requirements is frequently not understood. In specifying that joint approval must be obtained for interdisciplinary programming, or for work in another field, some catalogs convey the impression that the approval process is complicated or that the practice is not looked upon with favor by the departments. By failing to clarify what is meant by "options," "equivalents," or "exceptions" to certain requirements, some catalogs fail to inform students who might qualify for waivers or for making alternate choices.

The disparity in departmental requirements is so great that the value of a single graduate catalog is open to question. Some departments prepare separate catalogs, pamphlets, or supplementary materials to distribute to applicants, but unless the applicant specifically requests these he may not see them until he arrives on campus. In some cases information in the supplementary literature is contrary to that in the general catalog. In other cases it includes new or revised information.

Among the supplementary materials that were supplied by department secretaries as review material for this study were several graduate student handbooks and faculty handbooks. In general, these were formal departmental publications which stated in precise detail the policies and procedures governing the degree process and award. In several instances graduate student organizations had collaborated with the department in preparing guidebooks for graduate students, and in still other cases informal guidebooks were prepared and distributed by graduate student organizations. In addition to covering the departmental program and policies, the student club guidebooks often offered straightforward advice on strategies for success or survival in graduate school. Some included faculty evaluations. In their open-ended statements student respondents frequently mentioned that the student handbook was an excellent source of information about the department and its program.

In a few cases students seem to have developed a rudimentary underground press. For instance, in one institution students in sociology published a newsletter which was circulated at irregular times to keep the graduates informed of issues that affect their welfare. To this end the letter includes a calendar of special seminars, meetings, social events, or items of general interest to students. It also includes information on new courses, staff appointments, or research activities in addition to exchange, want-ad, or complaint columns. The substance of graduate student newsletters reflects a growing solidarity between students in different departments on the same campus or a line of communication with students in the same field who are on other campuses. In some cases, collective bargaining organizations provide a house organ for teaching or research assistants. Reporters and editors for the various student publications appear to cooperate closely with their counterparts in other universities. This may foreshadow a movement to organize on a broader base to promote actions of common interest to graduate students.

Ph.D.
Requirements

7

The extent to which the Ph.D. degree has been standardized is reflected in its requirements. Under the aegis of the Association of Graduate Schools in the Association of American Universities, which serves as both an advisory body and an overseer of graduate programs, practically all Ph.D. programs uniformly specify that the doctoral student meet six requirements: satisfy a residence requirement; demonstrate a reading proficiency in one or more foreign languages; master the substantive background offered in a series of courses and seminars; successfully complete a written qualifying examination and an oral examination; secure the approval of a faculty committee on his choice of a research topic and of the method to be used in its study; and write the results of his research in a form approved by three or more members of the graduate faculty. Ostensibly, each of the requirements is postulated on the theory that it contributes to the scholarly development of the student. Presumably, successful completion of the requirements marks the individual as an educated scholar. Thus, in practice, the requirements serve as benchmarks by which to measure a student's progress and evaluate his prospects.

Faculty respondents expressed a general conviction that at the doctoral level formal requirements serve a useful function *only* if they induce genuine interest and excitement in the realm of exploration and discovery. On the assumption that when requirements are precisely defined some students will settle for their precise fulfillment rather than use the experience to test the full measure of their own potential, many of the faculty members favored a relatively unstructured and unspecified academic program over a set of standardized requirements. Many preferred to build a program around the goals and needs of the individual student. While some argued that students at the graduate level are mature enough to play a decisive role in planning a course of study, the majority were convinced that some degree of structuring by the department was necessary to ensure quality control. Table 3 shows the percentage of faculty members in each discipline who thought that the present requirements in their institutions should be changed.

Graduate faculties generally assume that they and their colleagues are better judges of the essential knowledge needed for understanding and mastering their disciplines than are new graduate students. On this rationale they generally designate a series of courses intended to provide the knowledge base upon which advanced seminars are built. Not infrequently the courses so identified are institutionalized as "required" for all new students. Basically, the foundation requirement appears logically sound, but in practice it is often psychologically unsound. Autonomous and mature students expressed resentment of the "packaged program." They claim that by excluding them from program decisions at this level, the faculty cuts students off from involvement in their own academic plans and puts them in a position redolent of their impersonal undergraduate setting in which they were "told what was good for them."

In commenting on their course requirements some students stated that the time and energy consumed by heavy course demands forced them to live on the sidelines of the intellectual and cultural

Table 3

Percentage of Faculty Favoring Changes in Ph.D. Requirements, by Disciplines

Discipline	Residence	Courses	Seminars	Written final exams	Written qualifying exams	Foreign language	Oral exams	Dissertation
Biochemistry	17.1	37.0	25.9	31.9	31.6	37.8	25.0	4.9
Chemistry	19.2	45.0	22.9	22.3	30.0	46.8	27.9	5.7
Economics	23.9	47.9	30.6	21.7	30.1	56.8	33.8	10.6
English	24.8	48.8	30.7	40.1	37.3	40.8	47.1	20.1
French	22.1	40.0	28.8	37.0	34.0	32.2	29.3	12.1
History	18.8	58.2	39.0	26.4	30.2	32.0	25.0	8.8
Mathematics	26.9	29.2	28.0	23.1	26.3	23.6	24.4	13.3
Philosophy	17.4	61.2	55.1	31.7	39.6	34.1	36.4	10.0
Physics	22.2	35.4	20.7	20.1	21.8	42.5	16.9	3.0
Physiology	15.9	58.9	42.9	39.4	34.3	44.9	24.3	9.7
Psychology	33.7	63.5	35.9	39.3	48.1	57.5	27.1	15.5
Sociology	27.3	62.7	39.3	33.0	38.0	47.3	35.9	6.1

excitement which the university offered. Some establish a pattern of social isolation at this stage which becomes a fixed part of their later life style. Many students denounced the basic course requirement as an administrative device for handling the overload of first-year students. In admitting this strategy some faculty members defended the practice on the grounds that by screening out the weak and the dilettantes on the basis of their performance in the basic courses, the time and services of the department can be husbanded for the able and committed students. It was clear from the open-ended comments of faculty members and students that a uniform foundation requirement for all students is debatable. In spite of the fact that many basic courses are of high quality and are taught by exceptional teachers, others are not. The unevenness in course quality and the repetitiveness in their content make required courses the target of sharp criticism. Small numbers of students and faculty members attempt in devious ways to circumvent taking or teaching them.

In terms of recommendations for curriculum reforms some faculty members were reluctant to dispense with basic course requirements. However, agreement was fairly broad that because a course or activity is labeled "required" it does not follow that it is required for all, or is necessarily required for all in the same form. For this reason, most departments agree that students should be allowed to waive the requirements under certain conditions. This agreement appears to be honored more in the breach than in practice. It implies that some students might be admitted laterally into the program. To so admit him requires an evaluation of his previous work. Since this involves time or a formal petition for a waiver, both students and faculty are inclined to make a literal interpretation of the regulations. What was designed as an assurance of preparation becomes a particularized precept. Opponents of the general courses requirement claim that the heavy demands in this requirement leave little time during the critical first year of study for students to explore, think about, or test other areas of academic interest. They would prefer individually designed programs or the option to do independent study in the "required" areas.

When faculty members were asked whether there was a need

for change in the course requirements in their departments their responses indicated an almost equal division between those who believed that present course requirements should be retained (47.1 per cent) and those who believed that they should be modified (47.2 per cent). An additional three per cent were in favor of their elimination. The remainder reported that their department had no formally prescribed course requirements or that the requirements had recently been substantially modified or changed.

Normally, three fairly specific examinations are required for all Ph.D. students—a qualifying examination, a written comprehensive examination, and an oral examination. The first of these is used by some departments to certify that the student has acquired the basic knowledge in his field and is qualified for advanced work; the second is usually given at the completion of course work and is intended to test the student's mastery of the research in his field; and the oral examination is designed to test not only his knowledge of his field but also involves the examination of his proposed plan for his dissertation research. Upon successful completion of his examinations the student is advanced to candidacy. In a few institutions successful completion of this stage is certified by a Candidate in Philosophy Certificate or degree.

In addition to measuring the student's grasp of the knowledge in his discipline the comprehensive examinations are designed to measure his ability to organize, synthesize, integrate, relate, and express ideas clearly and coherently. Usually the written examinations are read and evaluated by two or more members of the faculty and the oral examination is under the direction of between three and five examiners. Only two institutions require an oral examination on the completed dissertation. In general, students reported that the written examinations are more helpful to their development than is the oral examination. This probably reflects the fact that students have few formal opportunities to express themselves orally and are uncomfortable when required to do so. For those who have little talent for verbalizing, the experience is often stressful.

Many faculty respondents apparently lack confidence in the Ph.D. examination system. Some 34 per cent felt that the qualifying examination requirement should be modified or dropped, 31 per cent would modify or drop the written comprehensive examination, 30 per cent thought that the oral examination should be modified, and 5 per cent voted to drop the oral test altogether.

The foreign language requirement in the Ph.D. program dates back to the origins of American scholarship. Until the late 1800's American scholars were obliged to go abroad to the German and French centers of learning if they were interested in advanced study. On their return to this country they often assisted in the development of graduate education here. In planning advanced programs, their knowledge of French and German enabled these early academic planners to keep in contact with the research ideas of their colleagues abroad. In this sense their knowledge of these particular languages became a research tool. It was almost automatic to expect that those who wished to pursue graduate work would need an ability to read in French and German, the languages in which most of the research was published. To certify their preparedness for advanced study, Ph.D. applicants were required to demonstrate a reading facility in these languages. Later the requirement was modified to permit students to acquire their language tools after admission to graduate study, but before acceptance as a qualified candidate. This practice is followed today in many institutions, although other languages besides French and German may now be substituted if the student's research field justifies a different choice.

Probably no other aspect of the Ph.D. program has been so vigorously denounced as the foreign language requirement. Serious questions have been raised about its purpose in a period when excellent English translations are readily available to researchers, but the most compelling arguments against the requirement seem to rest on moral grounds. Describing the fitful preparation, low level of proficiency required, temporality of the skill acquired, and the lack of utility for foreign languages in current academic programs, critics view the requirement as an institutionalized ritual or as an ornament in the Ph.D. program for which, in many disciplines, no rational justification or relevance can be documented.

Some institutions have begun to relax the foreign language requirements in fields where it no longer serves as a research tool. But tradition holds firm in most cases: 91 per cent of the respondents from private institutions and 90 per cent of those in public institutions said that they had been required to demonstrate their ability to read in one or more foreign languages in order to qualify as a candidate for the Ph.D. In cases where substitutions for the language requirement were permitted, the options included courses in computer language, statistics, mathematics, work in interdisciplinary fields, and in a small number of cases field work or participation in community projects.

The imbroglio in which the foreign language requirement continues to operate in Ph.D. programs is reflected in the data which show that 58 per cent of those who completed this requirement reported that it did not contribute to their intellectual development. Only 6 per cent said that it had contributed a great deal and 30 per cent said it had contributed somewhat. A chorus of gratuitous comments criticizing the foreign language requirement accompanied the students' responses. The most discordant notes were sounded by those who resented the requirement because they were never obliged to use the skill which they had (sometimes painfully) acquired and because the acquisition of that skill had, in many cases, delayed their progress toward the degree for one or more years. For some students the requirement took on a moral dimension because of the superficiality of the proficiency required or because learning a foreign language "to pass the examination" was not only lacking in integrity but encouraged rote learning rather than appreciation or insight. Findings previously reported by Berelson (1960), Elder (1958), Hansen and Graham (1968), Heiss (1964), Weitz et al. (1963), and Graham and Hansen (1968) that the *use* of a foreign language is seldom required in graduate work were confirmed in the questionnaire responses of doctoral students in the institutions in this study. While 90 per cent said that they were required to demonstrate their ability to understand one or more foreign languages, 58 per cent reported that they never used the languages for course work, 38 per cent never used them for research, and 45 per cent never had to use them in outside reading assignments. An additional 21 per cent said that they "seldom" used a foreign language for any of these three activities.

Slightly more private institution respondents than public school respondents reported that they used their foreign language skills in course work (8 per cent to 5 per cent), in research (17 per cent to 15 per cent), and in outside reading (11 per cent to 7 per cent). Among those who reported that they used their foreign language facility "a great deal" were 7 per cent who used it in course work, 14 per cent who used it for research, and 7 per cent who used it for outside readings. When student responses to this item were analyzed along departmental lines, the variation in their usage of foreign languages was pronounced. As expected, the department of French reported the highest usage (41 per cent). However, 33 per cent of the respondents in French reported that they never used their foreign language skills for course work, 17 per cent never used them for research, and 23 per cent said that their outside readings were almost exclusively in English. An additional 11 per cent of the respondents in French reported that they "seldom" used a foreign language for these three activities.

Psychologists, physiologists, physicists, economists, and sociologists represented the highest percentages of non-users in the sample. Seventy-seven per cent in this group reported that they never used their foreign language skill in their course work, and 60 per cent never used it in their research or outside readings. These data may reflect the fact that with the exception of the department of physiology all other departments provide for substitution in the language requirement. For example, 55 per cent of the economists, 50 per cent of the sociologists, and 41 per cent of the psychologists said that their departments permitted the substitution of math or statistics courses for one or more of the language requirements. Psychology and sociology also allowed options in computer language, interdisciplinary course work, and research methodology in lieu of the language requirements. Although the French and English departments do not permit substitutions in the language requirement, all other departments report some movement toward greater flexibility in this requirement.

The universities in this study generally require that Ph.D. students spend from one to two years "in residence" but they vary in their interpretation of this regulation. For example, while some define residence in terms of numbers of quarters, terms, or semesters, others define it in numbers of course credit equivalents. And while some require that all of the students' work must be in full-time continuous residence, others indicate that a certain minimum number of successive terms, quarters, or semesters will satisfy the requirement. In a few cases all of the residence must be spent on campus, but in others provision is made for credit to be gained while the student is "in residence" elsewhere. Although only one of the institutions in the study specifically states in its graduate catalog that "exceptions can be made for employed students" several of the institutions accommodate the employed student by scheduling late afternoon or evening courses or by permitting students to register for independent study in order to fulfill the residence requirement. Approximately three-fourths of the graduate faculty were satisfied with the residence requirement as it is currently applied by their institutions. Fifteen per cent suggested that it should be modified. Among the latter were many who believed that the minimum number of course units should be raised. Others supported the idea that the time period should be extended. Approximately ten per cent thought the requirement should be dropped.

In terms of its rationale, the residence requirement is quite defensible. It is based on the assumption that by withdrawing from mundane responsibilities and "residing" for a block of time in the university community the student will be in the company of persons and in the proximity of resources and facilities which can enrich his intellectual development and expedite his progress toward the degree. In this environment, presumably, he can learn directly— from literature, from his models, or from a wide variety of cultural and intellectual experiences—the discipline and life style of the scholar. Of equal import is the fact that his instructors can learn from and about him. An important component of the rationale for the residence requirement is that it provides the faculty with opportunities to evaluate the quality of the students' intellectual promise as they observe it over an extended period.

In practice, the residence requirement has serious deficiencies. As enrollments increase these deficiencies threaten to become so great that the requirement per se will be impossible to enforce because it cannot be implemented. For one thing being "in residence" is based on the premise that one has the amenities of a "place to hang one's hat"—or his books and papers. It assumes that he will have space—living, library, laboratory—for learning. None of the public institutions in this sample and few of the private universities can promise these amenities to all of the students who are technically in residence during the regular school year (although most might provide it during summers).

Though it is not possible to estimate the waste and discontent sparked by the lack of study space—and by the lack of informal space for discussing ideas with fellow students—few would doubt that it is great. Even a casual walk around any of the campuses in this study reveals the crowded and distracting conditions under which many doctoral students work. Those who hold teaching or research assistantships sometimes are assigned office space, but others must shift for themselves. A few of the respondents in this study volunteered the information that they accepted a research or teaching assistantship largely because it included work space and other in-service amenities. If the residence requirement is to have meaning, the university must be equipped with means to provide the benefits it promises. Otherwise, it becomes a frustrating and expensive economic debenture in which the student has no assurance that the university will fulfill its obligation to accept him as one "in residence." It is this requirement which, in the words of one graduate dean, "prevents the graduate school from becoming a correspondence institution."

GRADING SYSTEM

Traditionally, academic achievement has been evaluated on a grading system which uses alphabetical or numerical ordering. Recently that system has come under sharp scrutiny and widespread attack. In addition to the lack of confidence which many faculty members have in the reliability of the system, there is a mounting body of evidence to show that grading often encourages poor study and learning habits, produces underachievers as well as overachievers, and leads to unhealthy competition among one's peers. Thoughtful persons question the morality of a system which specifies that instructors evaluate a student's performance in terms of symbols which few regard as meaningful, especially when those symbols become part of the student's permanent record.

It is probably this question of closure or finality that makes the grading system seem repressive to many members of the faculty. The notion of a "final" examination in any branch of knowledge

today seems fatuous, and the practice of grading the student on discrete fifteen-block units of knowledge (or ten under the quarter
system) often leads to a lack of open-endedness about education as
a lifelong process. The mere acquisition of an A or a D conveys
little information about the student's growth since entering the
course and offers him little solid evidence on which to assess his
potential. Because the letter grade says nothing about the quality
of his mind or the modes of thinking he used to achieve the grade,
it reveals little about the student as a learner. Because it fails to include measures of his nonintellectual interests, it says nothing about
him as a person. This method of evaluation utilizes a large part of
a faculty member's time yet yields questionable results. The need
for a more defensible system of evaluation seems clear when one
speculates on the importance that is attached to grades and on the
disparity in standards, the errors in judgment, and the flimsy, sometimes false evidence on which grades are assigned.

Some faculty members believe that the grading system in
higher education cries out for reform not only because it is a misuse
of the teacher's time but because it touches the lives of individuals
with such finality. Decisions which determine the future career opportunities and judgments of an individual's ability are sometimes
predicated on the difference between a minute deficiency in his
grade-point average and the school's minimum grading standard.
Many faculty members believe that the grading system sets up and
perpetuates a practice which is reprehensible in a democratic society, for it often leads to a marking off of the "haves" from the
"have nots," or the dominant group from the minority. Some said
that, in conscience, they avoid participation in this practice by giving the same passing grade to all. The lack of consistency in grading
standards is matched by a lack of consistency in the rewards grades
bring. For example, in many fields women tend to get better grades
than men, but department chairmen report that women graduates
rarely get commensurate consideration in terms of job offers or
salaries.

A few institutions in this sample have begun to experiment
with variable grading systems. For example, in some cases a student
receives a letter grade for all work in his major field and a pass
or not pass for all work outside of his major. In other cases the

student receives a "progress" notation on his record until he has completed his course work. He will then take a series of comprehensive examinations on which his overall achievement will be evaluated and recorded. The rationale in the latter case is that evaluation is more open-ended. Because it provides a developmental measure of the individual's style or modes of thinking, and shows his growth in his ability to organize, integrate, and relate ideas, it is a better measure of his growth potential than are discrete grades.

There is a strong belief among test and measurement experts that faculty time is utilized poorly and a great deal of student discontent is generated through our present more or less standardized grading systems. It is possible in some institutions that a student may go through four years of college never having had a face-to-face discussion with any professor about his progress or promise. Unfortunately, the same conditions may prevail in the first years in a graduate program.

When graduate faculty members were asked to indicate whether grading provided a reliable means of evaluating a student's Ph.D. potential, 63 per cent agreed that it did, 25 per cent thought that it did not, and the remainder were undecided about its effectiveness. Over a third of the faculty members felt that grading tends to place emphasis on the structure of the degree program—that is, on credits and grade-point averages—rather than on knowledge as the primary goal. A slightly higher percentage believed that the integrative-synthesis aspects of scholarship are lost when students must be evaluated on their knowledge of discrete segments rather than on broad bodies of knowledge. According to 42 per cent of the faculty respondents, the competition generated by the grading system tends to encourage "grade getting," especially among those who strive to be identifiable on the lists from which prospective assistants or award recipients are drawn. Since "the ability to pull down an A is the criterion for eligibility for graduate awards," some students are compelled by economic necessity to focus on meeting the grade required. The price exacted by expediency is incalculable.

Practically every faculty member can relate an incident in which his relations with a student became strained when the student's course grade did not coincide with his self-evaluation. At the doctoral level this can be a serious impediment to collegiality and scholarship. Equally obstructive are situations in which students pressure for a grade rather than for an understanding of the rationale on which it is assigned. In this study, 20 per cent of the faculty members agreed that the grading system tends to destroy the collegial relationship which normally obtains between the Ph.D. candidate and his sponsor, 67 per cent thought that it did not, and the remainder were undecided. In their free comments about the grading system, faculty respondents were inclined to admit that they had little faith in grading as practiced but in the absence of a better alternative they were disposed to tolerate it. Others noted that they were opposed to the present system because the narrowness of the grade distribution—usually A or B—was not sufficiently discriminating or because the grade measured but one aspect of the scholarly composite.

According to most of the faculty respondents, the selection, orientation, and supervision of graduate students is as crucial an aspect of excellence in graduate education as is the quality of the graduate faculty. In addition to the need for better student selection techniques than are now available, respondents expressed a pressing need for evaluative measures which could "assure protection for the profession" by separating out the weak students and identifying the special needs of the strong. Some suggested that an intense evaluation should be made after the first year of graduate work. On the basis of his performance at that time, the options that are available to the student should be made clear.

Several respondents recommended that in lieu of using rigidly set or standardized criteria to test the ability or potential of graduate students, an assessment should be made of their native bent, interests, and skills. They argued that too many students, in order to meet the departmental standards, adopt what they perceive the professional image to be and in doing so lose their own individuality. Others noted that less motivated students "ride out of graduate school on the coattails of their eminent professors" without demonstrating their own creative ability. Table 4 shows the doctoral students' appraisal of the extent to which the various evaluative methods had been helpful to their self-development.

Nearly a fourth of the doctoral respondents in each institution and in each department reported that they had not found

Table 4

STUDENT APPRAISAL OF VARIOUS METHODS OF EVALUATION
(in percentages, N = 3162)

	Most Helpful	Somewhat Helpful	Not Helpful	Not Used or Offered
Grades	15	55	24	6
Conferences with faculty	20	31	10	39
Professor's written comment on assignments or lab work	15	37	17	31
Evaluation by other graduate students	12	39	15	35
Evaluation by research committee	6	13	8	73
Self-evaluation	54	40	3	3

grades to be helpful indicators of their academic progress; 16 per cent described them as "most helpful," and 55 per cent found them "somewhat helpful." Only 6 per cent of the respondents reported that their departments did not evaluate doctoral students on a grade-point system. Grades, apparently, are the chief media through which the faculty communicates to the student its assessment of his achievement. The message is usually interpreted by doctoral students as an assessment of their promise rather than (or in addition to) a measure of their performance.

The detachment implied in the use of a grade symbol serves to mask the nature of the involvement between the evaluator and the one evaluated. While it may only be a façade, it is this apparent detachment which doctoral students decry. Some wrote derisively of the coldness in the evaluation process, others wrote of it skeptically. It is of interest that many students in mathematics (who probably appreciate the limitations of symbolic rhetoric) and in sociology, psychology, and biochemistry (who possibly appreciate the influence of the affective on cognition or the afferent on the efferent) did not consider grades to be helpful devices for assessing scholarly growth or progress.

The use of the conference as an evaluation device was described as helpful by most of the students who had had such an experience. However, 40 per cent of the respondents reported that their professors did not use conferences for feedback purposes. Students and professors alike appear reluctant to seek face-to-face encounters in order to clarify questions pertaining to the student's progress or to his past performance. This is especially true of many first-year students. Some students convince themselves that the instructor is too busy or too inaccessible, and so they do not press for a conference. The professor, on the other hand, often feels that at the graduate level the student should make the initial step if he wishes a conference. Many who conscientiously post and maintain office hours find themselves sitting alone during those hours; others find that many who come in are interested in "small talk" rather than in a serious discussion of their goals or needs. Because a meaningful conference involves a considerable investment on both sides, it can be a most valuable evaluation experience for the student and for the instructor. Often it becomes the vehicle for humanizing the evaluative process and for a rewarding faculty-student encounter.

Judging by the comments of doctoral respondents, the evaluation process has its greatest value when it includes both sides of the human equation. If, as Rogers (1967) notes, there are genuineness and trust on each side, even a brief encounter can be critical but constructive and of immeasurable value. In describing such encounters students sometimes attributed the beginning of their commitment to the fact that "Professor X really took my ideas apart but he also gave me the help, encouragement, and the freedom I needed to put them together in a more reasonable form."

Apparently large numbers of the faculty view their written assignments and examinations principally as a base on which to validate the student's grade. Approximately 37 per cent of the respondents said that their instructors did not add written comments to substantiate their grading or to point out the errors or faulty reasoning in the written work. Among the remainder 50 per cent said that they found their instructors' comments helpful and 18 per cent reported that the nature of the comments was not helpful. A few cited examples of caustic and demeaning evaluative comments which had shaken the recipients' self-confidence.

Eighteen per cent of the respondents said that they had

profited from the evaluations made by their research committees. There were substantial differences in the ways this assessment was conducted and basic differences in the function of these committees. In some institutions an advisory committee is appointed at the start of the student's program and is responsible for helping him to select a program of study and for assessing his progress at certain stages. In other instances the main work of the committee is to approve the academic respectability of the graduate's proposed dissertation. Once his prospectus has been approved, the committee does little more than act as signatories to his finished research. In other cases committees are held responsible for critically guiding the candidate through each step in his research. Presumably, these committees serve a check-and-balance function over the quality of the student's research but they also serve as mechanisms through which surveillance can be maintained over departmental standards.

Doctoral students play a strong and often supportive role as pace-setters for one another and in many cases find evaluation by their peers a more helpful gauge of their progress than evaluation by the faculty. Fifty per cent of the respondents in the study reported that they had found the critiques of their fellow students valuable stimulants to self-examination. Some described their association with groups of students who had, with an intelligent self-interest in sharing knowledge, organized informal rump sessions or mock examination panels for the purpose of testing ideas and receiving feedback. Some respondents described these encounters as "inquisitorial" or "fiercely competitive," but they observed that the absence of the "grading syndrome" made the sessions non-threatening and highly provocative.

Seminar presentations were also regarded by students as opportunities in which to submit oneself to rigorous examination by one's peers and by the faculty. Many respondents found the critiques of fellow students to be helpful in terms of the insight they provided, but among some students the atmosphere was tense and hostile due to the intellectual one-upsmanship behavior of the more aggressive or more verbal students. Shy and insecure students were more likely to withdraw and become silent in these situations rather than suffer being "put down" by those who were prone to attack rather than to offer positive guidance.

As a general rule, doctoral students say that they profit most by self-evaluation. In assessing their progress and prospects they generally analyze the variety of verbal and nonverbal clues that are projected consciously or unconsciously by the faculty. The attitudes and behavior of the faculty toward students are carefully observed and the nuances in any word of commendation, or in any recognition—such as an R.A. or T.A. appointment—are carefully weighed. The rise or fall of other students in the department provides important guidelines on which individual students estimate their own chances for success. The failure or "washing out" of one can be a source of stress for all others, as the following comment indicates: "One of the teaching fellows who read our first-year papers was washed out after two years in the program. All of us were shaken by this event—especially since we didn't know much about the circumstances. We all wondered if we were 'next'—I kept comparing my chances against his."

There is a general belief among students that grading and evaluation are haphazard and mechanical. This is disillusioning for those students who entered graduate school expecting to receive specific and personalized evaluations of their intellectual strengths and weaknesses. Although evaluation at the dissertation stage comes close to the tutorial model which most graduate students appreciate, the sheer numbers of first- and second-year students in some departments precludes the use of this model for beginners. Some institutions attempt to compensate by encouraging small group conferences, colloquiums, or informal meetings at which students can obtain feedback and comparative information on the quality of their work.

In view of the almost insurmountable task involved in evaluating the large numbers of doctoral students who are currently enrolled, the problems of assessment are almost destined to accelerate. Because the value of the Ph.D. is so intimately dependent upon the quality and fairness of the evaluation process, deans and graduate advisers expressed deep interest in the resolution of this problem. The use of qualified outside or affiliated examiners is seen in at least one institution as a partial answer. Professional persons who are often found within the radius of a major campus sometimes assist as members of oral examining committees or research committees. To the extent that such persons represent prospective associates of the doctoral student, valuable consequences can follow for all parties. This practice can also avert the criticism that academic men tend to be self-authenticating judges of their own productions.

DISSERTATION

The dissertation is the crowning point in the Ph.D. program. In it the student demonstrates his ability to identify an important idea in his field about which more information is needed, and his ability to design and execute a plan for obtaining the missing knowledge.

According to Engel (1966) the origin of the thesis as a scholastic requirement dates back to the thirteenth century, when applicants to religious orders had to present and defend a point of doctrine in an interchange with their future colleagues. It was then adopted by the medieval universities (which frequently absorbed the ceremonials of the cathedrals upon whom they were dependent for space, financial support, and political protection) for use as a public ceremony in which the teaching ability of a man could be judged before the title "doctor" was conferred upon him. Thus, from an entrance examination, the thesis gradually evolved into a ceremony which purported to protect the public from charlatan physicians or from poorly prepared teachers and theologians. With the ascendancy of the German universities as innovative centers for the creation and diffusion of knowledge, Wissenschaft became the new mode of inquiry and a new model of the scholar-researcher emerged. With their interests heightened by the discoveries of Newton, Voltaire, Bell, and other "exact scientists," the German universities began to develop a new kind of graduate student—the specialist, who, according to Helmholtz (1893), "should add at least one brick in the ever-growing temple of knowledge."

Historical accounts show that in the centuries intervening since its inception, the thesis as a valid device for evaluating intellectual competence has been suspect. During its oral tradition, several Popes complained of the shallowness and lack of rigor in the substance and manner of the thesis examinations that were used to screen applicants for the doctorate. More recent critics deplore the concept of the thesis as "a contribution to original research," claiming that it should instead be taken only as satisfactory evidence of a candidate's training and potential as a *becoming* scholar. Ashby (1958) inveighs against "the very melancholy things that are perpetuated in the name of research." Kidd (1959), Babbige (1962), and Heiss (1963) have demonstrated that an insistence upon originality in thesis research has forced professors to become dependent upon outside funding and to seek financial assistance for their students—a phenomenon which takes its toll on the time, energy, and morale of the faculty, militates against their teaching, and operates as a questionable influence on the research interests and creative drive of graduate students.

Dissertation requirements appear to be consistent, if not virtually the same, for all institutions in the sample. Each university stipulates that the dissertation or thesis must embody significant ideas, be the product of independent investigation, and make a valuable contribution to knowledge in the field. It is expected to be of such scope and skillful presentation as to indicate the candidate's command of his subject, ability to contribute a fresh outlook or fresh knowledge, and demonstrate his mastery of the research methodology in his discipline. In most cases the dissertation must be judged "as having substantial merit" and be passed by a committee of at least three members of the graduate faculty including the major professor. In its directive on this requirement, one institution explicitly states that the topic must be "one of significance to the candidate's field but at the same time must not be beyond his experience or ability." Most institutions imply this limitation in their informal communications.

Judging by student comments on their experiences in the dissertation process, the challenge of being more or less independent and on their own as researchers has positive and negative aspects that can be far-reaching. These will be discussed in more detail in Chapter Nine, which includes departmental analysis of the graduate students' observations on their programs. Table 5 shows their responses to the question: What degree of independence did you enjoy in the dissertation process?

Serving as the capstone in the Ph.D. program, activities leading to the culmination of the dissertation requirement such as

Table 5

DEGREE OF INDEPENDENCE STUDENTS ENJOY IN THE
DISSERTATION PROCESS
(in percentages, N = 3153)

	As much as I wanted	More than I wanted	Less than I wanted	Not applicable
	(Percentages)			
Selection of faculty adviser	58	2	17	23
Selection of dissertation adviser	70	1	4	24
Selection of research topic	65	6	8	21
Writing of research design	44	5	5	46
Writing of dissertation	38	4	4	54

the selection of a topic, the preparation of a prospectus, the collection, ordering, and analysis of data, and the actual writing of the dissertation contributed more than any other experience to the development of the doctoral respondents in this survey. The travail that frequently accompanies the all-consuming demands of the dissertation is apparently mitigated by the satisfactions the student feels over his independent effort.

The length of the dissertation is becoming a critical matter, both for those who write them and for those who read them. In his analysis of the increasing lengths of Ph.D. dissertations, Allen (1968) notes that while the first Ph.D. dissertation at Yale in 1861 was composed in 6 pages, today 53 per cent of English Ph.D. dissertations are 151 to 300 pages in length, 32 per cent are 301 to 500 pages long, and 6 per cent are over 500 pages long. Commonly, the oral examination on the dissertation is at present limited to an evaluation of the student's proposed research rather than to the presentation of his results. Although departments still retain the right to require a final oral examination, most of them operate on the theory that a presentation before a seminar, a professional group, or a public forum will serve a better purpose than the traditional oral review before a faculty research committee.

On the whole, graduate faculty respondents were more satisfied with the dissertation requirement than they were with any other Ph.D. requirement: 88 per cent expressed approval of it as presently required, 9 per cent thought that it should be modified, and less than one per cent thought it should be dropped. Faculty members in English departments were least satisfied with the dissertation as required, and those in physics, mathematics, chemistry, sociology, philosophy, physiology, and history were most satisfied. When faculty members were asked to what degree their departments emphasized originality in research for the dissertation, 30 per cent responded that they expected a high degree of originality, 57 per cent expected a satisfactory degree, and 13 per cent said that their departments did not stress originality enough. More faculty members in economics and English than in other fields were disappointed, and more mathematicians, chemists, physicists, historians, and philosophers than others were satisfied or highly satisfied with the degree of originality required of their students' research effort.

In commenting on the dissertation requirements several faculty members suggested that a drastic overhaul in this requirement was needed and others suggested that it needed more modest reform. Among the modifications recommended was the replacement of the customary long reports by two or three published papers or a brief monograph. Several suggested that in some disciplines students might be required to develop an exhaustive review of the literature as a separate preliminary part of the requirement. In the next stage of his research he would be expected to contribute some net addition to that literature. Other respondents felt that students should be encouraged to publish some parts of their research even before completing the whole project.

Faculty members had five main suggestions for improving the quality of the dissertations produced by students in their departments: higher standards of excellence; more emphasis on individuality; greater diversity in form or structure; more interdisciplinary emphasis; and independent investigations in which the student is responsible for designing, planning, and executing the entire research process himself. This last suggestion was aimed at the criticism that Ph.D. students often use data already collected or plans designed by others and thus do not learn to do research "from the ground up." Some respondents proposed that in disciplines which justify the practice, a student might be permitted to present as his dissertation a separate segment of a team effort for which he had major responsibility, but in these cases he should do a smaller pilot study to ensure that he gains experience with all aspects of the research process.

Characteristics
of Faculty

8

Many current problems of graduate education are inextricably related with the fact that the responsibilities of the university faculty have changed considerably over the past two decades. Although the rate of change in the life styles and career patterns of professors has been uneven among the various disciplines, it has accelerated in almost all disciplines. Some types of faculty responsibilities have been eliminated, some have been combined with other professional groups, and some new roles and fields of study have been added. Some of the fields of study have merely changed their labels; others have emerged which did not exist in any previous form.

The biographies of many senior members on today's faculties trace a transition in their life style from that of the semimonastic scholar contemplating the life of the early Greeks to that of the scholar in the urban grant multiversity who spends his time studying the inhabitants of Carnaby Street or the Haight-Ashbury.

Viewed from any angle this represents a change that has been basically additive. In discussing the trends as they affect their disciplines, many department chairmen referred to the impact of these additions to faculty roles. As the primary producers of research, universities contributed substantially to the threefold increase that has occurred in knowledge over the past one or two decades. Concomitantly, as the main transmitters of knowledge, the instructional responsibilities of their faculties have appreciably increased. Department chairmen noted that these increments have resulted in more instrumentation, more facilities and services, more contacts with national and international scholars, more involvement with off-campus agencies, and more researchable problems for the faculty. At the same time, the size and diversity of the college-going population have made it necessary for most instructors to modify their teaching style and methods in some basic manner.

Analysis of the interview comments of the deans and department chairmen concerning the role of the faculty as change agents indicates that most of the change has occurred in faculty members themselves. When the interview comments were paraphrased, a composite profile of those changes emerged. Basically, as he looks at his career, today's university professor finds that with the great influx of students his relationships have been greatly altered. Most noticeably, he sees that the distance between himself and his students has widened to attenuate their relationships and to limit his influence with them. He notes this same phenomenon in his relationships with his colleagues in other departments. Increased numbers have decreased his opportunities for collegiality. More and more, he finds that his circle of associates has narrowed to those in his special field. He has moved from a period in which the role of the scholar was to synthesize and reflect on a body of knowledge already possessed, to a period in which the scholar is expected to advance knowledge of the unknown and to apply his findings to the development of technology for improving human living. He has seen universities become great by bringing together brilliant professors and allowing them to gather a group of colleagues and students who will pursue their own lines of research, but he notes that this has introduced some divisive elements and created powerful baronies. He has experienced a phenomenal increase in available research funds, travel grants, and stipends for his students, and, joy-fully, he has found that in a thirty-year period his salary has quad-rupled. But he also notes that many of his fresh Ph.D. students are able to draw considerably more financial compensation than he.

While he still finds some colleagues who are reluctant to adopt aggressive roles, he notes that they are gradually being re-placed by men who believe that initiative and the competitive spirit in the intellectual sphere are just as valid as these same qualities in the economic sphere. Those who hold this latter view sometimes startle him by their opportunism and lack of institutional loyalty, but he has come to realize that grantsmanship is an acceptable way of life for the scholar in the multiversity.

The use of the professor as an expert has become common-place. It has drawn thousands of them out of the university environ-ment and into the local and national arena. College and university professors now serve on external councils, committees, and commis-sions and participate actively on programs, panels, seminars, and symposiums which examine problems ranging from aerospace tech-nology to zymurgy (wine chemistry). They also serve as policy-makers on numerous boards and as heads of administrative units. A few have their own laboratories, others direct research centers or institutes. Still others have part-time responsibilities in affiliated in-stitutions. At any given point in time approximately 15 per cent are on academic leave. As knowledgeable persons in their fields, faculty members are called upon to testify before legislative or other com-mittees, to conciliate conflicts, and to adjudicate disputes on and off campus. They serve as advisers to presidents, governors, founda-tions, and to foreign as well as domestic institutions. As consultants and counselors in an almost infinite variety of situations, they leave their impact on the community. Increasingly they are becoming in-volved in the political world.

The popular figure of the gentle scholar who is deeply con-cerned about each one of his students has been replaced in the image-making media by the professor as an anti-hero: a man so busy publishing that he is unaware that the world around him is perishing—or worse still, as the man who created forces that now threaten to destroy mankind. To some, the works of the academic man are suspect because as he discovers and organizes new intelligence, he demonstrates again and again that the university is a force for "skepticism, emancipation, and pluralism." Some who knew it as a place for reinforcing old beliefs and values are threatened by this openness to change.

If there is one compelling lesson that emerges from the current state of confusion in higher education, it is the fact that the role of the university professor is grossly misunderstood by a large segment of the American public. Some see him *in loco parentis* and as such expect him to protect and transmit their values; others see him *in loco padre* and so want him to give counsel and support to their beliefs; still others see him *in loco politico* and these pressure him to adapt his teaching to their platform or to remain neutrally silent. The professor himself may see his role as that of a co-partner with his students in their common search for the truth in these various values, beliefs, or platforms. He often finds himself under attack by those who expect the professor "to know it all," but not to teach it "like it is" if in so doing he conflicts with their particular bias or belief system.

Attempts to define or to delineate the role of the professor usually result in dreary platitudes or glittering generalities. The guidelines offered for his various roles are either so circumscribed or so fluid as to make them useless. Books on the role of the college teacher offer little more than exhortations or injunctions about "the effective teacher." While their authors give minute details making for "tidiness" in teaching, they fail to come to grips with the nature of teaching itself. In short, they fail to consider what teaching *is*. Still less do they examine the existentialist concept of the *becoming* teacher. This is an area in which research is sorely needed.

The early years of a university instructor's career are often his most difficult. During this period in a large institution he may be "on" the faculty but he is not "of" it. Full acceptance is contingent upon his productivity. This almost invariably means published research. Until he has published, his status as a member of the scholarly community is on trial. His security as a member of the faculty is tentative. In a small institution the beginning year of a young professor may be difficult because he often is given a heavier teaching load than a senior member of the staff. If his doctoral program failed to teach him how to organize his material for teaching and gave him no background in the psychology of teaching and learning, he finds it difficult to adjust to the demands that teaching imposes on him or he imposes on himself. He has—besides lectures to prepare, papers to grade, records to keep, students to see, and meetings to attend—a life of his own to live. If he wants to spend that life in the groves of academe, he must keep his mind on his production. As he gains experience in the academic life he is given more and more administrative or non-teaching responsibilities. These enlarge his view of the academic world but often further drain his energies from his instructional responsibilities.

If one looks to the educational horizon, he can observe a new breed of college and university professors emerging. As yet, their numbers are far from legion, but the signs all portend that their tribe will increase. A profile based on the open-ended comments of professors in this sample shows that the new breed disavows the "institutional timidity" with which the academic community traditionally infused its members with respect to the scholar's role in social and political matters, and have reversed the non-involvement posture of their older colleagues. Whereas many of the latter are conditioned—and content—to assume the role of the social critic passively, the members of the new breed are inclined to take an active role in designing and reformulating plans for the improvement of the human condition. Rejecting the old sanctions of an academic culture which imposed a reserved life style on the scholar and rendered him ineffective on the action front, the new professors view the university as an institution without walls. More and more they eschew the library as the prime source of information for learning in favor of the "total environment."

Many, although not all, of this new group have their academic backgrounds in the liberal arts rather than in a professional field. A few are from the sciences. Using the methodology of the liberal arts, they tend to use what has been described as the "interconnectedness of knowledge" in their approach to the discovery of self, of man, and of society. They are, essentially, "interdisciplinary persons." While they accept and are quite capable of using the new technologies, they sometimes raise questions about the ethical and social consequences of such inventions as they affect the lives of men and women. Though fundamentally humanists and optimists, they often wear the faces of discontent when they observe or comment on existing conditions in society.

Some of the new breed are newcomers to teaching. The bulk of the others are junior members of faculties with three or four years of experience. A few have taught longer. Some of the newcomers are veterans of the dissent and the student protest movements that have swept college campuses the world over. Others were drawn into college teaching on the belief that education is the key to many, if not most, of the problems which beset man's relationships with himself and with other men. Almost all are committed to the ideal that the unexamined life is not worth living, thus they continually question the relevance of old knowledge and old values to new situations and new systems.

Some joined the new breed because the nature of their graduate programs prepared them to become action-oriented. Others who had been prepared in the traditional approach to knowledge say that they rejected its methods on the grounds that the university and its scholars are instruments for social change and, as such, neither can afford to fiddle over esoteric matters while Newark, Detroit, Watts, and Washington burn. Some are convinced that the needs of the present generation require a revolution in teaching methods. Others press for a total reorganization of the existing structure.

The nature of the institution's commitment and the objective interests of its faculty are the major determinants of how faculty subcultures are structurally induced on any given college campus. These are also the determinants of how the faculty member perceives his role and socializes his students. Clark (1963) found that faculties in small elite colleges and those in great research institutions hold quite different interests, attitudes, and values, and spend their time quite differently from those in less prestigious or nonresearch institutions. Table 6 shows the activities that were listed by the faculty respondents in the ten institutions in this sample in answer to the open-ended question: From what aspect of your academic work do you derive your greatest personal satisfaction? Inferentially, these data provide insight into the kinds of models that doctoral students observe as they are socialized into academic careers. While the responses serve as commentary on the work prefer-

Table 6

ACADEMIC ACTIVITIES MOST ENJOYED BY THE
GRADUATE FACULTY
(in percentages, N = 1290)

Activity Enjoyed	Number	Percentage
Research with faculty or students	283	22
Teaching and research	257	20
Teaching, writing, interaction with others	207	16
Research and teaching	196	15
Teaching (no qualification)	166	13
Research and writing	47	3.5
Contact with students	35	2.7
Teaching graduates	30	2.3
Other	69	5.5

ences that some faculty members express when asked to make a choice. Table 6 shows that the categories of preferences are not necessarily exclusive.

Two other determinants of faculty culture and utilization are the size and complexity of the institution and the extent of its integration as a total environment. In large-scale institutions, faculty subcultures generally form along similar or closely related disciplines. Although some faculty members move in and out of several groups with ease, most tend to be at home in, or to limit their work to, a single department. Research has demonstrated that faculty cultures are rarely found in pure form on most campuses, but that highly autonomous institutions tend to have distinctive cultures of their own. This may be partly because in the best institutions departmental walls are low or semipermeable. It may also indicate that their scholars feel little compunction about breaking through "administrative conveniences" if the demands of scholarly interaction or progress indicate the need.

In his studies of the activities of college and university faculties, Gouldner (1957) conceptualized as "locals" those who exhibit strong loyalty to their institution and tend to devote their primary labors to it. On the other hand, those who show greater loyalty to their profession, or those who are devoted to outside reference groups, he classified as "cosmopolitans." When faculty members were studied on the basis of their commitment as locals or cosmopolitans, and on the basis of their interest in pure versus applied studies, Clark identified four types of faculty orientation: the teacher, who is a "local" committed to disinterested or pure studies and to the college and its students; the scholar-researcher, a "cosmopolitan" interested in the production of general ideas but little concerned with their application and practice; the demonstrator, generally a "local" professional who on a part-time basis serves the college in a clinical, supervisory, or technical capacity (for example, the doctor, teaching supervisor, or industrial technician); and the consultant, who has a national reputation as a professional man, is very mobile, and is primarily interested in the application of knowledge.

Universities utilize all four types of faculty orientations in their operation. Because they have a heavy commitment to undergraduate studies, these institutions seek faculty members with a teaching orientation even though they rarely give rewards for it. The university's dominant need, however, is for the cosmopolitan scholar whose research produces new knowledge on which innovations can be predicated, and whose standing in the academic community reflects glory on the institution. Universities also use large numbers of demonstrators and consultants, especially in their various professional schools. Consultants often serve as bonds or intermediaries between the educational institution and the professional associations. Frequently their expertise is utilized in questions of influence or in matters concerning jurisdictional control over professional practice. Consultants are currently in increasing demand by governmental and civil agencies which attempt to redress social imbalances or to improve the quality of the environment. They play a crucial role in the development of urban universities which plan to put increased emphasis on their service function.

The graduate school is charged with the responsibility to prepare graduates for these pluralistic roles. It generally attempts to offer that preparation in a single academic program, the Ph.D.

Deans and department chairmen reported that, broadly stated, the university teacher is expected to use his skills in instruction, research, and service to his college. The assigned classroom teaching load of the graduate faculty member is approximately half that of the undergraduate staff member. This reduced load is to allow time for research and other scholarly activities. A sizeable portion of time must be allocated to coordinating the various activities or persons associated with his projects, with reading research related to his interests, and in communicating with scholars who are conducting similar or related studies. According to descriptive data collected by Wilson and Gaff (1968), the remainder of the faculty member's time is spent on approximately seventy different activities related to his academic role. These include preparing (or revising) lectures, reading lists, or teaching materials; developing examinations; reading and grading student papers; conferring with students about both academic and non-academic problems; preparing student records; holding office hours; answering correspondence; supervising students engaged in independent study; participating on faculty or student-faculty committees; attending department or general campus meetings; acting as an adviser to a student organization; and reading the journals in his specialty.

In addition to their teaching responsibilities, members of the graduate faculty prepare and evaluate the comprehensive or qualifying examinations of M.A. or Ph.D. applicants, serve on oral examination committees or thesis committees for their own degree students and also for students in related fields, advise doctoral candidates on their programs, sponsor and direct dissertation research, conduct their own research and report it to their discipline, serve as visiting speakers for their colleagues' seminars, attend and occasionally present a paper in a colloquy or symposium on some academic or campus-wide issue, and supervise one or more post-doctoral fellows.

In addition, graduate faculty members may serve as members of advisory committees that are associated with the graduate division, the research council, the chancellor's or president's office, or participate as resource persons on an ad hoc basis on matters before the board of trustees. They also serve on personnel committees in which appointments and promotions of colleagues are weighed, frequently supervise one or more junior staff members, and arrange contacts for teaching assistants who need help in finding placement. Some carry on an extensive correspondence with other researchers and may frequently be asked to serve as hosts to visiting scholars from other countries. They may, in addition, participate as members of accreditation teams, or represent their institutions in national meetings or public ceremonies.

There is an increasing amount of presumptive evidence to support the statement that the American university professor is becoming more and more like his Latin American counterpart with respect to his off-campus professional involvement. This may be seen in the fact that, as one department chairman observed, "ten per cent of the faculty are 'in the air' and another twenty per cent are off campus at any given point in time." Although many of these are involved in university-related activities during this time, a significant number are not. Department chairmen reported that many of their faculty members hold joint appointments elsewhere, have regular consulting offices off campus, or hold appointments in a research center or institute. A few write syndicated columns for commercial publication. A few others who are in great demand as speakers use agents to handle their bookings, and still others hold appointments as directors or associate directors of governing boards in organizations related to their specialty.

In many cases, the use of part-time staff members represents an accommodation to the lack of regularly budgeted full-time faculty positions. It is not unusual for a department which lists thirty or forty faculty members on its roster to have the full-time equivalent services of only ten or fifteen. In such cases, the full-time staff may be overburdened with administrative or committee assignments and students find the faculty inaccessible for adequate supervision. Thus, while the use of part-time staff enables the university to offer a wider range of special course work, the net results often militate against the guidance needs of students.

Explicitly and implicitly, major universities make it clear to their non-tenured faculty that unless they publish within a specified period of their appointment, their chances of retention are extremely remote. Tenured members face this same denouement with respect to the criteria for their advancement. Thus, as regards the university, only the productive scholar need apply. This policy has given credence to the statement that unless a university faculty member publishes, his life as a member of the faculty will be short or shortened. For many popular critics of higher education, the catch phrase "publish or perish" serves as a ready whipping post on which to hang the problems of college and university instruction. Those who suggest that the curtailment of research would serve as a quick solution to instructional problems apparently overlook the fact that 80 to 90 per cent of all college teaching is done by non-researchers and by those who do not publish. The probability is high that the quality of teaching would improve if commensurate rewards were offered for excellence in both of these academic responsibilities, and if the preparation of Ph.D. students included education in the art and skill of synthesizing and relating the knowledge produced through research.

The profile of the Ph.D. origins of the faculty respondents as shown in Table 7 suggests that the institutions in this sample educate staff for one another. As products of top-ranked institutions themselves, faculty members in the sample tend to orient their best students to expect placement in institutions at the top. As shown in the profile for the twelve departments, 636 of the respondents received their Ph.D.'s in one of the ten institutions in the sample. Four hundred and thirteen of the remainder received their degrees in seven additional institutions that were also ranked by Cartter as "distinguished," "strong," or "very acceptable" but which, for practical reasons, were not included in this study: Harvard, 151; Chicago, 84; Yale, 53; Princeton, 52; Massachusetts Institute of Technology, 30; Minnesota, 23; and California Institute of Technology, 20. Twenty other U.S. institutions awarded Ph.D.'s to four or fewer of the respondents and ninety received degrees from foreign universities.

These data provide insight into the dynamics of introducing innovation (or of maintaining the status quo) within a university. In their efforts to assure quality, top universities strive to recruit their influential or tenured appointees from among the graduates or faculties of a narrow group of institutions which are perceived to be in the same elite circle. As the appointees bring their acquired educational philosophies, academic ideas, and styles to their employing institution, the institution reinforces its position in the circle by taking on more and more of the characteristics the members value in common. Attempts to modify those values often meet internal resistance.

Table 7

Number of Faculty Members Who Received Ph.D.'s in One of the Institutions in the Study, by Disciplines

(Number in Discipline)

Institution	Biochem.	Chem.	Econ.	English	French	History	Math	Philosophy	Physics	Physio.	Psych.	Socio.	Total
Berkeley	4	15	15	10	3	12	6	5	16	4	12	7	109
Columbia	9	7	10	16	7	21	4	4	8	2	9	16	113
Cornell	4	0	3	4	1	5	6	6	12	5	2	1	49
Illinois	3	6	3	4	2	7	11	1	4	3	8	0	52
Johns Hopkins	1	1	2	12	2	1	4	0	2	5	0	1	31
Michigan	1	3	5	8	4	3	8	3	4	5	34	12	90
North Carolina	1	0	4	6	3	3	3	0	0	0	7	7	34
Northwestern	3	1	3	4	0	2	0	0	0	4	1	4	22
Stanford	3	0	7	3	1	6	9	2	4	1	16	2	54
Wisconsin	12	10	10	7	7	12	4	2	9	5	2	2	82
Total	41	43	62	74	30	72	55	23	59	34	91	52	636

The urge "to be like Harvard, Berkeley, or Columbia" usually arises at the departmental level. Occasionally the urge has been given substance by "loading" the faculty with graduates of the institution the department wishes to emulate. Some department chairmen reported that their departments represented schools of thought which on "certain special issues became tight little islands or voting blocks." Referring to Gardner's (1968) observation that in an ever-renewing society the appropriate image is the balanced ecological system in which each change in the system is brought into line with its purpose, one department chairman said that his problem was to convince the faculty that the educational system really was changing. Another described his staff as "a mutual admiration society of Ph.D.'s from X University who reinforce the ideas they learned there years ago." One dean reported that certain strong departments under his supervision had extensive interlocking relationships which enabled them to virtually control "the shape of the discipline for the next ten years" by their ability to move or to obstruct proposals for academic change and appointments.

The heavy impress of "an" academic style, as Aydelotte (1944), Riesman (1958), Drucker (1968), and others have warned, can, in an age of radical change, be a formidable impediment to reform. Drucker's observation that we are in an age of discontinuity—that is, a time in which change is so radical that the experiences and programs of the past offer little guidance in helping man to cope with present problems or future demands—applies to the struggle for reform and survival which modern universities face when they fail to staff for educational diversity or points of view.

In accepting an appointment in the institutions in the sample, 96 per cent of the faculty respondents said that they were influenced in their decision by the general reputation of the university and by the research opportunities available. Other highly important considerations included the reputation of the department (93 per cent), the reputation of individual faculty members (91 per cent), the atmosphere of freedom prevalent in the university (92 per cent), and the autonomy of the faculty (82 per cent). Of somewhat lesser importance were such factors as the quality of its students (78 per cent), the nature of its program (76 per cent), the salary scale (73 per cent), and the geographical location of the institution (65 per cent).

In this sample, 80 per cent of the faculty respondents from public institutions and 69 per cent from private institutions reported that they hold tenure appointments. The range extends from a public institution with 85 per cent of its respondents on tenure to a private institution with 56 per cent of its representatives tenured. Since 1915, when the American Association of University Professors was organized for the purpose of safeguarding the principle of academic freedom, academic tenure has been widely accepted as a correlative principle. However, because the system supports the former while often withholding or denying the latter, tenure has become a separate issue of considerable import to the university. Hofstadter and Metzger's perceptive and incisive *History of Academic Freedom* (1955) and the writings of Barzun (1968), Veblen (1965), and others are rich with examples of the fine irony and scathing prose which have been used to criticize some of the results of the tenure system. Among the indictments are the charges that once they "make" tenure many individuals cease to be productive, so that tenure protects mediocrity, and the charge that the common practice of having tenured members co-opt those to be tenured is tantamount to a guild system or to a priesthood, which perpetuates itself by a laying on of hands. Both of these charges are related to the question of academic viability. If the indictment that tenured members tend to nominate to their rank persons with whom they identify in terms of ideas, interests, values, and other affinities were in fact valid, academic conformity might ensue and the flow of academic ideas into the university might be inhibited.

In an attempt to measure faculty opinion on this issue, an item was included in the questionnaire which implied that the system of co-optation does inhibit change. Respondents were asked to indicate by a check-mark whether they agreed or disagreed with the statement. An invitation to comment freely on the issue evoked a considerable number of controversial and debatable responses. Much of the commentary pertained specifically to the term "co-optation." Some questioned its meaning (the omission of the hyphen through a typing error apparently perturbed some); others questioned its use.

The substance of the remaining comments suggested that, at least for some, the central issue was obscure or ambiguous. Some added responses which pertained only to the first part of the thesis, which referred to the selection process. Others pertained to the effect of the tenure process on the flow of new ideas into the university. Because it was not possible to decide whether a checked response related to one part of the statement or to the whole statement, an analysis of the data must be considered tentative or open to further question. However, for practical purposes of analysis, it was assumed that a checked "agreement" or "disagreement" represented a response to the central issue, whereas the qualifying remarks were seen as references to that part of the statement which touched a responsive chord in the commentator.

Sixty-seven per cent of those who responded to this item disagreed with the statement, and the remainder agreed. Among the former were many who qualified their disagreement with statements which implied that although the tenure system has inherent weaknesses, the respondent knew no system that worked better. In effect, these individuals raised the rhetorical question: What is the alternative? Appointment by trustees, legislatures, students, presidents, deans? It was clear from the tenor of the commentary that none of these alternatives was acceptable or palatable. Among the 33 per cent who agreed with the statement, those who qualified their agreement tended to do so in the direction of disagreement. That is to say, while they rejected co-optation as undemocratic, they defended the principle that the community of knowledge was the only reliable and relevant community to whom the selection and promotion task should be given. Their main complaint was that the range of academic ranks normally represented in the balloting on appointments and promotions was too narrow.

The substance of the comments made by those who rejected the inference that the tenure system inhibits innovation ranged broadly. Some said that they saw no evidence of that effect in their institutions, others argued that because ideas are always fluid in a "good" department or a "strong" institution, tenure is unrelated to innovation. Still others insisted that a *primary* purpose for tenure is to promote change. Some who approved the system aligned themselves on junior versus senior sides. Among the latter were those

who stated that most senior (tenured) faculty are quick to recognize
new ideas and to evaluate them soundly, whereas in the judgment of the respondent, "some junior faculty are rigid or narrow-
minded." The gist of many comments suggested that "given man's
inherent pettiness no other system *qua* system would work any better, therefore the imperfections in the present system must be borne."

While there was a pervasive and often explicitly stated premise that the competition among top universities has reduced the
importance of tenure, several positive admonitions emerged from
the analysis of the open commentary. These included the suggestions
that promotion committees should be representative of all ages and
all levels, avoid exercising an "establishment mentality," review
frequently, and whenever possible promote rapidly.

Advertently or inadvertently the institutions in this sample
seem to have achieved an interesting balance in the age distribution of their graduate faculties. Among 1464 who gave their ages,
34 per cent were 35 years old or below, 45 per cent were between
36 and 50, and 21 per cent were 51 years or older. Fifteen per
cent were below age 30 and 8 per cent were 61 or older. Table 8
shows the age distribution among the various disciplines. It is interesting that while the natural sciences as a whole have the largest
percentage of young faculty members, 42 per cent of the philosophy
and 40 per cent of the psychology departments are filled by persons
below 35. This may reflect the fact that psychology as a discipline
is fairly young and that philosophy—while a very old discipline—
has been rejuvenated by the flood of new reflections and new information in this field. Also of interest is the fact that biochemistry,
a current "glamour" field, is staffed by a larger proportion of men
over 35 but below 60. The latter figure may relate to the fact that
biochemistry is a new field; however, the smaller percentage of
younger staff members is more difficult to explain in view of the
excitement generated over the past two decades by research in this
discipline. A partial explanation may lie in the somewhat amorphous state of the field, but it may be more plausible to speculate
that biochemists have broad interdisciplinary opportunities in medicine or other fields on the campus, and that younger men tend to
select these connections in preference to a career in "pure" biochemistry.

Table 8

Age Distribution Among Faculty Respondents in Twelve Disciplines
(in percentages, N = 1464)

Discipline	30 or below	31–35	36–40	41–45	46–50	51–55	56–60	61 or over
Biochemistry	6	15	24	26	17	9	2	1
Chemistry	17	24	14	15	11	7	3	9
Economics	22	15	20	11	14	3	8	7
English	9	17	21	12	8	9	8	16
French	10	17	7	14	14	8	10	20
History	10	23	20	15	16	7	3	6
Mathematics	25	17	17	13	8	8	6	6
Philosophy	26	16	10	12	8	6	12	10
Physics	17	18	24	18	10	4	2	7
Physiology	3	11	23	19	19	13	7	7
Psychology	16	24	14	12	12	11	5	8
Sociology	16	20	27	17	7	4	7	3
Total	15.2	18.9	18.7	14.5	11.5	7.4	5.5	8.1

Women academicians were poorly represented in the sample for this study. Only 2.6 per cent of the faculty respondents from public institutions and 3.1 per cent from private institutions are female. Among doctoral student respondents 80 per cent were male and 20 per cent were female. The teleological statement expressed in these figures is clear to those who are concerned about the problems of the educated woman: the university is a male-oriented society. It remains so by imposing variable controls against the entrance of women. The major control is that of gate-keeping. By limiting the access of women to the Ph.D. program, the argument that "few women are chosen to faculty ranks because few are available" can be sustained. Other forms of control are supported more by mythology than by verifiable data. Some are designed to induce self-control. These are generally introduced to females early in the acculturation process and are transmitted in such messages as: "scholarship negates femininity," "certain fields are not suitable for women," or "women are ruled by emotion and men by reason, hence only males are equipped for life in the academy." In spite of the fact that data from other countries refute these statements, they have been repeated so frequently by male authorities that they are used to justify the blatant control exercised by one department in this study which states in its catalog that "preference is given to male applicants."

Comments added to both the student and faculty questionnaires by women respondents constitute a great cry of loneliness. Coupled with their isolation is their frustrating awareness that no matter how well they perform academically, most are foredoomed to a status secondary to their male counterparts. The chairman of a large English department described this reality when he mentioned that although he could easily place a male Ph.D. recipient of average ability in the best universities those same universities refused to consider appointing his superior women graduates. Some chairmen made off-the-record statements during the interviews in which they said that in their need for "warm bodies" to staff the undergraduate instruction and faculty research projects, they had appointed more women than they normally do. This admission was almost invariably followed by an expression of apprehension about "what effect the increased numbers of women would have on the department." A few implied that their private clubs had been invaded.

While some female faculty members wrote poignantly of having resigned themselves into accepting fewer rewards than their male counterparts, others were not so passive or sanguine. In fact, the militancy evident in the comments of women respondents forebodes a growing restlessness and a thrust on their part to gain greater recognition. Some reported that they had become active in the various women's organizations such as the National Organization for Women (NOW) and the Women's Liberation Front. Others had participated in women's caucuses within their professional organizations. In general, the goal of these movements is to disprove the notion that women are not as well equipped as men to cope with the world of ideas. The substance and form of the dissent movement among other minorities have given women the impetus to seek a hearing for their problems. Some observers expect that the decade ahead will see a revolution among creative and highly educated women.

At the graduate level the academic adviser plays a key role in the graduate student's progress. Most of the universities in the sample have institutionalized the role of the graduate adviser, although in at least two cases in this sample graduate advising is somewhat informal. Formal advisers are faculty members who are appointed by the graduate dean to act as his deputy within their departments. While he serves as a liaison between the graduate office and the department chairmen, the primary function of the adviser is to serve as a channel through which student matters are processed and student needs are served. In large departments a committee of advisers may be needed; in this case, one member may be appointed the coordinator or director of graduate studies. The large amount of paper work and record keeping entailed in this responsibility sometimes requires the services of a departmental graduate secretary or administrative assistant. From the students' point of view, it is important to cultivate this contact. If the secretary has empathy for students she can do much to expedite their progress and reduce their anxiety. On the other hand, if the secretary is protective of the faculty, the student may find her a formidable barrier to his access to the adviser.

Deans and department chairmen complain that faculty members are, as a rule, notoriously disinterested in the details associated with procedures, requirements, schedules, and other forms of administrative bookkeeping. On the other hand, faculty members admit that they purposely do not keep abreast of degree requirements on the theory that they would prefer to relate to students through discussions of substantive issues or research. Some successfully combine the students' needs for intellectual dialogue and casual conversation by holding informal social meetings in their homes. Judging by the comments of students who had been invited to these gatherings, they often provide memorable and enriching experiences.

There are growing indications that the heavy layer of professionalized personnel which the university uses to service student needs—for example in admissions, advising, housing, counseling, financial assistance, health, records, placement, and scholarships—have virtually insulated faculty and students from each other and thus inadvertently contributed to the growing discontent with education that is not a spontaneous and stimulating encounter.

Appreciable numbers of faculty members have reservations about the amount of guidance the doctoral student needs or should be given. Many agree with Veblen (1965):

The student who comes to the university for the pursuit of knowledge is expected to know what he wants and to want it without compulsion. If he falls short in this respect, if he has not the requisite interest and initiative, it is his own misfortune, not the fault of his teacher. What he has a legitimate claim to is an opportunity for such personal contacts and guidance as will give him familiarity with the ways and means of higher learning—any information imparted to him being incidental to this main work of habituation. He gets a chance to make himself a scholar, and what he will do with his opportunities in this way lies in his own discretion.

Approximately 21 per cent of the faculty respondents felt that graduate students often criticize the university and its faculty for deficiencies for which only the learner can be held accountable. In commenting on this point, respondents expressed impatience with students who articulated no clearly perceived goals, lacked independence, or failed to strike out on their own for the help they needed. Most of the faculty respondents view the role of the adviser as a critical resource which the student should seek when he needs guidance or direction. Some seem to have great distrust of the student who would like the adviser also to be a friend.

On the premise that the student-sponsor relationship should be based on compatibility of interests, temperaments, and respect, doctoral students are usually expected to choose their own sponsors. However, in some cases, the graduate adviser may assign the sponsor. In this event, an effort is made to match the expressed interests of the student with those of a staff member. In other instances, a member of the faculty may invite a student to become his advisee. This happens more frequently in the sciences than in the humanities and usually implies that the student will become an apprentice or research assistant to the sponsor. According to some student respondents, to be selected as an advisee "can be a kiss of death for one's own plans." On the other hand, it may signify that the student ranks high in the opinion of the faculty. For some, selection by the right man is tantamount to an invitation into future guild membership. To be known as Professor X's student can have great significance within the professional field. The converse may also be true.

The quality and character of the relationship between the doctoral student and his major professor is unequivocally the most sensitive and crucial element in the doctoral experience, for it not only influences the graduate student's scholarly development but also has far-reaching aftereffects. In an earlier study the writer interviewed one hundred doctoral students who were asked to describe the role they thought their major adviser should play as he guided them through the degree. Their answers indicated that they saw him in many roles. Essentially, they expected him to be a critic but a constructive counselor, a relentless taskmaster but a supportive colleague, a model of scholarship but an understanding tutor. They can accept the adviser in the character of a benevolent martinet, but they consider "the attitude of the master sergeant toward the private uncalled for in the academic environment." As a group, respondents were critical of the major professor who dictated rather than directed. Students said that they wanted advisers to be knowledgeable about the degree process but also personally aware of the

student and his needs. Over 80 per cent said that the ideal adviser
was one who briefed them on the hurdles they would encounter in
the program as well as on the strategy through which the hurdles
could be overcome successfully (Heiss, 1964).

The selection of a dissertation sponsor is often a complex,
anxiety-producing experience for doctoral students. Large numbers
of the respondents in each of the institutions in the study reported
that they did not as yet have a sponsor. Some of these students had
been in the program for nearly two years. It is not uncommon for
students in the nonscience fields to defer the selection of a sponsor
until after they have satisfied the basic requirements in their departments. Theoretically, this allows the student to be selective in match-
ing his interests with a faculty member whom he knows and respects. It also provides the faculty with a record of accomplishment
and with a longer period over which to observe the quality of the
student's mind. In practice, delaying his selection may militate
against the student—particularly if he is shy. If he is "nobody's
man" during this orientation period he may fail to gain a personalized view of his discipline. This may negate his chances for identifying himself to those who are in a position to enrich his academic
experiences and prospects.

Students apparently do a considerable amount of shopping
around for a sponsor and there is much transferring from one sponsor to another. Not infrequently transfers are made by mutual agreement. In some cases, a change in sponsorship may be recommended
on the basis of the fact that some other member of the faculty can
be more helpful to the student because he is doing research in the
area in which the student wishes to do his thesis. In other cases,
transfers are necessary due to faculty resignations or because the
sponsor's sabbatical leave coincides with a critical stage in the student's program. In still other cases, the sponsor and student may
find that their interests or personalities are not compatible and one
or the other breaks the relationship. In general, institutional arrangements can be made for the student to continue with his sponsor once his dissertation has begun even if the sponsor moves to
another institution. Internal adjustments may be somewhat more
difficult. Students who "fall out" with their sponsors are sometimes
suspect by other members of the faculty among whom they must

seek a replacement. The degree of difficulty this poses may account for the fact that 26 per cent of the respondents said that, given another chance, they would select a different sponsor from the one they had. These data may point to an important source of doctoral student discontent. They also point to the need for a careful analysis of the procedures used in the selection of a sponsor.

The data in which doctoral student respondents evaluated their dissertation sponsors are shown in Table 9.

Table 9

STUDENTS' EVALUATION OF THEIR DISSERTATION SPONSORS
(in percentages, N = 2003)

	Yes	No	No Answer
Gave more direction than I wanted	6	88	6
Gave less direction than I wanted	28	66	6
Scheduled regular meetings with me	19	76	5
Expected me to request meetings	82	13	5
Helped me to select a research topic	67	30	3
Expected me to select my own topic	49	45	6
Helped me to prepare for examinations	40	54	6
Accepted me as a junior colleague	60	33	7

In the folklore of academic life the university is often depicted as a community of scholars. Despite fundamental alterations in the life style of academicians and in the character and scope of university organization, the impression persists that the academic world offers a communal environment which is distinguished by an intellectual esprit de corps. Presumably, this spirit is infectious in nature and capable of inspiring the faculty to transcend its specific interests and inclinations in favor of an interest in institutionally valued goals. Ideally the campus-wide infusion of this spirit serves to unify the educational effort, generates collegiality, and produces an environment in which men and women are respected for the quality of their minds. Presumably, doctoral students are important members of the academic community. In theory, it is the responsibility of the faculty to introduce students into its membership and socialize them to its values. It accomplishes this formally through advising and orientation programs and through the recommendation of awards, fellowships, or admission to candidacy, and it finally seals their admission into the academic community by granting the appropriate degree. Informally, many members of the faculty attempt to provide an atmosphere in which students are accepted as junior colleagues before their formal acceptance as members of the academy.

In appraising the sense of community which existed in their departments, 20 per cent of the faculty members registered disappointment in its quality and 80 per cent registered satisfaction. Respondents were considerably less confident that students were sufficiently included in the department's communal relationships. Seventy-four per cent of the faculty respondents thought that their departments should make greater efforts to provide more opportunity for collegiality between faculty and students than they currently do. Inferentially, many of these suggested that the department should provide some mechanism which would induce collegiality. Others were convinced that collegiality was basically an infectious spirit, a phenomenon which the student "caught" when, through his own discovery, he identified with the goals of his department or with the ideals and interests of one or more members of the faculty.

Some measure of the degree to which the various disciplines succeed in providing a sense of community for future scholars may be seen in Table 10, which shows the student's response to the question: Does your department provide adequately for the interchange of ideas between faculty and students? These data show that the humanities and social sciences failed to provide a sense of community for at least 50 per cent of the respondents in those fields. Although 14 per cent of the students said that they had "no basis for judging" the meaningfulness of the interaction which students had with the experts in their fields, and 11 per cent more described these interactions as "rarely meaningful," 75 per cent reported that they had found their interactions "very meaningful" or "moderately meaningful." In their extended testimony on this point, students frequently praised a particular faculty member who had stimulated their research interests, shared his own research data with them, or

Table 10

DOCTORAL STUDENTS' APPRAISAL OF DEPARTMENTAL PROVISIONS
FOR THE INTERCHANGE OF IDEAS AMONG STUDENTS AND FACULTY

		Percentage		
Discipline	*Provisions Adequate*	*Provisions Inadequate*	*Uncertain about Adequacy*	*Number*
Biochemistry	67	26	7	198
Chemistry	69	23	8	422
Economics	48	41	11	252
English	33	56	11	295
French	35	51	14	150
History	37	51	13	345
Mathematics	68	22	10	272
Philosophy	53	35	12	196
Physics	56	28	16	327
Physiology	67	16	17	106
Psychology	61	31	8	364
Sociology	44	42	14	254

put students in contact with other researchers or resources which enriched their interests or gave meaning to their work. Apparently there are faculty members in all departments who relate well with students and find their work with them as rewarding as working with their faculty colleagues. Approximately 80 per cent of the students believed that members of the graduate faculty respected them as graduate student-scholars and showed an interest in their advancement.

Students were less conscious of a sense of scholarly community than were the faculty. This may be the result of the variations in their degree stages or it may be a facet of the competition which is prevalent when fairly large numbers of students are competing for attention and recognition from a small number of faculty members. Wide variations were found in their response to the question: Do advanced students serve as models for those who are not yet advanced? As seen in Table 11, students in chemistry and in the laboratory fields in general show a greater solidarity than do those

Table 11

PERCENTAGES OF STUDENTS WHO ACCEPT OTHER STUDENTS
AS MODELS, BY DISCIPLINES

| | *Percentages* | | |
Discipline	*Accept*	*Do not accept*	*Not sure*
Biochemistry	69	19	12
Chemistry	79	11	12
Economics	40	23	37
English	44	37	19
French	44	40	16
History	44	37	19
Mathematics	49	28	23
Philosophy	41	38	21
Physics	55	24	21
Physiology	65	19	16
Psychology	65	19	16
Sociology	51	29	20

in the humanities and social sciences. The fact that students in the latter fields tend to work on research which does not involve them directly with other students probably accounts for some of the differences. It may also be true that the scarcity of fellowships and grants in these disciplines forces students to become competitive rather than cooperative. In some cases, the price of faculty recognition is rejection by one's peers. This can have serious consequences for the student. As one respondent observed, "In our future careers we will be judged largely by our peers so it is important that we be accepted by them now."

The prevalence of an intellectual esprit de corps among doctoral students was more evident among respondents in chemistry (65 per cent), psychology (62 per cent), mathematics (61 per cent), and physics (60 per cent) than among students in other fields in the sample. It was least observable among students in French (45 per cent), English (49 per cent), and sociology (50 per cent). In their comments on this item, students frequently described their interaction with fellow students as more challenging than their classroom experiences or their brief out-of-class encounters with professors. The assimilation and identification of part-time students into peer groups is apparently problematic. Approximately 25 per cent of the respondents felt that these students do not identify with their disciplines, 19 per cent thought that they did, and the remainder were uncertain.

The majority of doctoral students evinced a healthy respect for the intellectual ability and commitment of their fellow students. Sixty-three per cent described them as committed to scholarship, 12 per cent thought that they were not, and 25 per cent were unable to make a judgment on this point. When students were asked to evaluate the graduate faculty as a whole on certain aspects of their roles as mentors, they responded as shown in Table 12.

Dramatic differences in the characteristics of the new generation of college students and previous generations motivated some professors to question whether they can or should attempt to lead today's student. Differences in cognitive types and in personality characteristics among today's doctoral candidates, and differences in the structure and amount of knowledge they must master, caused some respondents to conclude that the old rules, regulations, and requirements for the Ph.D. are no longer tenable. Originally intended to insure minimum standards of application and achievement, those standards are now often surpassed before the student reaches graduate school. And, in some areas of knowledge or expertise—such as computer usage—the student, not his professor, may be in the lead. For this reason, some departments impose a bare minimum of prescribed requirements in favor of providing an environment where free exploration is possible and individual creativity can be expressed. This does not necessarily mean that the student does not take a full program of courses. It merely means that he is given greater freedom in selecting them.

Faculty members who adhere to the traditional notion that all graduate students should be "put through the paces" find it difficult, if not traumatic, to accept the fact that those paces may no longer lead to scholarly purposes. The concept of the professor as a model and the student as an apprentice persists among appreciable numbers of the graduate faculty. According to department chair-

Table 12

STUDENT RATINGS OF GRADUATE FACULTY AS MENTORS
(in percentages, N = 3173)

	High	*Average*	*Low*	*No basis for judging*
Accessibility	50	36	12	2
Helpfulness and support	40	40	14	6
Interest in students	39	44	15	2
Evaluation of written work	27	49	10	14
Promptness in returning written work	25	54	11	10
Constructive criticism	33	45	16	6
Respect for divergent viewpoints	38	41	12	9
Respect for student's autonomy	46	37	10	7
Accuracy in assessing student's academic ability	28	51	6	14
Knowledge of student's academic ability	25	52	12	11
Knowledge of student's academic progress	26	44	21	9
Interest in student's research	32	37	14	17
Interest in student's development as a college teacher	12	28	39	21
Respect for graduates as becoming scholars	34	46	11	9

men, there are still significant numbers of professors who do not accept graduate students as co-partners and many who find it difficult to approach an assistant professor and admit that they lack the knowledge or newer technical skills needed to resolve a problem. They are even less reluctant to approach their graduate students with this admission.

Faculty assessment of graduate students varied somewhat from department to department, but their overall assessment as shown in Table 13 offers a profile of general faculty opinion about their Ph.D. students. In addition to the improved quality of their

Table 13

FACULTY OPINION OF TODAY'S GRADUATE STUDENTS
(in percentages, N = 1431)

Today's graduate students	Agree	Disagree	Undecided
Are among the best graduate students in the country	67	25	8
Are better prepared for graduate education than students five years ago	68	13	19
Are committed to a life of scholarship	41	34	23
Are concerned about the consequences of research	58	21	18
Are highly competitive 'grade seekers'	34	52	13
Are interested in interactions between related disciplines	47	35	16
Go beyond the requirements in independent search for knowledge	29	60	9
Criticize the university and faculty for deficiencies for which the learner only can be held accountable	21	56	20

preparation for graduate study, the characteristic most frequently mentioned when the faculty compared their current students with past generations of graduate students was the fact that today's student "lacks the fear of falling on his face." In the words of one department chairman: "They are the same bumbling students we were but they have more brass. They are to be admired because they wade in. We lacked that courage . . . as a result, I still fasten my seat belt whereas . . . the student and the young professors wade in." The cleavage in the so-called generation gap appears sharper between senior and junior members of the faculty of some departments than between doctoral students and the faculty. That is, some older members of the faculty use approaches or adhere to values that are categorically rejected by the younger members, and some younger members may be more knowledgeable in some areas, or skilled in methodologies, that are foreign to the older members in the same discipline. For the most part, the gap is accepted as a natural phenomenon and gracefully bridged by those who acknowledge and capitalize on their different skills. However, according to

department chairmen, some older faculty members operate on the
assumption that "history has taught the old what the young must
know" while some younger faculty members refuse to accept history
as a valid base on which to make assumptions about the present.

A *New York Times* writer has observed that crises on campuses have made student-watching a national pastime. Although
they would hardly describe it as a pastime, college and university
administrators in particular and professors in general spend an increasingly disproportionate amount of their time in student-watching—often under duress. This was particularly true of personnel in
those institutions in this study which have been centers of student
protest. Faculty members in these schools said that they were now
investing considerably more time as members of committees, boards,
commissions, and negotiating teams in their attempts to respond to
student protest than they do in instructional duties. The use of the
faculty's time in these tasks has the potential of bringing returns that
can have more important effects over a greater period, and for a
greater number, than the same time spent by professors in "covering" their courses. Although working with intransigent or recalci-
trant students often leads to frustration, diminishing returns, or to
a dead end, many professors find that this use of time gives them a
better understanding of where the education system needs revision
or strengthening, or where teachers themselves have failed to meet
the students' aspirations about the college experience. It would be a
serious mistake to underrate the importance of devoting time to
this activity. By now, most college personnel are sensitive to this
fact. Although many are still unprepared to meet the prospect with
élan, the probability is that faculties will spend an increasingly large
amount of time in out-of-class informal contacts with students or
student groups. In some respects this will lead to more, not less,
teaching and learning.

As a result of their united effort to seek solutions to the
global problems raised by the students, many college and university
professors have begun to reexamine the relevance of their disciplines
to today's problems. Some have reorganized their approach accordingly. For example, the chairman of a physics department noted
that many of his staff members had changed their research focus
from an abstract to a problem-oriented approach. Some professors
admit that they are learning for the first time of the great com-

plexity involved in organizing and administering a university in an era of rapid social and technological change. Sociologists, for example, who for years rejected Dewey's suggestion that the school system offers a ready-made institution for studying social change are now examining it from top to bottom, inside and out. Judging by the number of papers they write about higher education, many professors in varied other fields have been jolted out of their preoccupation with their own discipline and have turned their attention to concerns involving student discipline and freedom. This often brings them full circle back to a reconsideration of how they have used their teaching time.

Speaking from a university undergoing a serious crisis of student unrest and protest, faculty members who were interviewed for this study voiced deep concern about the need for university reform. Some felt that the faculty was in greater need of help and education than the students. Looking at the pressures within their departments caused by the rapid growth of knowledge, at student overload, at the lack of collegial amenities, at the dearth of administrative services, and at the financial strains on the graduate level, some saw little hope of relieving those "whose initial creativity was being ground down year after year in details which enervated, rather than energized, their morale and gave them little desire to try to generate an esprit de corps."

The comments of some faculty members reflected their accumulating frustrations with academia or with academic requirements. Wrote one:

After listening to the students' protests I, too, am for: (1) Anarchy—let's throw out the catalog or at least change the rules every two years or so. (2) Direct confrontation—let the senior staff regularly tell the junior staff just what they think of them and vice versa. A similar relationship would be the only humane way of relating to graduate students. (3) Discarding useless competition in favor of encouraging cooperation—just for the sake of fellowship—not by decree.

Another commented:

I'm writing this as the university is struggling to return to normalcy. Our department and our university have shown themselves unable to respond to powerful and legitimate student demands. Our graduate students want us to be more accessible; to be more willing to listen as well as to speak; to spend time happily rather than begrudgingly and in brief doses with students, to be a faculty which will learn with students rather than simply train them. When I was a graduate student here ten years ago I felt these same needs and communicated them to senior faculty members but the results were few.

A résumé of the general suggestions offered by faculty respondents toward the improvement of their relationships with doctoral students and for greater refinements in their roles as models included the organization of joint faculty-student seminars and informal social get-togethers, the development of a booklet about the faculty for use by the students, direct teaching as well as research experience so that on-the-job guidance and evaluations can be made, less caste and more collegiality in faculty-student interaction, and a philosophy which honors excellence or superior achievement in such a way so as not to imply rejection of the less gifted but basically well-qualified student.

Characteristics
of Students

9

Addressing himself to graduate students, Whaley (1967) suggested that each generation has an obligation to reassess for itself the state of its affairs. To this end he cautions that so long as graduate students do not question the models offered to them by the faculty, by professional and technical societies, or by those who employ Ph.D. recipients, they will be shortchanged in their intellectual development. In addition, Whaley contends, they will themselves have failed to contribute new intellectual components or patterns to society.

If the premise is to be supported that doctoral education represents both a generative and a regenerative process, continual renewal and evaluation of the ends and means of the process must be practiced both by its designers and by those who will, presumably, reflect its impact as they assume their various careers. It was in this spirit that the students in this study were asked to appraise their

Ph.D. programs. The overall characteristics and evaluation of the respondents are included in this chapter. Responses to certain specific aspects of the program are included in other appropriate places in the book.

BIOGRAPHICAL CHARACTERISTICS

Males outnumbered female doctoral student respondents by a ratio of eight to two. The only field in which female respondents were in the majority was French (53 per cent). The next most populous fields for women were English (35 per cent) and psychology (32 per cent). The fields which had the lowest numbers of graduate women students were physics (3 per cent), chemistry and philosophy (11 per cent), and biochemistry (12 per cent).

Marked differences are found in the ages of doctoral respondents in various disciplines. These are shown in Table 14. It is

Table 14

VARIATIONS AMONG DISCIPLINES IN THE AGES OF
THEIR DOCTORIAL STUDENTS
(in percentages)

Age Group

Discipline	*21–25*	*26–30*	*31–35*	*36–50*	*51 or over*
Biochemistry	28	60	9	3	0
Chemistry	44	50	5	1	0
Economics	26	62	9	2.5	0.4
English	26	45	17	11	1
French	28	37	21	12	2
History	19	57	16	8	0
Mathematics	39	53	6	2	0
Philosophy	26	50	14	10	0.5
Physics	33	56	9	2	0
Physiology	15	54	24	7	0
Psychology	30	54	12	3	0.8
Sociology	28	48	15	8	0.7

of interest to note that approximately 20 per cent of the student respondents were older than—or within the age range of—34 per cent of the faculty. Private institutions attracted a larger percentage of students between 21 and 25 (36 per cent) than public institutions (24 per cent). The latter also enrolled slightly more respondents who are 36 years of age or older (6.1 per cent) than did private institutions (5.2 per cent).

On the basis of their marital status, the respondents were distributed among the disciplines as shown in Table 15. If it can

Table 15

MARITAL STATUS OF PH.D. RESPONDENTS
(in percentages)

Ph.D. Discipline	Single	Married	Divorced	Widowed
Biochemistry	50.8	48.7	0.5	0.0
Chemistry	53.4	44.9	1.6	0.0
Economics	50.2	48.2	1.6	0.0
English	45.3	49.0	4.7	1.0
French	48.7	46.0	4.0	1.3
History	46.4	51.3	2.0	0.3
Mathematics	59.2	40.4	0.4	0.0
Philosophy	47.2	50.3	2.6	0.0
Physics	52.1	47.3	0.3	0.3
Physiology	36.8	62.3	0.9	0.0
Psychology	42.3	55.8	1.9	0.0
Sociology	39.0	58.7	2.0	0.4

be assumed that single students are freer than married students to make a commitment to advanced study, the respondents in mathematics, chemistry, physics, biochemistry, and economics appear to be in the best position. If the converse is true, students in physiology, sociology, and psychology are better prepared to make that commitment. At least for this sample, divorce appears to be more prevalent among graduates in the humanities and less prevalent among the natural scientists. In terms of marital responsibilities, number of children is probably the most important factor to compute in assessing the commitment the student makes when he decides to pursue the Ph.D. Table 16 gives data on the parental responsibilities of the respondents in the sample.

Table 16

PARENTAL OBLIGATIONS OF DOCTORAL RESPONDENTS
IN VARIOUS DISCIPLINES
(in percentages)

Number of Children

Discipline	None	One	Two	Three	Four	Five or more
Biochemistry	63.4	17.8	14.9	3.0	0.0	1.0
Chemistry	73.4	15.5	7.2	3.4	0.5	0.0
Economics	60.8	26.9	8.5	3.1	0.8	0.0
English	60.6	19.4	11.2	5.6	1.2	1.8
French	56.4	20.5	17.9	1.3	1.3	2.6
History	59.5	17.8	12.4	7.6	1.1	1.6
Mathematics	65.8	20.0	10.0	2.5	0.8	0.8
Philosophy	56.2	22.9	13.3	5.7	1.0	1.0
Physics	63.4	20.1	13.4	1.8	1.2	0.0
Physiology	44.9	30.4	15.9	4.3	2.9	1.4
Psychology	70.6	17.9	8.7	1.8	0.9	0.0
Sociology	61.1	16.7	14.8	4.9	2.5	0.0

There was considerable presumptive evidence in the doctoral student responses to indicate that financial security in the form of a grant, assistantship, or scholarship provided the recipient with rose-colored glasses. Almost all those who wrote favorable assessments of their graduate programs reported that the financial assistance provided by their department was adequate. The converse of this was true for many who were discontented with graduate education. The frequent complaints of the latter about the department's lack of a sufficient number of assistantships or other sources of financial aid were matched by complaints about the competitive spirit, gamesmanship, and favoritism in their department with respect to the allocation of assistantships and the equitable distribution of other sources of stipends or support for doctoral study.

The availability of a scholarship or fellowship was an important factor for 68 per cent of the respondents in their choice of a graduate school. Only 13 per cent said it was an unimportant factor. The remainder said that they did not have a scholarship. Several students volunteered the information that they would have selected a different institution for their degree programs had they been able to obtain assurance of financial aid from the institution of their first choice. Graduate deans and department chairmen expressed general concern about the financial uncertainties in the lives of graduate students. They noted that despite fellowship support many excellent doctoral candidates had had to drop out of the program or take a leave of absence because of financial pressures.

Spurred by Berelson's data which show the inordinate time spent by some of his respondents in securing their degrees, some universities recently introduced a five-year Ph.D. program. An enabling grant from the Ford Foundation permitted some of the institutions in this sample to subsidize for a maximum of five years a select group of students who agreed to commit themselves to full time study until the degree is earned. In commenting on the positive returns from this plan, some department chairmen were pessimistic about the ability of the university to uphold the five-year limitation after the Ford grant runs out. Some expressed the hope that federal grants or loans might fill the gap. Some deans noted that the inflationary costs of graduate education had made it necessary—particularly for married students with children—to supplement their stipends through outside employment. This not only negates their full time commitment but also delays their progress.

Faculty members appear to be more hopeful than deans about the availability of fellowships or scholarships for doctoral students. Forty-eight per cent expect the amount of fellowship support to increase, 34 per cent expect it to continue at current levels, and 17 per cent expect decreases over the foreseeable future. An average of 66 per cent of the faculty respondents in sociology, economics, and English expect fellowship support to increase. Faculty members in physics (39 per cent), chemistry (31 per cent), biochemistry (26 per cent), and mathematics (24 per cent) are more inclined to expect decreases in this support. These data may reflect the fact that the latter fields are already heavily subsidized or, given the present climate of opinion in federal financing, the respondents are pessimistic about the priority which research in their fields will receive.

The depressing or interfering effects of financial strain on the graduate student's progress and well being are probably incalculable. Many of the students' dissatisfactions, in reality or in fancy, seem to be related to financial pressures. And much of the loss in terms of numbers of those who complete all work but the dissertation is also traceable to this factor. The words of a student in philosophy illustrate the all-encompassing strain that financial worries impose on Ph.D. students.

> Worries help no one . . . yet financial pressures seem to hinder most of those with whom I've talked. I would be willing to work for less pay later on if I could reduce my worry about money and the sacrifice my family must make now, I'd like to be free to study: I don't want to be rich. My family and I lived very nicely on a $3,000 fellowship . . . We lived on it for 12 months but it has recently been cut by one-third. Now I must hurry to finish . . . Creative ideas don't develop in crash programs. I get upset because I must chop away at the requirements instead of satisfying a little of my curiosity about other areas of knowledge.

On the other hand a student in the sciences makes this observation:

> All students who are accepted are assured of financial support during their stay here. The faculty treats us as individuals not as so-and-so's protégés. Because of these factors, students cooperate rather than compete with each other. There is competition for grades of course, but it is relatively subdued and goes hand in hand with the sharing of class notes, resources, and knowledge.

Students in the humanities have fewer avenues of support for graduate study than do students in other areas. For this reason, more of them take teaching positions or other outside work while studying for the doctorate. Table 17 gives the U.S. Office of Education data on the financial status of graduate students in the U.S. in 1965. These data underline some of the inequities that occur in the allocation of graduate stipends. Although graduate deans spend

Table 17

AMOUNT OF STIPEND SUPPORT RECEIVED BY GRADUATE STUDENTS (in percentages)

Amount of Stipend	Biological and Physical Science	Social Sciences	Humanities
Less than 500	6	9	21
500–1499	7	14	13
1500–2499	24	31	24
2500–3499	36	26	23
3500–4499	14	11	12
4500 and over	14	9	7

Source: U.S. Office of Education, The Academic and Financial Status of Graduate Students, Spring 1965. Washington, D.C.: Government Printing Office, 1967, p. 30.

considerable time and effort in trying to achieve equitable balances, increasing costs and decreasing support make their successes seem small and transitory. Worry about the financing of graduate education was widespread among department chairmen. The following quote is typical:

> One of our greatest problems is that of finance. Because a very large part of our research is federally supported we worry about what Congress can do to cut it down or out of next year's budget. . . . We would be in great difficulties if we had grants expire that were up for renewal. . . . We raised 18 million dollars privately for a chemistry building without much trouble, but it takes 600,000 yearly for maintenance. These are the things we worry about. They are all of a piece with your interest and ours in keeping our quality high. The shortage of money keeps us worrying about our good students.

As they reflected on the immediate problems that are created by the decreasing availability of fellowships and other forms of student support, graduate deans commented on the long-range consequences of recent cutbacks in student aid. One major consequence was the problem of assuring future manpower needs in areas of knowledge that will be in heavy demand in the decade ahead. Several of those interviewed said that the urgency of the response that is needed to stem the degradation of man's environment virtually mandated that a dozen or more disciplines concentrate their attention on ecological problems. The result is that new fields of knowledge are forming that have begun to compete with the existing departments for the available funds. Deans and department chairmen expressed concern because scholars on whom departments had built their academic program are becoming so heavily committed to the resolution of national problems that the university finds it increasingly difficult to depend upon these scholars to staff the instructional program.

Most department chairmen said that they occasionally tried to spread their resources by dividing teaching assistantships into smaller units or by dividing the budget allocated for a full-time equivalent position into two, three, or four part-time appointments. While more students were subsidized in this way, their stipends were so marginal that some were forced to drop out. Some deans observed that the quality of the undergraduate program could be jeopardized if such partial funding persisted.

Deans and department chairmen alike were apprehensive about the effect that rising tuition costs and increases in out-of-state fees would have on the student mix. They described the increasing difficulty of being competitive nationally for top students unless the institution can assure the applicant of some source of support over and above that provided by his scholarship. They noted that students from other geographic regions or from foreign countries add an important dimension and character to the quality and work of the institution, but they added that this character fades with each increase in tuition. Table 18 provides the profiles of the native and foreign student "mix" among the respondents in the institutions in the study.

The decision to invest in doctoral study generally involves a long chain of individual decisions for the student. Most of the factors he must weigh can be subsumed under those which are academic and those which are personal. For the married person, the

Table 18

GEOGRAPHIC ORIGINS OF DOCTORAL STUDENTS
(in percentages, N = 3187)

Institution	Home state student	Out-of-state student	Foreign student
Berkeley	29	59	12
Columbia	45	46	9
Cornell	23	63	14
Illinois	28	65	7
Johns Hopkins	11	78	11
Michigan	24	68	8
North Carolina	17	76	7
Northwestern	22	71	7
Stanford	17	75	8
Wisconsin	18	73	9

decision almost invariably involves the problem of keeping his family well and happy on a subsistence budget for four or more years and of fulfilling marital responsibilities while literally detaching himself from his spouse at critical times. For the single student, the decision may mean cutting himself off from a normal social life, postponing marriage until he is economically able to undertake it, or extending the period during which he is dependent upon his parents. In addition, many males are confronted with decisions which relate to their draft status. Some are reluctant to begin a program which may be cut off in midstream. Others see graduate study as a delaying tactic. In addition to the psychological strain which these concerns exert, the prospect of spending four or more years in the role of a student has limited appeal. This is especially true for those who must decide whether to give up responsible positions to return to the disciplined life of the university student. The more mature the applicant, the more ego strength he may require for persistence in graduate school with its growing lists of rules and regulations.

An important factor in the decision to seek the Ph.D. is the student's desire to achieve personal advancement. This involves estimates of self-worth. For those who have doubts about their intellectual capacity, the fear of failure may loom large. Graduate students who hold vague ideas about the commitment required in the Ph.D. program generally find it difficult to make realistic estimates of their potential for success. For this reason, they approach the degree tentatively. As a defense against possible failure, some develop what Maslow (1967) refers to as the "Jonah complex" in which individuals avoid, or put off, testing the full measure of their aspirations or strengths. Various devices are used by students in this process. The most common is the pretense (generally held in reserve) that the M.A. is their principal goal.

The younger single student, who has less at stake, generally manages to meet his self-doubts head-on, but for those who risk the status they have already gained with family, friends, or professional associates, failure can be ego-smashing. Some doctoral students meet the specter of failure—at least in fancy—at every corner in their degree programs. As they successfully pass the various stages the fear may diminish but their anxiety reaches an apex during the oral examination and the dissertation periods. The student's self-doubts rarely disappear until he has the appropriate number of faculty signatures affixed to his research thesis. Some students attempt to cushion the blow of possible failure by pretending to make only half-hearted commitments to the intellectual life or to the discipline it entails. In many cases, this extends the process and often dulls the edge of intellectual excitement or interest. It may also lead to malingering. The fringe of every major campus is ringed with a conglomerate of those who, for one reason or another, can neither cut their ties with the university nor tighten them.

Evidence of the diverse goals of the Ph.D. seeker—and of the diverse uses he expects to make of his doctoral education—may be found in the data in which doctoral students stated their reasons for seeking the doctorate. Their responses show that the majority of doctoral students include college or university teaching high on their list of goals, but appreciable numbers keep their options open for careers outside of the academic community. Figure 3 shows the factors which students considered to be important in their decision to study for a Ph.D. Intellectual interests and the desire to achieve competence in a discipline were high on the list of purposes students gave for seeking the Ph.D.

It has frequently been said that individuals seek the Ph.D.

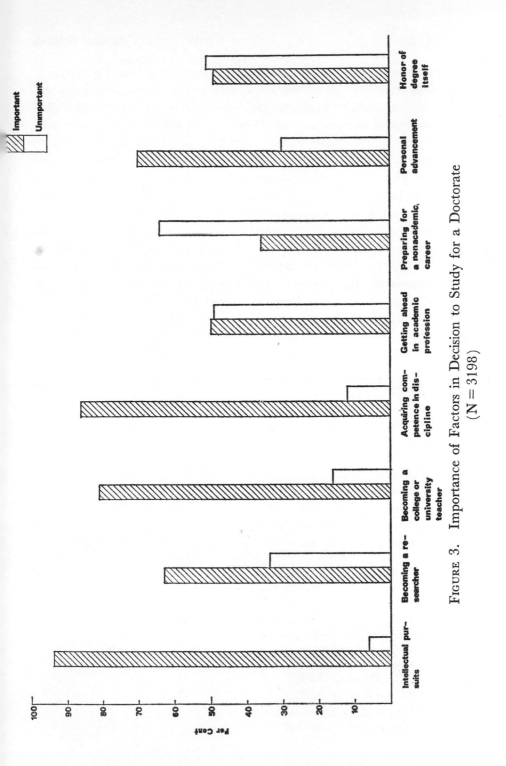

FIGURE 3. Importance of Factors in Decision to Study for a Doctorate (N = 3198)

mainly as a union card which gives them entrée into the academic brotherhood. This inference was accepted by 45 per cent of the student respondents in the humanities, by 23 per cent in the biological and social sciences, and by 20 per cent in the physical sciences who were asked to comment on the motives of students in their departments. Students in private universities were less inclined to regard the Ph.D. as a credential than were students in public institutions. The utility of the Ph.D. degree per se appears to receive greater recognition among doctoral students than do other awards the degree might bring. For example, while the respondents seemed well aware of the placement opportunities that were opened by the Ph.D., they were not inclined to think that their peers were impressed by the prestige the degree promised. Only 11 per cent thought that students were motivated by a desire for prestige, 57 per cent thought they were not, and 32 per cent were uncertain about their fellow students' motivation toward this end. Table 19 records doctoral students' appraisals of their peers.

Table 19

Doctoral Students' Appraisals of Their Peers
(in percentages)

	Agree	Uncertain	Disagree
They enjoy an intellectual esprit de corps	56	20	24
They are committed to scholarship	64	24	12
Advanced students serve as models	55	18	27
Part time students fail to identify with classmates	27	55	18
Some of the best students leave because they underestimated the rigor of discipline required	15	26	59
Some of the best students drop out because they find requirements too constraining	20	23	57
Many drop out because they don't like the competition	13	30	57
They seek Ph.D. chiefly for prestige	11	32	57
Most graduate students regard the Ph.D. as a "union card"	32	23	45

Studies at the Center for Research and Development in Higher Education by Heist (1968), Trent-Medsker (1968), Knoell-Medsker (1964), Watts, Lynch, and Whittaker (in press) indicate that mobility from one institution to another is becoming a way of life for many college students and is gradually becoming more common among graduate students. For example, 9 per cent of the respondents in this study had been enrolled in a doctoral program at an institution other than the one they were attending when they completed the Center's questionnaire. The range in the per cent of transfers was fairly narrow for public universities (8 per cent to 10 per cent) but somewhat uneven among private institutions (6 per cent to 14 per cent).

In both types of institutions academic reasons other than grades were cited as the most important factor in the decision to change. Some 61 per cent of the public school respondents and 47 per cent of the private school respondents who had transferred said that they had done so for one or more of the following reasons: their academic interests had not been challenged; they found a better program in the school to which they transferred; their major professor had moved taking his students with him; they had experienced dissatisfactions or disappointments with a specific requirement; or the quality of graduate education in their prior institution was inferior. Four per cent reported that they changed institutions after receiving a terminal M.A. from their prior graduate school.

Other major reasons given for changing institutions included "personal factors," which motivated 15 per cent of the changes made by public school respondents and 22 per cent of those made by private school respondents; "financial problems," which were cited by 4 per cent of the private and by 9 per cent of the public respondents; and "a combination of academic, personal, and financial reasons," which prompted 3 per cent of all the transfers. The remainder moved after deciding that it would be more stimulating or beneficial to move to another institution after reaching the M.A. level. Among the latter were some who transferred out of the first institution when their academic achievements made them eligible for their present institution.

Another form of mobility which was reported by the respondents was the shift to different academic fields. A profile of this movement indicates that approximately 8 per cent of the public university respondents and 6 per cent of those representing private institutions in the sample transferred to another field after they began their Ph.D. studies. The reasons given for these moves included positive academic factors which satisfied a new or broader interest and negative factors based on some dissatisfaction or disappointment with the program in their prior fields. Other reasons included the encouragement by a professor in the new field or the offer of a better scholarship or financial subsidy. Approximately 15 per cent changed fields for social or personal reasons. Some of these involved personality conflicts with advisers, others involved friendship patterns or the influence of peers. It is not known from the data to what extent changes in major fields of study were made to correct wrong choices resulting from inadequate advising or orientation. However, judging by the substance of the comments on this item in the questionnaire, both of these services were implicated to some extent.

As Tucker has documented, nearly one half of those who enter the Ph.D. program drop out at some stage in the process. Most Ph.D. holders can remember moments or stages in their own programs when they wondered whether or not the effort was worthwhile. Perhaps just as frequently they questioned whether the effort had not been misspent on activities and concerns which did not advance their intellectual growth. Questions of this nature have been debated in the literature by such persistent critics as West, who saw the Ph.D. becoming form with doubtful substance, and Arrowsmith, who regards the process as often dehumanizing for its participants.

The current widespread disillusionment with higher education at the undergraduate level, which prompts many promising students to terminate on or before receiving the baccalaureate, poses serious implications for graduate education in the future. Longitudinal studies by Heist (1968) and Mock and Yonge (1969) of the intellectual disposition of college students show that high-ability students have been dropping out of college in increasing numbers. The persisters, who are eligible to enter graduate school, may include relatively few of the very creative because these were lost at lower levels. The need for research on the causes of this phenomenon cannot be underestimated.

Over one-third of the student respondents in this sample reported that they had interrupted their studies or had been tempted to drop out of the doctoral program. In most cases, students ascribed their doubts to pressures which demanded coping mechanisms other than those used to resolve academic problems. For the most part, the pressures generated self-doubts that debilitated the respondent's interests or caused him to question the wisdom of investing his energies in the demands of the "system." The fatigue factor, which was cited by nearly 40 per cent of those who contemplated dropping out, probably masks other important factors. In a study of a small sample of graduate students at Yale, Hall (1969) identified two paradoxes which emphasize the fatigue or malaise factor:

(1) Yale students were selected for their outstanding intellectual competence and zest for scholarly pursuits. Yet these same students are often described by themselves and the faculty as being intellectually and emotionally "dead."

(2) Yale is one of the most exciting learning centers in the country, yet many students see the Yale experience as little more than routine work, heavy program requirements, or having little sense of intellectual community.

The following tabulation illustrates, in percentages, the response of 1285 students who were asked to indicate why they had been tempted to give up their quest of the Ph.D. Other reasons given in-

Academic problems	16.0	Poor relationship with sponsor	5.9
Lack of interest in field	25.2	Health problems	6.3
Faculty's lack of interest in students	26.0	Family problems	12.2
Stress of passing hurdles	37.0	Financial problems	22.5
Poor relationship with adviser	13.8	Tired of study	40.5
		Disillusioned with graduate education	44.4
		Uncertain about draft status	12.2

cluded: concern over social problems, department atmosphere or goals disappointing, over-specialization, questioned value of degree as means to personal goals, rejection of dissertation topic, personal problems. The statistics in this tabulation point to some serious de-

ficiencies, unmet expectations, and stress areas in doctoral study.
From the point of view of the student, they provide a base on which
academic reform must be initiated if the following observations of
student respondents are to be challenged:

> In connection with your question, many or most of the po-
> tentially "best students"—most able and interested people
> —never enter graduate school; they are disillusioned as un-
> dergraduates by incompetent teachers—both faculty and
> teaching assistants. It is well known, but rarely admitted,
> that the most capable, energetic, and creative people do not
> enter academic professions. Potential intellectual leaders
> who do decide to get a graduate degree do so in spite of
> what they must go through and who they must associate
> with, not because of these things. There are very few peo-
> ple who are really tuned in to the subject matter who also
> have the patience, perseverance, and "cool" to go all the
> way to a degree. The majority of graduate students fall into
> one of two categories: those whose quiet self-discipline suits
> them very well to getting a degree but who lack a genuine
> feeling for or interest in the field; and all of those turned-on
> people who never finish because they thought that getting
> the Ph.D. had to do with how bright you were and not how
> prudent. My department is full of students who aren't get-
> ting through because they haven't observed what it takes. It
> is my experience that the creative, original thinkers who pay
> little attention to personalities are often tripped up, while
> those who are long on strategy and short on subject matter
> can make it. As a result, those who do finish do so either be-
> cause they *like* the competition, the rankings, and the pass-
> ing of requirements and stages, and the rigor for the sake
> of rigor; or *despite* these things. Unfortunately there aren't
> many people whose devotion to the subject will carry them
> through the exasperating trivialities of academic life. What
> we have left are those whom the trivialities suit quite well—
> hardly the sort of people likely to inspire promising under-
> graduates.

> Of the dozen or so dropouts whom I personally know, in
> most cases the reason was insufficient attention to the nice-
> ties of obtaining an academic degree: filling one's schedule
> with stimulating courses unrelated to degree requirements;
> devoting all one's time to a T.A.-ship while neglecting one's
> own study; taking so long to prepare for oral exams that
> the committee eventually departed and a new committee

(imposing new requirements) was set up; preparing for a stage II requirement before stage I was passed; antagonizing a professor in class, etc. In all of the other cases, the students were even less motivated to finish—some went off to seek the meaning of life elsewhere; some got married and moved away; one girl chose not to exceed her husband's level of education (an M.A.). Evidently these people did not want the Ph.D., though graduate school suited them for a while.

In their free comments doctoral students often expressed their distress at seeing classmates or friends whose intelligence they rated high drop out of the Ph.D. program. Deans and department chairmen also expressed a similar concern during the interviews. Some of the latter observed that creative students—who may or may not fit the departmental image—are sometimes ignored or set adrift by the faculty. Others leave because the tight structure offers them no creative outlet. One dean observed that he had a filing drawer filled with letters from disillusioned dropouts who were academically strong but temperamentally disinclined to conform to rigid requirements or to the demands of particular faculty members. In their free comments many students expressed not only a deep concern about the fate of such dropouts but also noted that their loss reflected on the quality of those who persisted. Table 20 shows the percentages of those who agreed with statements in the questionnaire which implied that some of the best students drop out because the requirements are too constraining, the competition is too distasteful, or the student underestimates the demands that the degree process entails.

The high dropout rate among first-year doctoral students is sometimes attributed to their disenchantment with the research emphasis in the doctoral program. Students who are not decisive about their area of interests are sometimes tagged as "drifters" or not very serious scholars who will eventually drop out. Some do. Others collect credits and high grade-point averages but make no progress toward a degree because their collection lacks an integrated focus on a major area. In some cases the student himself fails to hone toward a goal. In others he is inadequately advised, and in still others the graduate system fails to accommodate him and other individuals

Table 20

DOCTORAL RESPONDENTS' PERCEPTIONS OF WHY THE BEST
STUDENTS DROP OUT OF THE PH.D. PROGRAM
(in percentages)

Discipline	Found requirements too constraining	Under-estimated rigors of the program	Disliked the competition
		(Percentages)	
Biochemistry	13	10	5
Chemistry	7	8	9
Economics	23	14	14
English	33	21	16
French	30	17	13
History	26	23	17
Mathematics	12	15	17
Philosophy	21	11	8
Physics	14	15	16
Physiology	18	18	6
Psychology	16	13	11
Sociology	45	15	15

whose interests change or span several areas. In some cases a student who expresses a negative interest in research in favor of an interest in teaching finds it difficult to acquire a sponsor who is sympathetic to his goal. In other instances, Ph.D. students "drift" into teaching as opposed to being drawn into it. A large number of these may remain indefinitely in the graduate program, treading water as far as their Ph.D. candidacy is concerned.

The argument that the Ph.D. dropout represents "waste" is more or less specious. Many so-called dropouts eventually make important contributions to society and lead very satisfying lives. However, the increasing numbers who have copped out, as well as dropped out, may represent a real loss to society. Rogers (1964) warns that if we value the person we must examine the weaknesses in the process which leads some to reject it or to be disillusioned with it. Such an examination might begin with the academic environment.

In one of their most frequent and cogent criticisms, doctoral respondents indicted their departments as unfavorable to or lacking in some of the necessary components of an intellectual environment. It seems clear from the data that one's impression of the departmental atmosphere depends upon where one is in the hierarchy. Departments which minimized the hierarchical nuances received warm praise from the respondents. Conversely, those departments which stratified and formalized their interrelationships were coldly denounced for exhibiting "colonializing" attitudes. While little reliable evidence is available on the efficacy of a warm versus a cold atmosphere on scholarly development, in the present climate of opinion in which the human being struggles for identity, it seems clear that doctoral students prefer some heat. Where they do not find warmth some have generated it on their own, as the recent history of higher education verifies.

The extent to which graduate students err in estimating the self-investment which the doctoral program requires are revealed in the data which show that an average of 28 per cent of the respondents in this study found the investment to be greater than they anticipated and 12 per cent found it to be less than they expected. The remainder said that they had estimated fairly accurately. The disciplines which apparently demanded more than the respondents anticipated were: history (37 per cent), English (36 per cent), sociology (35 per cent), physics (32 per cent), economics (30 per cent), and psychology (29 per cent). Those which demanded less self-investment than the respondents expected included French (18 per cent), philosophy (15 per cent), and economics (14 per cent). Whether the differential in expectations implies an indictment of the academic requirements, the orientation or advising process, the length of time required for completion, a failure on the part of the students to make adequate and diligent inquiry into departmental expectations, or errors in the students' judgment, cannot be ascertained from the data. Suffice it to say that the differences between expectations and actuality may be the source of some of the discontent and discontinuities commonly found among doctoral students.

When respondents were asked whether they would select the same field of study if they were to start their programs again, 87 per cent of those in both private universities and public institutions reported that they would. The range among public university respondents who would opt for the same discipline was from 84 to 91 per cent, and among private institution respondents it ranged from 79 to 92 per cent. Students who appeared satisfied with their choices were more frequently found in mathematics (93 per cent), psychology and chemistry (90 per cent), physiology, history, English, and biochemistry (88 per cent), whereas an average of 18 per cent of the respondents in physics, French, and economics were dissatisfied and would not reselect the same fields. The basic reason which students gave for their unwillingness to choose the same specialty included its preoccupation with research, lack of relevance, and rigid requirements.

Some measure of the student's satisfaction with his choice of a graduate institution may be obtained from the data which show that more than one fourth of the respondents in all institutions would not select the same institution were they to start their degree programs over again. The percentage of those who would not select

Table 21

STUDENT SATISFACTION WITH THEIR GRADUATE
INSTITUTIONAL CHOICES
(in percentages)

Discipline	Would select same institution	Would not select same institution
Biochemistry	74.3	25.7
Chemistry	83.5	16.5
Economics	68.2	31.8
English	69.3	30.7
French	69.9	30.1
History	73.8	26.2
Mathematics	77.5	22.5
Philosophy	69.7	30.3
Physics	72.4	27.6
Physiology	82.0	18.0
Psychology	75.3	24.7
Sociology	65.8	34.2

the same institution ranged from 19 per cent to 36 per cent among public institutions and from 21 per cent to 31 per cent for respondents registered in private universities. When the data were arranged in terms of the responses of students in various disciplines, the results shown in Table 21 were noted. The main reason that respondents cited for not selecting the same institution were its impersonality, bigness, rigid requirements, and their inability to find meaningful intellectual relationships with the faculty on problems within their discipline. Reasons for which respondents would select the same institution included the reverse of the above factors, the outstanding quality of the faculty and graduate students, the freedom and independence provided in the academic program, and the availability of a scholarship or grant.

The mailing of the student questionnaire was timed (and staggered) so as to ensure that the respondent would have had at least one full semester, term, or quarter in his doctoral program by the time he received the questionnaire. Table 22 shows the respondent's stage in the degree process at the time he completed the research instrument. These data demonstrate the early involvement in research which is fairly common among students in the laboratory sciences. In most cases students in these fields worked on research before they completed their course requirements or fulfilled the foreign language requirement.

When students were asked to indicate how long they expected it would take to complete their Ph.D.'s, the data shown in Table 23 were obtained. When their admissions dates and expected dates for completing the Ph.D. were plotted, students in physics expected to achieve their degrees in 4.4 years, biochemists and philosophers in 4.3 years, psychologists and students in French in 4.2 years, historians and English majors in 4.1 years, chemists and mathematicians in 4.0 years, sociologists and economists in 3.9 years and physiologists in 3.8 years. Approximately 0.4 per cent of the total respondents said that they had not set a target date for completing the Ph.D.

Students and other critics of higher education frequently allege that most academic programs lack relevance to the burning questions of the age. The emphasis which high school and undergraduate programs have placed on social issues and the expectation

Table 22

Stage of the Respondents in the Ph.D. Process
(in percentages)

	Completed required courses	Passed written exam	Passed language exam	Passed orals	Working on research	Writing dissertation
Biochemistry	76.1	51.7	74.3	46.6	81.8	18.4
Chemistry	76.2	60.0	63.8	41.0	85.6	15.4
Economics	77.8	58.1	72.4	27.6	55.7	39.9
English	76.8	47.6	74.1	31.9	43.5	32.2
French	75.7	56.7	77.9	39.4	46.6	43.7
History	79.4	49.5	83.0	44.1	55.2	29.9
Math	74.7	62.3	62.4	47.7	59.3	23.4
Philosophy	73.0	62.2	66.9	27.7	37.8	44.9
Physics	77.6	77.2	65.1	51.2	69.3	16.4
Physiology	75.5	43.7	70.4	45.9	82.7	21.6
Psychology	77.3	57.0	56.3	27.2	71.2	23.6
Sociology	78.0	33.9	59.3	19.8	53.4	23.3

Table 23

STUDENTS' ESTIMATE OF TIME REQUIRED TO ACHIEVE PH.D.
(in percentages)

Discipline	Six years or more	Four or five years	Three years or less
Biochemistry	11	78	11
Chemistry	5	78	17
Economics	6	58	36
English	14	46	40
French	18	42	40
History	19	55	26
Mathematics	9	66	25
Philosophy	20	60	20
Physics	21	70	9
Physiology	9	55	36
Psychology	11	72	17
Sociology	12	52	36

that graduate study and research will focus on their correction leads many graduate students to become disillusioned when they find that research in their field is designed to embellish the discipline rather than to provide knowledge that might alleviate man's concerns. The extent to which student respondents agree that study in their disciplines is related to current issues is shown in Table 24. In contrast, in response to the question "To what degree does your department provide relevance in its graduate curriculum?" the faculty responded as shown in Table 25. The frequency with which students commented on the imperfections in man's environment implied a deep commitment to action. The passion in their remarks leads to the speculation that ecology will become a new testing ground for confrontation or a new call for collaborative action in the immediate future.

The compelling nature of some recent confrontations between students and the university faculty and administration seems to have led disparate segments of the academic community to organize for united action. Among these groups are found a number of graduate student (and ex-graduate student) clubs or organiza-

Table 24

STUDENT IMPRESSIONS OF THE RELEVANCE OF THEIR PROGRAMS
TO CURRENT ISSUES, BY DISCIPLINES

(in percentages)

Discipline	Agree	Disagree	Uncertain
Biochemistry	8	62	30
Chemistry	5	55	40
Economics	40	41	19
English	12	66	22
French	10	71	19
History	34	38	28
Mathematics	10	55	35
Philosophy	13	62	26
Physics	5	65	30
Physiology	16	49	35
Psychology	29	47	24
Sociology	49	35	16

Table 25

FACULTY OPINION ON THE RELEVANCE OF THE CURRICULUM TO
SOCIAL CONCERNS

(in percentages)

Disciplines	To a high degree	To a satis- factory degree	To a dis- appointing degree
Biochemistry	40	44	16
Chemistry	62	31	7
Economics	23	49	26
English	27	48	23
French	34	53	13
History	36	49	15
Mathematics	39	54	8
Philosophy	21	52	27
Physics	34	49	17
Physiology	49	38	12
Psychology	46	40	13
Sociology	22	45	30

Table 26
ACTIVITIES PROVIDED BY GRADUATE STUDENT CLUBS
(in percentages)

	Communication among students	Student-faculty communication	Communication with administration	Communication between related fields	Conducts colloquy	Scholarly activities	Contact with current research	Informal social programs
Biochemistry	93.1	78.6	46.5	62.1	64.3	64.3	51.7	60.7
Chemistry	79.7	73.9	36.8	38.3	44.9	47.8	88.4	30.4
Economics	90.1	87.1	27.2	22.4	75.1	67.0	84.8	53.8
English	87.3	88.8	30.0	32.9	77.8	69.3	88.6	48.5
French	87.0	72.7	13.2	26.4	65.5	56.4	73.6	50.9
History	85.6	83.7	30.8	42.8	80.8	73.8	89.5	53.8
Mathematics	92.7	95.6	57.4	44.7	79.4	74.2	89.7	72.4
Philosophy	84.3	77.0	10.3	25.7	94.6	78.4	81.9	77.0
Physics	94.4	84.9	43.4	71.2	77.0	53.9	54.7	78.8
Physiology	97.1	84.6	29.0	35.9	41.0	38.5	89.7	43.6
Psychology	90.6	91.3	60.0	25.9	41.3	49.3	90.6	36.1
Sociology	90.4	86.5	28.6	37.3	69.7	60.0	89.1	47.0

tions. Some clubs are formed along departmental lines. Others are campus-wide. Some are designed to give the graduate student a more effective voice in academic change. Others are frankly political. Still others have a primary interest in their disciplines or in improving the social interaction between students and the faculty. Among respondents in this study, 43 per cent reported that their departments did not have a graduate club. Thirty-six per cent of the respondents in the departments that had clubs were members, and the remainder were non-members. Students in the humanities and the social sciences were more inclined to form and to join clubs than were students in the sciences. Among the activities and interests provided in some degree by graduate clubs were those shown in Table 26. In a few cases graduate clubs are organized as collective bargaining groups and are run on a committee structure "to protect student interests or to assure that graduates have an effective voice in student matters."

Student Appraisals
of Ph.D. Program

10

On the last two pages of their questionnaire—which were left blank —graduate students were invited to add any additional comments they wished to make about their graduate programs. Seven hundred and eighty-five students used the space for this purpose (some added pages to supplement the space provided). The dispersion of the positive and negative comments among departments is shown in Table 27. In reviewing their free comments for clues about the quality of their doctoral experiences, it must be conceded that graduate students vary on a great many dimensions including, among other things, their motivation, interests, and commitment to the discipline required in the Ph.D. program. For this reason it would be impossible to establish the reliability and validity of the respondents' assessment without additional knowledge about them as individuals. On the other hand, it must be assumed that these institutions had secured reasonable assurance of the ability, interest, and commit-

Table 27

CHARACTER OF PH.D STUDENTS' OPEN-ENDED RESPONSES ON
THE QUALITY OF THEIR PROGRAMS, IN NUMBERS

Discipline	Positive response	Negative response	Total number in sample
Biochemistry	31	10	199
Chemistry	43	29	425
Economics	12	66	253
English	28	99	296
French	13	56	151
History	36	118	349
Mathematics	10	32	273
Philosophy	13	57	196
Physics	20	34	328
Physiology	13	51	106
Psychology	45	91	365
Sociology	14	59	256

ment of their doctoral students prior to their admission. On this premise, and allowing for a certain amount of *ad hominism,* the remarks of the 785 students who commented separately on their graduate programs were viewed as written in good faith and are therefore illuminating for purposes of this study. At the same time it was conceded that the absence of commentary may imply a general satisfaction with graduate study. Each of the comments was read by three persons, two of whom made a preliminary classification of the points they covered; the final analysis was made by the project director.

In general, the agony and the ecstasy of scholarship were revealed in the open-end statements of doctoral students. While many wrote appreciatively of their education, many others wrote poignantly of their disappointments. Among those who commented critically, the great majority expressed their criticism in thoughtful and temperate language. However, the sharp and acrimonious character of some statements implied that the respondents wrote in anger and in deep disillusionment. A number of the latter added the information that they were dropping out of graduate school. If those who are responsible for graduate education reflect seriously on the substance of the students' appraisal they would probably find that most of their suggestions could be profitably implemented and that most of their problems are resolvable. A profile of the students' comments is included here.

When the statements were classified on the basis of their positive or negative content, the negative observations outnumbered the positive by nearly two to one. The only department about which proportionately more positive than negative comments were made was chemistry. Those departments which received the highest number of negative comments were philosophy, French, and sociology. When the nature of the free comments were categorized they tended to fall into five broad areas: the atmosphere of the department, its goals and policies, faculty-student relationships, the curriculum, and the financial support of graduate study.

Positive comments concerning departmental goals and policies cited such factors as the interest of the faculty in student needs, the availability of financial support, the flexibility of the program, the independence and freedom accorded to students, the informality of the academic atmosphere, and the quality of the graduate students. Negative comments centered on such aspects as the department's size, impersonality, inadequate orientation to graduate study, insufficient supervision and guidance (especially at the dissertation stage), overemphasis on research, failure to provide teaching preparation, and the absence of a sense of community.

In their positive statements about the faculty, students praised their competence as scholars, their personal interest in the financial or academic needs of their advisees, their social consciousness, and their efforts to make needed research resources available to graduate students. Negatively, respondents faulted the graduate faculty for poor teaching, overemphasis on research, preoccupation with publishing, inaccessibility, distant and formal attitude toward students, failure to provide adequate guidance or direction, and favoritism toward the brilliant or "favored few."

Comments regarding the curriculum were nearly all negative. These indicted the course and foreign language requirements, the mechanical manner in which grading and evaluation were conducted, the lack of options or opportunity for creative approaches to learning, the high specificity of the program, and the restrictions against study in related fields. There was wide disparity in the respondents' comments regarding the department's part in providing financial support for graduate students. Some commended the department for supplying generous fellowships which made no demands on the recipient's time. Others said that although they had been able to underwrite their educational expenses with their teaching or research stipends, the responsibilities of these appointments made severe inroads on the time they could devote to study. Still others were critical because their departments had been seemingly insensitive to the financial plight of its doctoral students.

In their free comments, it was noticeable that in form as well as in substance students in the humanities appear to be more attuned to the art of criticism than students in the sciences. The fact that, by and large, the latter are basically interested in quantitative phenomena while the former are motivated toward qualitative (and therefore ambiguous) ideas and problems may account for the fact that the criticisms of students in the sciences were direct and unembellished whereas those of students in the humanities were reinforced by examples, extenuating conditions, causal relationships, and reflective thought that was often personalized to self or to someone known to the commentator. In contrast to the natural and physical science students, the objects of whose scholarly interest are basically non-human, the comments of students in the humanities revealed the emotional investment which their disciplines exact. The former appear to experience few problems in responding objectively to their disciplines. On the other hand, for the humanist, who is interested not only in "What is man?" but also in the more complex question *"Who* is man?" detachment poses as a contradiction. The nature of their struggle to resolve this dilemma was revealed in the evaluative statements which students in the humanities made about their Ph.D. programs. In analyzing those statements it must be assumed that while a sharp statement might spotlight a graduate student's problem, it might also be expressive of a scholarly style.

SOCIAL SCIENCES

Respondents in the social sciences—economics, history, and sociology—tended to write their impressions of graduate education in copious sweeps. Many of their critiques exhibited a high level of thoughtful sophistication about the problems inherent in graduate education. Some wrote in anger. A few appeared to have written in despair. Generally, their comments were more expressive of the recent student protests than were those of respondents in other disciplines. However, their references were frequently directed against deficiencies in the larger society (with which, in their judgment, graduate education was not grappling) rather than to the graduate program per se. Of 113 statements appended to their questionnaire responses, 36 were favorable and 77 were unfavorable. Possibly because of its size, the history department received the largest number of comments. All three social science departments received high praise for the intellectual opportunities they made available but in many cases respondents said that "you find your own path and follow it—mostly alone." As one student noted: "One feels isolated because one is always in one's area. Your friends tend to be in the same field. You can see people losing perspective—they tend to stop living."

Contrary to the impressions given by students in other disciplines, students in small social science departments tend to complain that smallness militates against the student. This was particularly the situation in one institution in which the faculty represents a single school of thought and in another wherein course work is sparse because of the small staff. In some of these instances, respondents reported that the Ph.D. program required an "almost compulsive devotion to the sterile library" rather than an exposure to the "challenging confrontation of minds pursuing solutions to problems." On the positive side, students in three private institutions commented appreciatively on the small size of their departments. Conversely, students in each of the public institutions complained frequently of "overcrowdedness," "factory-like procedures," and of a long list of deprivations which resulted from the heavy demands placed upon the limited resources of personnel and physical facilities at their institutions.

Students in economics and sociology sometimes volunteered the information that they had been deeply involved in what they defined as "student politics." Some forwarded with their completed questionnaire copies of statements, petitions, pamphlets, reports, and other materials which they and their peers had prepared for presentation to their faculties in an effort to initiate changes in their academic departments. Most of the messages conveyed in these publications pertained to changes students wanted in the mechanics of their programs, but some included suggestions for improving faculty-student relations or requests for a redefinition of the role of the graduate student in the structure and goals of the department. A few were written in the form of demands in which the department was denounced in sweeping rhetoric and top-to-bottom academic reforms were asked. Judging by the numbers who reported that their departments had responded positively to the students' requests for academic reform, the graduate faculty is in most cases responsive to the reasonable or "due process" requests of students.

Professors in the social sciences were described by some respondents as distant, inaccessible, and often out of touch with student problems. While some excused this behavior on the grounds that there were many outside needs for the professor's expertise, others referred to the faculty as "part-time employees" or as "moonlighters." The remarks of one graduate student incorporated the thoughts of many when he wrote pessimistically about the effects of the Center's study on the "publication syndrome":

> Suppose you discover that graduate faculties don't give a damn about their students or the quality and relevance of their graduate courses. Then what? Are the "sinners" when they see the results of your survey going to change their ways? . . . Not the graduate faculties in the social sciences where I know them . . . They moonlight as much as possible. By which I mean, they try to give as little of their time as possible to teaching, preparing lectures, keeping office hours, meeting informally . . . They moonlight even when they don't think they do. "Publish or perish" is moonlighting . . . So, if you find in your survey that student-faculty relations do not please the graduate students, matters will probably not be improved by discovering that fact . . . Rather you will have to find some way of rewarding the professor more than do they for whom he moonlights.

Respondents in economics who elaborated on the quality of their doctoral programs often spoke positively of the high quality of their faculties, but their criticism was more frequent than their praise. Those who were critical charged that a prior interest in publishing and consulting kept many instructors in economics both out of reach and out of touch with doctoral students. Students in this field described their advisers as too busy, their classes as too large, the requirements as too rigid, and the grading as too arbitrary and mechanical.

Citing the large size of the student body and the rigid course of study, some students saw the economics department as analogous to "high-priced tool factories." Describing their departments as "production oriented," doctoral students said they were forced to stifle their interest in making a critical analysis of the quality of that product in order to hone in on the "deadening requirements." Many were disappointed because the department's heavy emphasis on quantification prevented them from exploring other methods which might permit a more meaningful attack on the problems which confront economists. Some accused their departments of having more interest in "doing research" than in interpreting it, teaching it, or using it.

Students in economics appear to be indirectly or directly drawn toward activism. In at least three institutions in the sample respondents in this field reported that they were involved in contributing to academic reforms within their disciplines. Some were critical of the slow rate of that reform. In one case, students reported that the "touted reforms in their department were part and parcel of a complex political struggle between the older and younger members of the faculty." The experience was described as a "trying business" for students who found that their advice about reform had not been accepted. Because communication between faculty and students had been severely strained by this experience instead of correcting the inadequacies in faculty-student relationships, the changes which the faculty initiated caused a greater distance to arise between them. Students in this institution reported themselves confused and angry because they had not been consulted or advised about the change. The atmosphere in this department was described as hostile and tense. In contrast, students in two private universities described their economics departments as informal, friendly, noncompetitive, and low pressured. Noting the excellent opportunities for interdisciplinary relations and active informal faculty-student colloquium, students in one of these institutions reported that they were treated as junior colleagues and respected for the quality of their minds.

Respondents in three of the ten institutions in the sample who commented on their Ph.D. programs in history described their experiences in graduate school as reasonably satisfying. They ascribed their contentment to the small size of the department, its outstanding faculty, the interest displayed in the students' development, the excellent opportunities provided for supervised teaching, adequate financial support, and the high caliber of students.

In the remaining institutions, students in history characterized their departments as plagued by overenrollment and understaffing. Respondents expressed their unhappiness with this situation by saying that graduates in their departments were processed by "assembly-line techniques"; assigned, rather than permitted to choose their advisers; received relatively little guidance and learned quickly during the first year of study that any resemblance between the ideals depicted in the rhetoric of the graduate catalog and the reality of graduate study depended more upon happenstance than design. The most persistent complaint was against the impersonality of large departments. Although some unevenness was evident in the degree of satisfaction reportedly experienced, most of the commentators felt that their orientation to and guidance to history was cursory and inadequate. A few charged that only a favored few received the attention of the faculty. The latter were the students who were awarded assistantships.

Complaints about the length of the Ph.D. program varied. In some institutions students said that they were rushed through too quickly whereas in others the program was reported as so extended that most students had grown tired, lost their first flush of enthusiasm, or had become jaded and cynical about the scholarly life. Some inferred that functional careerists or less capable students often moved through the program in history without trauma, while the creative, committed, or critical students constantly fought the temptation to give up. Other criticisms of the Ph.D. program in history included the rigid course and the foreign language requirement, the overemphasis on "period history," and the department's lack of attention to current social ideas and issues. In addition, some indicted the faculty for failing to tie history into an interdisciplinary framework. Several respondents reported that in reaction against their department's "intellectual and ethical emasculation of society" they, and some of their peers, had become campus activists. In this role they protested against the "super-professionalism" of their professors and against the failure of the department to emphasize the role of the historian in formulating climates of opinion or ideological conflicts.

The encomiums expressed for some professors in history were glowing. The professors in one institution were praised for the interest they showed in the education of teaching assistants in preparation for their future roles as college teachers. Students in this institution described their professors as men who teach "where the students are." They do so by selecting topics for research or discussion which spring from the life problems of students rather than from their own concerns. As these problems are subjected to intellectual analysis and to the methods of scholarly inquiry, "the gap between ancient canon and modern historiography is reduced."

In responding to the invitation to make additional comments about their graduate programs, students in sociology replied in appreciable numbers and in strong, direct language. For the most part, their observations reflected negatively on the organization of the department—its size, factory atmosphere, rigid course requirements, "crash" programs, "frivolous" research emphasis, and poor student-faculty relations. If their comments can be assumed to be reliable, all sociology departments seem to suffer from having more students than their faculty and physical resources can accommodate. As a result, many comments were directed to problems associated with "overcrowding and bigness." In addition (or possibly as a result), departments were described as disorganized, operating in the absence of clearly defined objectives, and pragmatic in their approach to the problems inherent in sociology. Some respondents reported that the lack of unity in the academic program and the "separateness" of its various schools of thought operated against students whose examination committee included faculty members with "contradictory biases."

Students in this field voiced concern about the disparity between talk and action in faculty behavior. While some noted that they found dogmatism among their professors, others made sharp and sophisticated references to their instructor's tendencies to pursue esoteric or "off-beat" research instead of examining social problems that threaten to destroy modern society. Students in sociology were prone to report that they had experienced limitations on creativity, interdisciplinary exploration, and opportunities for teaching. Impressionistically, it appears that students in this field are often unhappy with their models. However, their frequent allusions to "playing the game" imply the willingness of some to make a pretense of accepting the models in order to achieve an immediate, personal goal. Some become activists and try to change the models. Still others reconcile their conflict by resolving to devote themselves to modifying the model after they have received the Ph.D., when they will be in a decision-making role.

In their positive comments, doctoral students in some departments of sociology praised the looseness of the program, the high levels of intellectual enthusiasm generated by some of the faculty members, and the department's outstanding competence in research. In two institutions the atmosphere of the department appears to be warmed by its informality and by the high esprit de corps among graduates; these are sustained and sparked by highly organized student clubs.

BIOLOGICAL SCIENCES

Students in the biological sciences, as represented by the departments of biochemistry, physiology, and psychology, dispensed nearly equal amounts of praise and reproof in their evaluations of their Ph.D. programs. However, there were greater imbalances in their appraisal of institutions and departments than the quantitative data suggest. For example, in two private institutions all the added comments about the biochemistry department were favorable, whereas in two other private schools all but one or two comments were unfavorable. For the same department in public universities few or no comments were added.

In general, student appraisals of the department of biochemistry portrayed it as a warm cocoon. In most cases departments were small, faculty members were friendly, all students held research assistantships, stipends were adequate, good facilities were available to students, and peer interaction was healthy. Respondents conveyed the impression that the biological sciences were on top of the knowledge explosion and that students shared in the reflected glory of the faculty's research. Unfavorable comments about departments of biochemistry included the charge that the research interests of the department were too narrow. This posed problems for those whose interests were broad or different from those of the faculty. Some of the commentators indicated that they received greater satisfaction in working with clinicians in the medical school than with the faculty in biochemistry. Others were critical of the teaching, the inadequacies in advising, the rigidities in the oral examination and, in one case, the fact that retroactive changes had been made in the curriculum, which created delays for students who were already well advanced.

Although physiology students appear reticent about their graduate experiences, there was a general feeling of satisfaction among those who did comment. This arose, as they put it, from the superior quality of the faculty, the intellectual curiosity of graduate students, the diversity of approaches encouraged, the excellent opportunity for interdisciplinary work, and the good communication within the department. The relatively few unfavorable comments were directed against the length of the program, the rigidity of examinations and, in two cases, the lack of identification with the department due to a medical school orientation in its research.

In addition to their questionnaire responses, 133 graduate students in psychology added free comments about their graduate programs. Eighty-three wrote critical statements and the remainder wrote approvingly. Often, opinions varied broadly within the same department. For example, in one large public institution, about which 31 statements were made, two-thirds of the respondents praised the quality of the faculty, the atmosphere of freedom within the department, the opportunities to work independently, and the good student-faculty relationships. Others in the same department reported that the faculty were narrow in their approach to research and that the burden of required courses during the first two years made graduate study dull and uncreative. Some students were scath-

ing in their charge that the field which studies creativity as a phenomenon does little to induce or encourage creativity at the graduate level. There were frequent complaints about the "structured
nature" of the Ph.D. program and charges that the department did
not respond to the psychology of "real life."

Many respondents in this field wrote sharp and incisive critiques of the department's overemphasis on research at the expense
of alternate career interests which psychology offers. In some cases,
students attributed the loose structure of the program and the apparent freedom within the department to the faculty's lack of interest in all but the most brilliant students. According to respondents
the latter were generally co-opted into the faculty's research projects. In these instances some students gained valuable collegial experiences but others found themselves in the role of "technicians."
For the brilliant student who is interested in ideas, the latter view
of research can be disillusioning and disheartening. While respondents frequently stated that they were glad to have the opportunity
and freedom "to do their thing" independently, their resentment
about the lack of counsel and guidance they received, and the sense
of alienation they experienced was reflected in their rhetoric. Their
disappointments were often expressed in statements in which the
writer implied, "I'm checking off the list of requirements and getting through as fast as possible."

Although some of the large departments in the sample received commendations for their atmosphere and their management,
students in small departments seemed, on the whole, to be more
content with their Ph.D. programs. Since they approached the ideal
student-faculty ratio, the image of the small department, as projected by graduates in it, is much less harried than that of larger
ones. Whether serenity correlates high with scholarship is debatable.
Nevertheless, on a purely personal basis, students in small departments perceive themselves as well off, and students in large departments idealize small ones as more conducive to scholarship. The
latter's frequent references to the "factory atmosphere," "the bureaucratic policies," "the pressures on the faculty to be researchers
rather than teachers," and the numerous service personnel who must
be dealt with "in place of the faculty" document this idealization.

HUMANITIES

The comments contributed by students in the humanities (as represented by the departments of English, philosophy, and French) documented not only their skill in expressing their personal reactions to the Ph.D. program but also their ability as critical observers and analysts of graduate education in general. The pervasive theme in the observations of students in English was the fact that their departments enrolled an incredibly large number of students for whose intellectual development a relatively small number of faculty members were available. This imbalance may account for the long list of problems they enumerated in appraising their degree programs. Heading the list of particulars was the lack of time that was available in the program for conferences and consultation between students and faculty members. Some students said that they feel guilty when they take up their professor's time because he has so little of it to give. The frequency with which this situation was described by students in English (and by the faculty in their questionnaire) conjures the image of harried students and harassed professors who avoid confronting each other even on a friendly basis.

Respondents in both private and public institutions observed that their departments of English lacked warmth or a sense of community, imposed heavy workloads and thus left little time for reflective thought, engaged uninteresting teachers to teach irrelevant courses, and neglected the creative aspects of the discipline in its stress on technical competence or on "stuffy" requirements. The tragedy which lies concealed behind the avalanche of negative comments from respondents in this field is that in every institution students commented about brilliant and inspiring teachers who generated high intellectual excitement. However, the heavy demands of teaching in this department made it impossible for most instructors to respond to students on an individual basis.

Because graduate catalogs sustain the mythology that each Ph.D. student will receive the personal counsel, guidance, and supervision of one or more mentors of his choice, the student's high expectations are rudely dashed when he finds that his faculty contacts are limited to the classroom, or formalized by appointments

which must be cleared and scheduled through the department secretary. This has the effect of stifling spontaneity and of forcing the
student upon his own resources. Sometimes his greatest enrichment
comes from his peers. If he respects them for their intelligence they
may actually become his chief source of intellectual stimulation and
criticism. If he finds them uninteresting and concerned mainly about
"the requirements," he generally withdraws unhappily within himself or drops out of the program.

It would appear from the tenor of the comments from respondents in English that these departments are so deeply engrossed
in the theoretical or technical aspects of communication that they
find no time or opportunity to practice it. Examples of gross lack of
sensitivity to the importance of good communication were common.
In one case students were notified in a *form letter* that the department had tightened and changed its evaluation standards, applied
its new ones retroactively, and advised recipients of the letter that
they could not register for the next term because they failed to meet
the new standards. In other cases requirements had been changed
and communication of the essential information regarding the
change was limited to a notice posted on the department bulletin
board. In another case the financial stipend for teaching assistants
was cut by two-thirds and students said that they were notified of
the cut so late that they had no way of obtaining funds in time to
underwrite their next registration.

The aspects in the Ph.D. program in English which evoked
positive comments from students included: its creativity, the freedom and independence it allowed in the selection of courses and
research topics, the excellence of the library, and the opportunity
which the program offered to gain supervised teaching experience.
Obviously, not all institutions were cited as praiseworthy in all
these areas. The negative comments included the reverse of these
factors plus a long list of more specific complaints about the length
of the degree program, the difficulty of selecting a research topic
that wins committee approval, the department's failure to impart
an enlightened methodology on which students might rely, the loneliness of dissertation writing, and the lack of education for teaching.
In addition, students in English reported that the pleasure of scholarship becomes obscured by financial worries. Many reported that

they must take low-paying jobs or mortgage their future by taking loans to finance their dissertations because their departments have no funds to support graduate students.

Students in French who supplemented their appraisal of their programs in written statements tended to be in total agreement that the time required to obtain the Ph.D. was too long. Some attributed the protraction to inaccurate advising during the preliminary period. These students said that they often took unnecessary courses or got involved in work which did not advance their progress. Others complained of heavy workloads and of course work that was dull, pedantic, non-specific, and poorly presented. Some respondents described their French professors as narrowly specialized, out of touch with the contemporary world, unequal in their treatment of doctoral students, and more concerned about publishing than about teaching. Several made nonspecific comments pertaining to departmental "politics." Because these were sometimes associated with comments about the paucity of financial aids for students, they implied that there was favoritism in award practices.

On the positive side, a few students observed that their departments were free, intellectually satisfying, and organized as a community of scholars. One commentated that while the program was rigid, "one had the feeling that he deserved the degree when he finally got it, and the degree was worth the getting." There was little substantive difference in the statements of private university respondents and public university respondents who were majoring in French.

Of fifty-seven free comments contributed by Ph.D. students in philosophy concerning their degree programs, only seven were favorable. The positive comments praised the small size of the department, the freedom to select courses independently, and the opportunity to work closely with one's adviser. Judging by those who commented unfavorably, students in both private and public universities see the atmosphere of their department as clouded with tension, sometimes hostile, lacking in community and communication, and inadequate in its orientation program and advising service. The curriculum in philosophy was described as rigidly structured, dysfunctional for present philosophical concerns, overprofessionalized, lacking in opportunity for creative dialogue, and "crippling" in its course requirements and workload. As in other departments within the humanities, financial aid for students was scarce in all philosophy departments. In some large departments, according to respondents, this has the effect of creating strong competition among students. Some of those who received teaching assistantships complained that their heavy workload made it impossible to finish the degree within the three-year period prescribed in their subventions. Those who held research assistantships also found that the duties involved interfered with their own progress. Students in philosophy reserved their most biting criticism for the faculty. The gist of the comments impugned their ineffectiveness as teachers and advisers and their "self-centered one-upmanship." In one large private university department, about whom 19 philosophy students wrote unfavorably, faculty members were accused of "breeding a cult of yes-men," "acting as petty tyrants," "playing God," and being "purveyors of pettifoggery."

PHYSICAL SCIENCES

Analysis of the free comments added to the questionnaire by doctoral students in the fields of chemistry, physics, and mathematics indicated that students in these fields experienced greater satisfaction in their doctoral programs than did students in other fields. This was particularly true for students in private institutions, who frequently expressed appreciation for the small size of their department, its high morale, and the friendly and informal interaction between faculty members and students. With some exceptions, respondents described the faculty in these three fields as highly competent, oriented toward research, and concerned about the graduate students' development. Although their strong and sometimes acerbic comments about the intense research emphasis in their programs seemed to connote criticism, students often balanced their negative observations by praising the high quality of the faculty's research output. And while some respondents wrote resentfully of the faculty's preoccupation with its own research, they often ascribed this preoccupation to the "publish or perish" injunction which institutional mores placed upon the faculty, rather than to the faculty's disinterest in students.

In spite of some criticism of the great emphasis on research, it seemed clear that students in the natural or physical sciences perceive the Ph.D. program as preparation primarily for a career in research. Those who are given a role as a research assistant, or as a fellow in the research effort of the department, appear to be content with this emphasis. They often expressed their satisfaction by commenting on the challenging responsibility, first-class treatment, opportunities for learning, or perquisites they enjoyed as members of the research team. On the other hand, because of the dearth of research assistantships it was apparent that many graduate students in these departments are observers rather than active participants in the department's research effort. Among those not selected as research assistants, feelings of discontent, insecurity, diminished interest in the field, and resentment against the "favorites" quickly generate. First-year students in large public institutions appear to experience these feelings more than students in private institutions. The latter can offer practically all of their graduates some form of subsidized participation. Since the subsidy is tied to a member of the faculty, some of these problems can be avoided.

The disparity in the allocation of financial aid is a raw issue among graduate students in the hard sciences. According to some respondents, the competition and rivalry that develop in the scramble for assistantships "may bring out the best but it also brings out too many of the worst qualities" in students and faculty members alike. Some respondents found their sense of justice offended by professors whom they described as "weight-swingers," "private entrepreneurs," or "raiders," who, because they are heavily funded, can entice the best students and command the best resources.

The sympathies of the respondents were sometimes extended toward less well-supported but equally competent professors in the department, and to the students who were caught in the web of the entrepreneur's research to the neglect or detriment of their own. Commentators inferred that such professors belong in private enterprise rather than in an academic institution. Judging by the frequency with which respondents described their education as overspecialized, lacking in interdisciplinary contact, insulated from the impact of their discipline on humanity, there appears to be a growing trend among students in the sciences toward an expanded social consciousness. This was expressed in the words of a student in chemistry who wrote: "Academically, we have been social hermits, but recently extensive revisions were made in the program which exposed us to excellent outside speakers. Their fresh ideas and challenging, humanistic approach have changed the atmosphere in the department to one of optimism and greater contentment."

From the tone of the comments made by doctoral students about its program, the chemistry department may be a model department. It is usually close-knit, has a good communication system between students and faculty—and between students themselves—and provides a liberal amount of personal guidance in the students' development. The atmosphere in some departments appears to be warmed by a spirit in which "everyone helps each other" and faculty members are interested in all of the students, not just in those whom they sponsor. The quality of instruction in chemistry may be a clue to student satisfaction. Despite the department's heavy research emphasis, teaching in chemistry was frequently described by the doctoral respondents as excellent. In all but two departments, teaching in chemistry was described as creative and stimulating. The overall requirements in chemistry were usually described as minimal although there was much criticism of the heavy course prescriptions during the first year and of the foreign language requirement, which students describe as useless.

The primary criticisms made by students in chemistry included its narrow specialization, overemphasis on grades and examinations, restricted freedom in research, and limitation on independent thinking. In a few cases, respondents implied that students in chemistry were tolerated only because they helped with faculty research. Students in two institutions criticized some members of the faculty for playing politics within the department and for treating students as technicians. Unlike students in mathematics, who described their programs as fairly inflexible, students in chemistry generally praised their departments for the freedom and independence they experienced in planning their study programs. However, students in two institutions implied that freedom and independence were operative only if choices were made within the bounds of the discipline; walls were quickly erected if one expressed an interest in work outside of the department.

Respondents in mathematics were less inclined to extend

their comments about their graduate experiences than were students in other fields. Forty-two statements were received, ten of which reflected favorably and thirty-two of which reflected unfavorably on the math program. Most of the favorable comments expressed an overall satisfaction with the program. In a few cases, specific praise was recorded for the outstanding faculty and for the quality of students in the department. However, most of the criticism was aimed at the faculty's lack of interest and concern about students because of their preoccupation with their own research interests and personal motivation. Other unfavorable comments suggested that classes were too large, competition for grades and other awards was excessive, and thesis topics often had to be developed in complete isolation or without the assistance of one's sponsor.

Some mathematics students described their professors as so "boxed in" by abstract research interests that they treated students as "un-persons" or responded to student needs formally and pre-emptorially. As advisers some were so vague about and disinterested in the academic requirements that they sent students to department secretaries for advice on the program. In one institution the student grapevine advised math graduates that if they hoped to survive they should select their programs on the "personality or the impersonality of the instructors." Teaching in mathematics was alleged by respondents to be poor. This was ascribed to poor planning or to the professor's obvious preference for research. Students also complained about frustrating examinations and about the obscure ways or means that were used to evaluate the candidate's performance.

On the whole, students in physics described their Ph.D. programs as satisfying because the atmosphere of their departments was free and relaxed. While an appreciable number wrote critically about their departments, students in this field seemed to neutralize their negative comments by balancing them with positive observations. For example, statements about the heavy research emphasis, poorly prepared lectures, or isolation of the physics student from other disciplines were often conjoined with statements about the heady research atmosphere, the excellence of faculty research, or the close camaraderie within the physics "group." References to a lack of financial support for graduate study and for meaningful research were directed against two institutions in the open-ended responses of physics students. It may be inferred from the positive comments made by students in the other eight schools (or from the absence of commentary on this point) that support for these purposes is reasonably adequate.

Some statements contributed by Ph.D. students in physics reflected the impact of the small size of their departments on the comprehensiveness of their academic programs. In one case respondents noted that because of the limited number of course offerings and research facilities it was impossible to plan a course of study or a dissertation topic selectively. Some respondents from small departments remarked that students failed to gain broad perspective in physics because everyone worked on the same general problems. Others commented that the closeness of the department sometimes resulted in "faculty and students getting to know each other too well."

Possibly because research constitutes their initial or primary interest, students in physics have fairly mature (if fatalistic) expectations of their role as apprentices and most of them accept it uncomplainingly. However, the number who questioned the nature of that relationship and the extent to which the responsibilities of the apprentice contribute to his development substantiate Ashby's contention that graduate students are no longer content to be "hewers of wood and drawers of water" but want to be substantial partners in a scholarly pursuit. The comments of one student epitomize the thoughts of many who see themselves being used as mere technicians:

> The high level of project-directed Federal support for the physics department (my major department) in recent years appears to have transformed the department into a research institute in which graduate students are tolerated if they don't get in the way too much. I have read that the primary purposes of university graduate research are to advance knowledge and to introduce graduate students to the art and science of research. Here, the emphasis is on the project and on research results. In the interests of efficiency, graduate students are used mostly as technicians. Nonthesis research (or working as a technician) is not a formal requirement, but it is a requirement for all practical purposes. The graduate student grapevine tells from time to time of stu-

dents who were failed in their oral exams because they were not diligent enough in their non-thesis research. One of the frustrations in the non-thesis research is that we may be given a problem without being told why the problem is of interest or where it fits into a research program. Questions as to why the professor wants to do something are not encouraged.

Students in physics, as in other fields, expressed a growing concern about the alienation of their discipline from society as its research becomes more and more specialized and more and more obscure. Some raised rhetorical questions about the direction of research in physics while others addressed themselves to the question of "whether the country needs Ph.D.'s in physics." Implied in these comments was the feeling that the discipline had isolated itself from "applied fields where the action is more socially productive." Some commentators expressed disappointment and disillusionment with the field of physics because it had failed to engage in a vigorous exchange of ideas with the society which constitutes its environment, or because its scholars had failed to explicate their research goals.

Preparation
for Research

11

All universities look upon their Ph.D. degrees as certification of competence for research. For this reason they regard the academic program as the means through which future knowledge-producers are developed. The literature on the Ph.D. is heavy with criticism of the imbalances which its requirements encourage between research preparation and preparation for teaching. It is also criticized for being preoccupied with the esoteric and for failing to provide students with opportunities to encounter the everyday problems to which the discipline can lend expertise. The inference is often made that preparation for research is actually preparation against teaching or against other interests and needs of scholars.

These criticisms may be valid for students in the humanities, where teaching and reflective writing are the expressive forms of scholarship. However, in the physical and biological sciences the criticism is less accurate. The students who elect these fields tend to be attracted to research and view it as a major activity in their future careers. Thus they are, with some minor exceptions, content with the program's research emphasis. The social sciences face more complicated problems in providing research preparation. Because their methods are derived from both the sciences and the humanities, Ph.D. students in these fields spend a considerable portion of their time acquiring a broad base in research methodology and struggling with ambiguity as they attempt to design their own research programs.

The weakness in most Ph.D. programs seems to center on the fact that while the program professes to *educate* for research, in reality it *trains* for it. Jencks and Riesman (1968), Sanford (1962), and others observe that by emphasizing research almost exclusively students are steered toward research careers armed with a set of approved methods, skills, and techniques. In this sense students are professionally geared but they are not always prepared to think innovatively about the researchable problems in their field. Sanford (1962) observes that the prescriptive requirements in the Ph.D. process often cut off the edge of wonderment and curiosity which the student brings with him by depriving him of the chance to explore other pathways independently.

In a sharp denunciation of what he labels "the shame of the graduate school," Arrowsmith (1966b) charges that the humane fields are being dehumanized because they have designed their programs to emulate the scientific methods and the narrow specialization of the sciences. McConnell (1969), another critic of narrow specialization, notes that educational programs which accept systematic cognition or reason as the only legitimate instrument of knowledge fail to understand that "reason is capable of reducing human experience and human values to juiceless formality, lifeless logic, and unfeeling abstraction." In this study these views were amply supported by the responses of both faculty members and students, as the following statements indicate. The first was submitted by a doctoral student in literature in a large public institution, but it epitomizes the thoughts expressed by students in other fields and in other places.

In general, I have objected to the "professionalism" inherent in graduate studies. The role of a scholar as a technician rather than as a teacher and human being receives emphasis here. The idea that the greatest researchers make the best teachers is accepted on faith and disproved every time classes are given. Researchers tend to be dull, unprepared for classes, and disinterested in students other than as disciples of their particular "gimmicks" for publishing. It is stressed and demonstrated that the road to success lies through publication; promotion and tenure follow the production of one or two books and a spate of articles.

In a variant on this theme a student in a private university wrote:

It is true, there is no excuse for muddy thinking, and insofar as "professionalism" insists on clear thought based on empirical evidence, it is to be commended. But when the Establishment faculty enforces a program of study dedicated to memorization of bibliographies and knowledge of secondary criticism rather than literature, a scribal tradition worthy of the most dogmatic religion has arisen. In a recent issue of the *New York Review of Books* Richard Ellmann defended the research scholar against attacks in periodicals beginning with Arrowsmith's article over a year ago. Granted, research scholars may feel unjustly accused. They and a few of their fellows have made complete successes of themselves. With endowed chairs, every third year off, graduate assistants, and light course loads, they have the best of all possible worlds. They are "scholar-adventurers" (to borrow the cant of "introduction to literary studies" courses) poaching on the lives and works of novelists, poets, dramatists; in the trail of their safari runs a horde of scrabbling sifters and bone-picking hyenas fighting among themselves over "banks and schools" or "banks and shoals" of composition A versus composition B. These are the same scholars who identify students by number instead of name so they "won't get involved"; they can't spare the time from collation of the first and second editions to wonder what the poor writer really had to say. And these are the men who train the next generation of teachers, today's graduate students. Thanks for the podium.

Ph.D. preparation for research in the sciences also has its share of critics. In his analysis of the epistemological aspects of scientific knowledge, Polanyi (1958) challenged a number of assumptions on which education for a research career is generally predicated. He argues that graduate students are often presented the "false ideal" of research as a thoroughly reasonable, logical, and orderly enterprise, whereas in reality it is sometimes intuitive and often "messy." He also notes that because the language of scientific research is couched in precise definitions, other rich sources of knowledge are often cut off. He views science as "an art which cannot be specified in detail [thus] cannot be transmitted by prescription since no prescription exists." He strongly supports the idea of an internship in which "by watching his master and emulating his efforts in the presence of his example the apprentice unconsciously picks up the rules of the art, including those which are not explicitly known to the master himself." On the other hand, the comments of a faculty respondent in physics reflects doubts about the apprenticeship or the models it provides:

> Our typical graduate research program is an apprenticeship rather than a challenge to truly independent investigation—post-doctoral research is taking over the latter function and the process is probably irreversible. It is not at all clear to me that the health of physics as a discipline is favored by the intense straining toward novelty, brilliance, and reputation which now characterizes graduate study and research (as distinct from a more leisurely pace of thoughtfulness and even playfulness in the older tradition of scientific "amateurism"). Physics may have been injured by the way it has been supported.

Rabi, the Nobel Laureate, observes that faculty members in the sciences often fail to communicate effectively with beginning graduate students because they use a private language that is intelligible only to individuals at their own level of expertise. He suggests that in presenting their ideas and their work to graduate students, scholars should draw on biography, philosophy, history, and sociology, and in so doing help the student to connect the knowledge and tools of his discipline to the elements of life. This strategy could add clarity, meaning, and relevance to the student's program and also help him to interpret his own role in the scheme of life.

A long list of critics contend that the institutionalized "publish or perish" dictum which faces university faculty members is the main reason for the alleged imbalances in research preparation at the Ph.D. level. In many cases this emphasis serves the dual purposes of helping both the student and the faculty to advance professionally. In this sense the problems of doctoral students with regard to controlling the imbalances in their scholarly activities are but the extensions of their advisers' problems. The importance of research visibility to a department was expressed in the comment of a department chairman in the humanities who said that the Cartter report had the effect of putting extreme pressure for publication on the faculty in his institution. In his judgment, the effort expended in giving research higher priority left a vacuum in the department's instructional emphasis.

The recent growth in the research function of the university has considerably strengthened the differentiation of the university, but not without serious cost to the institution. Commenting on the consequences of the intensified and expanded research emphasis in universities, department chairmen said that the primary sacrifice has been at the undergraduate level, where cohesion and balance have been upset because instruction is increasingly being given by graduate assistants or by those who have a primary interest in teaching at the graduate level. In a study of academicians, Parsons and Platt (1968) found that while the faculty members in their sample wished to spend more time than they currently did in teaching, they expressed a preference for teaching at the graduate level.

The research assistantship is the primary vehicle through which students in the sciences and social sciences obtain research preparation. In some cases, the assistantship precedes the student's own research. In other cases it parallels it or his own research grows out of the assistantship. In the latter case, the project out of which his dissertation develops is directed by the student's sponsor or by a faculty member on his research committee. Almost invariably the assistantship involves a stipend. However, it is not unusual for a student to assist a professor with his research for the purpose of gaining experiences and contacts with active researchers in his field.

Thirty-three per cent of the student respondents said that they held or had held a research assistantship. The solitary nature of research in the humanities and the lack of support for research

in the areas of French, English, or philosophy problably accounts
for the fact that only a few respondents in these fields reported that
they held an R.A. On the other hand, relatively large numbers in
the sciences and in the quantitative fields of economics and mathematics held research assistantships.

Among the 1123 respondents who held research assignments,
33 per cent said that they had accepted the appointment because
it was a requirement in their degree programs, and 81 per cent said
that they accepted it as a means to satisfy their financial needs. In
terms of an academic rationale, 59 per cent wanted to further their
preparation for a research career, 53 per cent wanted to learn new
research methods, and 17 per cent sought the appointment because
they wanted to work with a certain faculty researcher. Respondents
in chemistry, mathematics, physics, and biochemistry sometimes reported that the title of Research Assistant was given automatically
to students at the dissertation stage. In these cases the appointment
involved no extra work for the student, for it was assumed that his
own independent research contributed to the departmental output.
Sixteen per cent of the student respondents indicated that their
thesis research was a part of a larger research project in the department.

An analysis of the response data of students in the twelve
disciplines who were asked in the questionnaire to appraise the work
they were assigned as research assistants shows that an average of
88 per cent of the respondents in chemistry, biochemistry, physiology, and physics found the work intellectually satisfying and challenging. In contrast, 39 per cent of the respondents in economics,
English, history, philosophy, and sociology, and all six respondents
who held research assistantships in French, failed to find it intellectually stimulating.

In evaluating other aspects of their assistantship activities,
83 per cent agreed that the experience had afforded sufficient independence, the opportunity to develop research knowledge and
skills under supervision, and an opportunity to work with other researchers. The assistantship contributed to the development of approximately 93 per cent of the respondents in chemistry, biochemistry, physics, and physiology, but 83 per cent of those in French

and approximately 17 per cent in all other fields reported that the character of the work involved in their assignment was routine "busy work" which did not add to their academic growth.

Although appreciable numbers of students in the physical and biological sciences indicated that they found their experiences as teaching assistants to be "very meaningful" or "moderately meaningful," a slightly higher percentage described their research assistantships in these terms. Duties and activities in research apparently contribute more to student morale than do duties associated with instruction. Respondents frequently commented on the enjoyment they felt in working closely with the faculty or with other assistants as they cooperatively pursued a research problem. Those who enjoy a close association with a faculty researcher report that they gain a phychological lift from the honorific status that the association bestows. Many report that the intellectual stimulation and the challenge posed by the give-and-take of the partnerships as they exchange or defend their ideas whets their appetite for research. Unfortunately, many students who do not receive research appointments develop poor self-images and experience psychological stress.

Since the relationship between project directors and their assistants generally approximates an interaction between junior and senior partners—or near co-equals—the atmosphere in the research laboratory is more informal than that found in a teaching assistant's interaction with his supervisor. Thus the R.A. is more comfortable in his role than the T.A., and he finds it relatively easy to identify with the interests and goals of his colleagues.

When the extended comments of research assistants in the physical and biological sciences were compared with those of respondents in the social sciences and humanities, the impression emerged that the physical activity required in laboratory research acts as a unifying principle on the intellectual and spiritual satisfactions the researcher derives from his effort. In the Aristotelian sense, the preoccupation of the intellect with observable phenomena—in contrast to the abstract nature of the involvement in "armchair" or library research—seems to imbue the learner with a greater sense of well-being and contentment. The differences in the ideas expressed by research assistants in the various disciplines for improving the research assistantship experience appear to be more than accidental. Research assistants in the humanities and social sciences would like more responsibility, research assignments which coincide with their interests, and more consideration as members of the project team. In the physical and biological sciences, respondents say that they would like more independence in testing out their own ideas.

The organization of doctoral students in the physical and biological sciences around continuing faculty research generates an esprit de corps which, if not based on friendship, is based on a regard for the contribution each member makes to the end product. This seems to have the effect of motivating the graduate student to compete with himself rather than with his peers. If he observes competition among the faculty (or between departments in "rival" institutions) he accepts it as part of the game called "discovery."

In contrast to the acrimony and malaise which seemed to permeate the comments of many respondents in the social sciences and humanities, something of the spirit behind the moon voyagers was evident in the comments of research assistants in the physical and biological sciences. The dramatic nature of the breakthroughs in science—and the infectious nature of the scientists' pride in their accomplishments—according to one student, "not only turns us on but opens the door for future research that will sustain the excitement for a lifetime."

Hidden in the remarks of doctoral students in all disciplines is the implicit idea that the most important breakthroughs—from the point of view of man's survival and progress—lie just inside the doors of the social sciences and humanities. Some contend that if these disciplines do not remove the trivia which clutters their doorways, both they and society will go down the drain. As one student noted: "The medium is only part of the message. Students are protesting against content as well as form. Brilliant trivia is, nevertheless, trivia. Some reforms will be made within disciplines but the meaningful breaks will be made by problem-oriented interdisciplines, which I think are rapidly forming." Some commentators noted with irony and some with despair that we have the expertise to create the "meaningful breaks" but that the resources needed to forge the keys—money and political wisdom—are being diverted to other purposes. "Thus," they argue, "researchers in socially critical areas must fiddle while the country burns."

An indictment that is frequently raised against the research assistantship is that it is sometimes exploitative of student talent. Some critics point to the large number of A.B.D.'s inhabiting the halls of academia who, as research assistants, become "hewers of wood and drawers of water" for the department's research, or "technical hacks" for a particular professor. In many of these cases the interests of the student are overlooked, neglected, deferred, or "indefinitely postponed" until the project is finished. Some students get trapped, others trap themselves. In an attempt to examine the extent to which an appointment as a research assistant interfered with the student's own progress toward the Ph.D., an item eliciting this information was included in the questionnaire.

An average of 28 per cent of the respondents in all fields said that the duties required in their research appointment had indeed interfered with their progress toward the Ph.D. The range for all departments was from 6 to 83 per cent. Although there were relatively few research assistants in the humanities, 83 per cent of those in French, 53 per cent in English, 35 per cent in history and in sociology, and 32 per cent in economics who held research assistantships reported that their own progress had been interrupted because of the demands of their research assignments. In contrast, only 6 per cent of the chemists and 10 per cent of the mathematicians and physicists reported that they had experienced delays in their own programs.

Although respondents were often sharply critical of professors whom they identified as "academic entrepreneurs" who made "technical hacks" or got "excessive mileage" out of their research assistants, there were frank implications that students mask their antipathy to such professors as long as it is counterproductive not to do so. Their frequent laconic references to "playing games," "beating the system," or to "the solidarity of the R.A. research group" implied a very active grapevine system which operates as a source of information on the idiosyncrasies of the various project directors who might be in need of assistants. In spite of their sharp criticism, many research assistants seem to make the mature judgment that the opportunity to work as a member of a team is worth the risks of delaying one's progress or working overtime for an irascible or demanding research professor. In the words of one respondent, "If he knows his field, and knows what he wants to know, I can overlook his lack of concern about my time schedule." Another, who criticized his mentor's lack of sensitivity to his overworked research assistants, excused the professor because "he is tops in his field, and while students grumble, the learning payoff is incalculable."

In straightforward testimonial statements 22 per cent of the respondents who held research assistantships reported that their experiences in this role were "perfect," "couldn't be improved," or made them "happy with it as is." Many students seem to learn early in their academic experiences that the excitement in research is, as Edison remarked, 2 per cent inspiration and 98 per cent hard, repetitive, and often dull work. Those who accept this fact have a better chance for survival in a research department. In general, research assistants convey the impression that their Ph.D. programs provide fairly adequate preparation for "doing" research. Its shortcomings seem to lie in the fact that it does not adequately teach the graduate how to identify the researchable questions.

When faculties were asked to assess the quality of the research facilities in their institutions they gave highest ranking to its library holdings. Eighty-one per cent of the respondents described this resource as "excellent" or "good" and 7 per cent rated it as "poor." The remainder rated their libraries as "average." During the interviews deans and department chairmen frequently attributed the quality of the institution's output to the general deployment of funds for library purposes during the institution's formative years. Many mentioned that by enabling the institution to attract and hold distinguished scholars, the university's long tradition of supporting a top-quality library was the initial impetus to its current high standing. Ninety-three per cent of the student respondents in the physical sciences, 83 per cent in the humanities and the biological sciences, and 77 per cent in the social sciences described their research and library facilities as adequate.

Despite the high rating respondents gave to their libraries there was some dissatisfaction with the quality of library services and organization. Deans (who apparently receive the complaints) noted that library budgets did not adequately cover their personnel needs. In some cases this created breakdowns in service or required the use of non-professional staff who did little more than check books in and out. In other cases the organization of the library was described as too cumbersome or monolithic to provide efficient service.

Huge enrollment increases and phenomenal rises in the amount and scope of their research activities has placed formidable demands on the facilitative resources and services of universities. Unlike institutional facilities, which are more or less fixed, research needs are in a constant state of flux. At any given stage in a research project very different kinds of facilities may be required from those needed in any preceding stage. As projects advance, facilities may have to be rearranged, replaced, or salvaged. Needs may be temporary, long standing, or show sharp rises and sudden falls. Some cannot be anticipated. Department chairmen reported that these uncertainties create the greatest strain on institutional planning.

According to those interviewed, coordinating and administering research resources for the department consume a very considerable amount of the chairman's time, energy, and persuasive ingenuity. Often the chairman must set priorities or mediate conflicting intradepartmental claims for support, services, or space. In large departments he may be assisted by a coordinator, administrative assistant, or a research committee, but these adjuncts do not necessarily relieve the chairman of the responsibility to respond to the needs and requests of individual faculty members. As the final arbitrator of competing claims, the department chairman often walks a narrow line.

In addition to the strain imposed on university property, the demands for research facilities can generate serious internal tensions. The nature and intensity of those tensions was revealed during interviews with graduate and academic deans and in open-ended comments in the faculty questionnaire through their liberal use of terms such as "grantsmanship," "empire builders," "research entrepreneurs," and "the cannibalistic tendencies of research groups." Apparently, chairmen must sometimes base their decisions on personality quirks or on the basis of "peace-keeping" rather than on the basis of educational priorities or balance.

According to Ph.D. students, the doctoral dissertation is one of the most critical stages in the degree process. Often it is the most protracted. For those who are motivated toward a career in research it has high intellectual appeal, though much trauma. For those who may be primarily interested in teaching or in non-research careers it may represent little more interest than the fulfillment of a requirement. Some students are dismayed at the inordinate amount of time required to center on a topic, get it approved by a committee, and once launched on the research, battle ambivalence at every turn. On the other hand, some enter the graduate program knowing in advance the topic they wish to research and experience no blocks in having it approved.

There is an incredible lack of balance in the amount of assistance sought or received on the dissertation. In some cases the dissertation is the outgrowth of a research position or assistantship in which the entire expense of the research is borne by a granting agency or a sponsored research project which, in addition, may provide the student with subsistence pay. In other cases the entire costs are borne by the individual, who must borrow heavily to underwrite his education and his research; it is not unusual for him to obtain his Ph.D. owing several thousand dollars. Sponsors and research committees vary widely in the way they view their role in assisting the doctoral candidate in his research effort. Some believe that the student is more or less on his own. In some cases, after the topic is approved they do not see the student again until he applies for approval of his finished product. At the other extreme some sponsors ride herd on the candidate on every point and end up— as at least one faculty member in this study admitted—practically redoing whole dissertations.

Student expectations of the sponsor and the research committee roles also vary widely. While the majority prefer to work on their dissertations more or less independently, they generally learn how to take advantage of the process of professional analysis and advice which the experienced faculty researcher solicits throughout his career. Students who are au courant learn to seek out resources, follow leads, and develop the relationships which will put them in contact with those who have researched the same topic or some related problem. If they are in doubt about a problem, they will use those members of the research committee who can provide the distance of an analyst and the guidance which, presumably, they are qualified to offer. On the other hand, some students do not seek the advice of their research advisers. Some refrain from doing so because of personality conflict problems. Others seem to resent criticism or prefer to muddle through on their own. Some find this period one of lonely isolation or deep frustration. Others waste much time, energy, or motion or become research dilettantes or malingerers. Some prefer to get advice from other students who "know the game" or only from those professors whose ideas confirm their own views. Many respondents appear content to have their research committees act as a rubber stamp.

It is clear from the respondents in this study that sponsors and research committees can be especially helpful to those who do not work well in isolation. Most respondents view their advisers as sources of information or helpers over the dissertation hurdle. Others value the sponsor as an audience on whom to test the soundness of their research ideas. At times the sponsor may be a catalyst or prodding agent. More frequently, he is a supervisor standing by or on-call as needed. One of his chief functions is to help the student confine his research within manageable limits. The rolls of A.B.D.'s are probably appreciably swelled by those who did not obtain or seek advice on the latter point.

An average of 82 per cent of the doctoral respondents in biochemistry, physics, psychology, and chemistry, 76 per cent in English, history, mathematics, philosophy, and sociology and 62 per cent in economics and French thought that their departments provided or demanded adequate research preparation. It seems clear from the responses of students who had reached the dissertation stage that many were disappointed with the lack of assistance, guidance, and collegiality they met in their relationships with their dissertation sponsors. Nearly 30 per cent said that they had failed to find these amenities to the degree they wanted them or hoped to experience them in their Ph.D. programs. Approximately one-third felt that they had not been accepted by their sponsors as junior colleagues and nearly 80 per cent reported that their advisers failed to schedule regular meetings for the purpose of checking the candidate's progress or needs.

In spite of the fact that the comprehensive written and oral examinations are crucial to the doctoral student's progress—and basically new experiences for most students—more than half of the respondents reported that they had received no briefing from their advisers as to what to anticipate in preparing for these exams. There were implications in their free comments that the normal stress aspects of the oral examinations was accentuated by the fact that students often approach them with little knowledge of their purpose, format, scope, or any previous experience in the oral defense of their knowledge or point of view. As a result, many students overprepare. The tension is heightened because "one puts his whole future on the line on the basis of a two- or three-hour performance before his committee." By failing to advise their candidates that they are to be examined on the quality of their ideas rather than on the mechanical recall of factual material, some sponsors and research committees convert this experience into an obstacle course instead of offering it to the becoming scholar as a stimulating model of collegial interaction.

It is possible that highly autonomous faculty members, such as are found in top-ranked institutions, want to protect the autonomy and independence of their students and so leave them largely on their own. On the other hand, most scholars do not work in the stark isolation which many doctoral students endure at the dissertation stage. The satisfactions in doing independent research would, judging by their responses, be enhanced and heightened for Ph.D. students by periodic expressions of interest on the part of the sponsor. Many students said that they would profit psychologically, if not professionally, by an occasional opportunity to check their progress or to talk about their research. These data imply that the contractual agreement between the institution and the Ph.D. student is sometimes broken unilaterally by the faculty. Students who invest in the degree program and arrive successfully at the dissertation stage should be assured of adequate guidance and direction. When these are unavailable or of poor quality, the waste of individual resources and morale tends to be high and the quality of graduate education suffers.

An index of the satisfaction graduate students received in working with their sponsors may be learned from the data which show that 26 per cent of the respondents said that they would choose a different sponsor if they were selecting anew. Higher percentages of respondents in mathematics (83 per cent), physiology (83 per cent), and chemistry (80 per cent) would select the same adviser compared with an average of 72 per cent in biochemistry, economics, English, history, physics, psychology, and sociology, and 68 per cent in French and philosophy who would make the same choice.

Among members of the university faculty, publications are the principal index of productive scholarship. This fact influences and directs most of the activities that are incorporated into the graduate program. Based on the data in this study, Ph.D. students are encouraged throughout their academic programs to contribute to the world of professional scholarship and activity.

The respondents in this study reported that in addition to the prescribed academic activities and their teaching or research assistantships they had also published a scholarly paper (19 per cent), delivered a paper at a professional meeting (14 per cent), and designed or performed original research that was not a part of their dissertation (45 per cent). Other types of activities which were performed by smaller numbers included lecturing or teaching in another college, serving as consultant, editing a graduate journal, and the preparation of an annotated bibliography. Fifty-six respondents said that they were in the process of writing an article or book at the time they answered the questionnaire. These data substantiate the early socialization of students toward the "publication syndrome."

More students in the laboratory sciences than in other disciplines reported that they had published during the period of graduate study. For example, 36 per cent of the psychologists, 32 per cent of the physiologists, 28 per cent of the chemists and biochemists, and 26 per cent of the physicists reported that they had had a scholarly paper published, in contrast to six per cent of the students in philosophy, 8 per cent in French and in mathematics and an average of 12 per cent in English, economics, history, and sociology. Reasons for the quantitative differences in publication rates may lie in the fact that papers in laboratory fields generally involve straight-forward reporting of observed phenomena or the descriptive report-ing of an experimental "piece" of research. On the other hand, papers in the non-laboratory areas tend to deal with problems of great ambiguity and depend upon data which require the writer's interpretative insight. Other factors may include differences in avail-able research tools or auxiliary services and differences in the "drive to publish." Heavy subsidization of research in the sciences generally enables students to have free use of laboratory equipment, comput-ers, typing and editorial services, whereas students in less affluent disciplines must often scrounge for these aids or subsidize them out-of-pocket. It is also possible, judging by student comments, that the "race between laboratories on the East coast and those on the West coast to get out reports on a problem they are studying separately" stimulates a higher publication rate.

The quantitative unevenness of publication between respond-ents in the humanities and in the sciences may also be attributed to the fact that the teaching responsibilities of the former may pre-clude the time or opportunity for writing. Unlike the research assist-ant, the teaching assistant spends a considerable portion of his time in service to undergraduates or in the preparation of materials which enhance his teaching but do not promote his development in schol-arly writing. If the seeds of the "publish or perish" dilemma are sown among teaching assistants they can produce a moral predica-ment. The following observation of a student in history describes the dimension of that dilemma: "I came to graduate school to pre-pare myself for teaching in the liberal arts. I have observed that teachers are second-class citizens in the academic world. I now want to do research because I have learned that that is where the prestige is. I consider this a moral decline on my part."

Because the reward system in the institutions in the sample is based essentially on "measurable criteria"—that is, research—professors who received their recognition under this system of awards are inclined to rationalize the importance of projecting themselves as research rather than as teaching models. Thus, as they bend their efforts toward preparing their graduates for the prerequisites of the system, they tend to socialize them into the life style of the researcher for whom publications are the sine qua non and teaching is often viewed as a distracting intrusion. While this policy has done much to support the university's research productivity, it has had some serious negative effects on the quality of college and university teaching.

Preparation for College Teaching

12

In democratic societies it is a generally accepted aphorism that the quality of life enjoyed is a reflection of the quality of the educational enterprise the society promotes and supports. This is predicated on a corollary principle: the quality of the educational enterprise is a reflection of the investment society is willing to make to prepare those who will bear responsibility for the cultivation and transmission of the knowledge and values the society possesses.

Since the cultivation and transmission of knowledge is a primary responsibility of the academic profession, it follows that the quality of education and of life is largely determined, in any given society, by that society's response to the question, How well are your teachers prepared for teaching? This is not merely to ask How well have your teachers achieved mastery of the knowledge in their teaching field, and how free are they to teach that knowledge to others, but how well have they been prepared in the art and skills

227

of teaching it? If we direct this last question to the preparation of college teachers, we receive some disquieting responses.

In accepting responsibility as the teacher of teachers, graduate institutions assume accountability for the most sensitive aspects of the whole educational effort. Success or failure at this level has repercussions and social consequences that are both manifest and latent for every other level and for almost every educational variable. As teachers of teachers, graduate institutions are in a pivotal position to influence the totality of life enjoyed by—or denied to—individuals and society in general. Their role in the preparation of college and university teachers is particularly crucial in the current period of soaring student enrollments and compelling social issues.

The growing interest in higher education as a universal right, coupled with the size and character of the population which currently seeks that right, has generated demands for changes in education which have definite overtones with respect to the future character of higher education and for the types of faculty orientations colleges and universities will need. In some cases the nature and magnitude of the demands would require replacement of the traditional evolutionary process of planning by revolutionary approaches that threaten to uproot suppositions and attitudes that are deeply planted. In other cases the demands are predicated on what are, as yet, indeterminate goals; hence, planning, at best, must be tentative. In either case, institutions of higher education are rapidly learning—sometimes the hard way—that educational theories that were appropriate during more normal periods of transition have little relevance in this age of rapid technological development and social change. They have also begun to realize that they cannot produce action-oriented ideas for change without in some way being involved in their implementation or implicated in their consequences.

Those who plan doctoral programs are faced with the dilemma of whether to educate scholar-teachers, teacher-scholars, or both. Usually they start with the basic question: Is any distinction necessary or desirable at this level? Until quite recently most planners rejected Newman's contention that "to discover and to teach are distinct functions and distinct gifts rarely found in the same person" in favor of Huxley's view that research informs teaching.

In either case, most graduate faculties have operated on the assumption that the process of becoming a researcher requires rigorous exposure to theory and practice but the art and skill of teaching "comes naturally"—or develops gratuitously when one is educated for research. Thus, the emphasis in most Ph.D. programs has been heavily weighted in favor of preparing students to discover knowledge, and only incidentally if at all on how to impart to others the nature and value of that knowledge. As a result, the American college teacher is the only high-level professional person who enters his career with no practice and with no experience in using the tools of his profession. Graduate faculties, who are responsible for the education of future college teachers, are generally disposed to hold the opinion that an intelligent, liberally educated individual who has achieved mastery in a subject matter field is thereby qualified to teach it. More recently student unrest provided the impetus for a reexamination of this belief, and there has been a noticeable increase in the number who are willing to concede that some teaching experience under the supervision of a master teacher has merit. However, a majority still reject the idea that any formal study of the art and skills of teaching, or the nature of the learning process, adds substance to practice. According to the American Council on Education report, *An Assessment of Quality in Graduate Education,* members of the graduate faculty see an almost perfect correlation between "teaching effectiveness" and "eminence in one's field." The emphasis from the point of view of the graduate faculty is on content, not teaching style.

Educational researchers contend that these beliefs are not based on any rational analysis of the complexity of the teaching process, the subtleties of the learning process, or the difficulty of teaching under the stressful conditions in higher education today. Instead those who hold such ideas assume, in effect, that teachers *qua* teachers are born, not made. They reason syllogistically: "I had no formal training; I am a successful college teacher; therefore, my students can become successful college teachers without training." This is the simplistic philosophy on which many members of the graduate faculty face the question of education for teaching. If they espouse any method, it is that of the apprentice observing his mentor—usually doing research.

In fact, graduate students rarely have an opportunity to observe the faculty in a teaching role because although in almost any given department members of the graduate faculty spend fifty or sixty hours a week on their professional assignments, they spend an average of only six to seven hours a week in a formal class. In some institutions there is simply no option offered to observe a variety of teaching styles and methods. At the graduate level practically everything is geared to research, which relies heavily on the seminar approach. In some institutions, a specific ranking system splits off the teaching undergraduate faculty from the research faculty. Thus isolated from teaching models, the bright ambience is research and the evocative pull for the student is in that direction. The cumulative effect of this is that teaching becomes increasingly trivialized at the graduate level. As diffusers or popularizers of knowledge produced by the scholar, the teacher rarely achieves parity with him. Graduate students taught in this environment go out and teach the only way they know how—for technical competence.

A review of the available reports on the preparation of college and university teachers yields some evidence of recent gains in the number of institutions which purport to provide education or experience for this career (Koen and Erickson, 1967). A comprehensive survey taken in 1967 by researchers at the University of Michigan reported that approximately 450 graduate institutions listed courses or programs of instruction designed to assist beginners in the art and skills of college teaching. Since then several other institutions have added formal training in this area. Approximately 80 per cent of the 450 programs are directed toward students who are working for the Doctor of Philosophy, the degree normally required for those who seek regular appointments on a college or university faculty. Among the remainder are approximately 30 institutions which offer the Master of Arts or Master of Philosophy degree or specialist degrees that have been designed to prepare junior college and undergraduate college teachers. Recently, four or five institutions have introduced the Doctor of Arts degree and a dozen more are preparing to opt for this degree for those whose career interests are in undergraduate teaching.

About half of the institutions which claim that they give their Ph.D. candidates preparation for college teaching publish no reports on how this experience is implemented. Among reports that are available on the remainder, there is little solid evidence that the high rhetoric used to describe the program is matched by viable educational experiences that are carefully designed to develop individuals in the art and skills of instruction.

The activity which most commonly serves as the core of the teaching experience for the graduate student is the teaching assistantship. The Michigan Center for Research on Learning and Teaching reports that 75 per cent of the 450 institutions whose programs it reviewed indicated that the teaching assistantship was their primary tool for preparing future college teachers. Ninety-five per cent of these institutions describe the assistantship as an opportunity for teaching under supervision and guidance. However, various other studies report that less than half of those who held this appointment in the reporting institutions received adequate, systematic, or continuous guidance from a senior member of the faculty. A sad commentary on the static nature of their programs may be found in the data which show that in half of the fifty institutions which produce 90 per cent of the Ph.D.'s each year, the program for teaching assistants had remained substantially unchanged during the past decade or more. Thus while spiraling increases have occurred in college enrollments to exacerbate the problems of guiding and training assistants, and unprecedented developments in teaching and learning technology have begun to change the character of teacher preparation, nearly half of our major Ph.D.-producing institutions have made no methodological changes to meet the new demands. The deep well of discontent with the character of undergraduate teaching today may have its source in these data.

Of the more than two thousand teaching assistants in this study the majority reported that they experienced satisfaction with the assistantship experience, but appreciable numbers found it wanting in some essential aspects. In reviewing these data it should be kept in mind that the respondents were pursuing their programs in ten top-ranked universities and that most of them enjoyed the security afforded by a four- or five-year grant from the Ford or Danforth Foundations or from a federal fellowship program. In some cases the institution, too, had received a grant for purposes of strengthening its graduate program. Included in the institutional subventions were funds with which to secure staff for the supervision of teaching and research assistants.

Although 87 per cent of those who held teaching assistantships said that they had accepted the appointment because they wanted to gain teaching experience, the financial need filled by the appointment was equally, and in some instances, more compelling. Ninety-one per cent of the public university respondents and 87 per cent of those in private institutions said that they had accepted the appointment as a means to finance their degree goals. Fifty-four per cent of the private school teaching assistants reported that doctoral students in their departments were "required" to have teaching experience compared with 36 per cent of the public school respondents for whom the teaching assistantship was a required activity.

Most universities in the sample have carefully defined their criteria for the selection and appointment of teaching assistants. Unfortunately, in their press to find enough persons to staff their undergraduate classes, departments sometimes have to wink at the criteria. The rationale for the "required" teaching assistantship is sometimes based on the fact that the institution's need for low-budget instructors to staff its undergraduate courses forces some departments to require teaching experience for all Ph.D. aspirants.

Teaching assistants are typically the raw recruits, first-year students in the graduate program. With the exception of students in the humanities, who usually hold the teaching assistantship for three years, the average length of time spent in training is from one to one and one-half years. A large number forsake the teaching assistantship in their second or third year to seek the more highly respected and coveted appointment as a research assistant. In some cases the best students never gain teaching experience; they are selected early for research assistantships and remain in them throughout their programs.

The duties and responsibilities of teaching assistants vary widely among institutions and among departments within the same institution. They may range in character and level from routine nonacademic details to full responsibility for teaching a regular course. In many cases the duties of a teaching assistant are unspecified: he fills in wherever his services are needed. In other instances they are broadly defined. For example, in the physics department in one large university in the sample, teaching assistants are given a written description of the office they will assume as an assistant. In this statement the graduate is advised that he has a three-part responsibility: to facilitate in every possible way the intellectual development of the individual students in his section; to ascertain and carry out the aims of the professor in the development of the plan of the course; and to further his own training and development as a physicist and teacher.

Some departments attempt to scale the tasks that are assigned to teaching assistants so as to make the degree of complexity and responsibility in the task consonant with the teaching assistant's background and level of maturity. But in many cases graduates are mustered into service without any basic training or without any attempts to match their skills with the responsibilities to which they are assigned. The size of the undergraduate classes in the humanities and in the mathematics department generally requires that departments use their teaching assistants as leaders in small discussion sections, as readers, or as auxiliary advisers for undergraduate students in the major. In science departments there is a pressing need for laboratory assistants, so first-year graduate students usually assume these duties.

The data in Table 28 show the types of experiences gained by first-year graduate students and outline the variations in the degree of responsibility students are given as teaching assistants. The data also document the important economic contribution the graduate student makes to the instructional program in his department. Those institutions which offer a systematic program in teaching preparation usually attempt to arrange a squential pattern of experience for their T.A.'s. However, in many cases the teaching assistant is given a limited number of routine tasks which have doubtful value for his developmental progress or growth.

Departments vary widely in the amount of responsibility they give to their teaching assistants. For example, 23 per cent of the respondents who were teaching assistants in English, French, and mathematics reported that they had total responsibility in planning the course they taught, 65 per cent held full responsibility for devising tests, and 8 per cent were responsible for grading all papers either in their own course or in the courses offered by their faculty

Table 28

Tasks Assigned to Teaching Assistants during Their First Year of Graduate Study
(in percentages, N = 1843)

Task	Biochem.	Chem.	Econ.	English	French	History	Math.	Philosophy	Physics	Physio.	Psych.	Socio.
Observation of classes	25	44	27	12	35	21	19	31	27	30	29	29
Assistance in non teaching duties (reading, setting up labs)	41	73	40	18	31	34	44	37	62	49	69	53
Teaching occasional class	31	37	38	31	34	45	49	39	50	30	52	57
Conducting lecture course sections	15	28	53	25	18	62	83	49	53	19	55	64
Teaching lower division course	15	29	36	54	89	30	60	17	38	39	31	32
Teaching upper division course	11	11	9	4	8	8	1	4	10	10	12	8
Advising undergraduates	5	12	16	11	0	25	7	14	8	11	21	19
Supervising other teaching assistants	0	3	4	0	0	1	1	1	2	3	3	1

supervisor. In addition, 76 per cent of the teaching assistants in these fields assumed total responsibility for assigning all final grades and 81 per cent were responsible for keeping all records associated with their teaching assignment.

In contrast, only 1 per cent of the respondents who were teaching assistants in biochemistry, chemistry, physics, and physiology had total responsibility in planning the course they taught or assisted in, 4 per cent were responsible for devising all tests, 37 per cent were responsible for grading all papers, 9 per cent assigned all final grades, and 21 per cent were totally responsible for the record-keeping associated with their teaching assignment. These data not only show the differences in the teaching experience provided by the various academic divisions but also illuminate the probable cause of the complaints by science students that the teaching assistantship fails to provide enough responsibility or realistic teaching activities through which teaching ability might evolve and mature.

The special educational features of the assistantship that were offered to T.A.'s in the ten institutions in the sample included orientation meetings ranging from two or three hours to two weeks, regulary or informally scheduled meetings of the teaching assistant and his supervisor, pre-service training, special seminars on teaching, and the evaluation of the assistantship experience by the participants. The data in Table 29 indicate the extent to which these experiences were available to the respondents in this study.

A third of the respondents who held teaching assistantships described the experience as very helpful, another 25 per cent found it moderately helpful, and 8 per cent described it as rarely helpful. The fact that 32 per cent said that they had no basis for judging the value of the experience as preparation for teaching is disconcerting because among this group were many who said that they were assigned routine, non-teaching tasks. Others who had been assigned teaching duties were critical because they had received no supervision and no evaluative feedback from their faculty supervisors. The programs that were rated most satisfying were those which provided experiences that were graduated in responsibility. Respondents were most critical of those programs in which a "sink or swim" philosophy prevailed, and of those in which the teaching assistant had little control over the instructional style or method.

Table 29

EDUCATIONAL FEATURES OF THE TEACHING ASSISTANTSHIPS
(in percentages, N = 1857)

	Optional	*Required*	*Not Offered*
Orientation-to-teaching meetings	13	58	28
Intensive pre-service training	5	10	85
Special seminar for teaching assistants	10	16	73
Regularly scheduled meetings with faculty supervisor	22	37	40
Regular but informally scheduled meetings with supervisor	37	27	35
Recommended meetings with sponsor	34	8	57
Evaluations of T.A.'s by their students	32	11	56
Provided the T.A. with a written statement of his duties and responsibilities	12	28	59

In their open-ended comments on the strengths and weaknesses of the teaching assistantship approximately 75 per cent of the respondents reported that the experience had increased their interest in teaching, and an equal number said that the experience had improved their instructional skills. In spite of the fact that 81 per cent reported good relationships with their supervisors, only 59 per cent felt that they had been given enough guidance. Seven per cent felt that they had been over-supervised. One per cent thought they had been given too much unsupervised responsibility.

When those who held teaching assistantships were asked in an open-ended question to offer suggestions on how their experiences might have been strengthened, 1238 responded. Among these, 33 per cent thought that teaching assistants should be given more responsibility, 26 per cent thought that their departments should emphasize the importance of teaching and provide education in teaching methods, 8 per cent recommended various structural changes in the assistantship, and 8 per cent thought assistants should receive higher pay. Others suggested that the teaching assistants should be accepted into the department as junior colleagues, and that the number of credit hours for which the graduate is required to register to be eligible for a teaching assistantship be reduced. The latter suggestion is based on the fact that some institutions require the teaching assistant to register for six or eight units of course credit during the period of his assistantship. Faced with the pressure to maintain his grade-point average as a Ph.D. student, he often finds it necessary to concentrate on his studies at the expense of preparing for his teaching role.

That there is a growing concern among college and university presidents for faculty who know how to teach is documented in Berelson's data which showed that over six hundred college presidents and academic deans rated "knowledge of how to teach" one of the primary skills they looked for in seeking staff. In response to this interest, 35 per cent of the current Ph.D. programs now require some teaching experience. Among faculty respondents in the institutions in this study, 68 per cent reported that supervised teaching experience was available in the form of assistantships and 39 per cent reported the availability of an internship for those primarily interested in teaching careers. Other types of preparation for teaching experiences included seminars on college teaching (23 per cent), and course work on college teaching (13 per cent). Another 7 per cent reported that a special program was available for those who were interested in careers in college teaching.

Fundamental to the practicum or internship is the assumption that teaching implies a certain behavior and, as behavior, one's teaching style can be subject to analysis, change, and improvement. A second important assumption is that teaching is an extremely complex kind of behavior involving the full range of thought, communication, and physical action. To this end, the intern's program is ostensibly arranged so as to provide opportunities for him to observe and analyze a variety of models whose styles and coping mechanisms are appropriate for college teaching. In addition, some programs attempt to provide the intern with opportunities to analyze and evaluate under realistic experimental conditions his own approach to teaching, his students' approach to learning, and the strategy and techniques for organizing the materials and preconditions for teaching. Generally, his program includes a basic foundation in psychology or sociology and in teaching methods that apply in his substantive field. In a few cases the program includes an interdisciplinary seminar in which problems of teaching are analyzed and compared. In the internship, practice is related to the student's course learning and is arranged sequentially so as to provide variable activities and responsibilities. In some cases, the student takes his internship on his own campus, and in others, the experience is gained in another institution with which the university has arranged his supervised teaching schedule.

As the need for more college teachers grows, and the criticism of undergraduate teaching becomes more vitriolic, the question "Is there a need for a new doctoral degree for college teachers?" becomes more pervasive. The issue has been debated frequently and heatedly. Spurr (1970) and Dunham (1969) document the dimensions of the debate and show evidence to support the need for new degrees for college teaching. In the data in this study there is evidence of growing faculty support in some fields for a special degree for those who plan careers in college teaching. Among faculty respondents representing the twelve academic fields in the study, 35 per cent favored the introduction of a teaching degree in their field. Another 20 per cent were not certain of the need and 44 per cent opposed such a degree. Those who favored the degree agreed that it should be offered by the substantive department rather than by the School of Education and that it should be designed for synthesizers and disseminators of research rather than for researchers per se.

These data indicate new thinking on the part of graduate faculties and may portend changes in future doctoral preparation. Up to now most proposals for a special degree for college teachers have been met with studied indifference on the part of the graduate faculty, most of whom perceive such a degree as a dilution or a diminution of rigorous scholarship or productive of a second class of scholars. Almost universally, the department chairmen who were interviewed for this study were inclined to correlate a degree that is different "in kind" with a degree inferior "in quality." It is clear that if a doctorate in college teaching is ever to emerge as a viable and respected degree, it will require strong and aggressive administrative leadership, effective representative support from the teaching faculty, and a political place and power within the university structure.

Almost everyone has a bad conscience about the injustices in the academic reward system and its effect on teaching, but deans and department chairmen insist that until some way is found to recognize teaching, the hortatory injunctions will do little toward changing the balance between preparation for teaching and preparation for research. Nor will formal programs of teacher preparation be in any great demand. Most students are no less sensitive than professors to the reward system. Few are inclined to elect a program of study which might jeopardize their mobility up the academic ladder or lessen their attractiveness in the academic marketplace. Thus present practice is perpetuated.

Many graduate deans agree that if no one is willing to speak for teaching, or if those who speak are defeated by the wall of silence which confronts them, patchwork efforts at reform will continue to be applied in place of new and different doctoral programs that might be designed to educate integrated teachers, not just specialized scholars. Although the graduate deans in this study generally support the idea of a teaching doctorate in principle, few are sanguine about its early acceptance in their institutions. Some believe that the internship or practicum in college teaching which some universities now offer may pave the way for a new program at the doctoral level. Others have hopes that the Candidate or Certificate in Philosophy will provide the necessary education. A few believe that degrees per se will lose their significance as the primary credential for college faculties.

The fact that 26 per cent of the teaching assistants who responded to the graduate questionnaire reported that they would welcome more emphasis on teaching methods may portend a shift in career interests among doctoral students. Judging by their open-ended statements, it appears clear that increasing numbers of the current graduate generation prefer careers in college teaching over university research careers. That this increase coincides with present decreases in the demand for research personnel may be fortuitous for the short-run. However, an imbalance in the direction of teaching interest at the expense of research interest could have very serious long-range consequences. At any rate, Ph.D. students in increasing numbers are insisting that teaching as a profession requires as much, if not more, solid, sensitive, and systematic preparation as does research. In some institutions they are making a concerted effort to acquire that preparation.

An assessment of the preparation of future college teachers would be incomplete without a consideration of the fact that students today make a sharp distinction between dedication to a career and commitment to one. This is reflected not only in their expressed attitudes about their role as teachers, but concretely in the figures which show that they are beginning to unionize for bargaining purposes. About 6 per cent of the 2040 respondents who are currently teaching assistants in the ten institutions in this study said that they are members of a union. Another 45 per cent said that they would join such a union if a local were available. Only 12 per cent said that they opposed teachers' unions on principle.

While 40 per cent of the respondents view unions primarily as media through which to negotiate for better salaries, approximately the same number would use the union to secure improved working conditions, standardized workloads, limitations on the size of the lab or the discussion sections that are assigned to assistants, or to obtain improvements in appointment procedures. Thirteen per cent believe that unionization is a means through which undergraduate programs eventually can be strengthened. Implicit in these and other data on today's students is the fact that "dedication" to teaching as an ideal is being replaced by the conviction that teaching involves a secular and not a sacred trust. In this sense it involves commitment, not sacrifice. If unionization of teaching assistants becomes a trend, it will probably have far-reaching influence on the attitudes of future teachers toward the concept of service. Also affected will be the institutional autonomy derived from the use of graduates as solutions to the problem of staffing undergraduate classes.

The American Federation of Teachers claims authorship of the educational revolution. By enlisting future generations of college teachers into its membership it insists that it will hasten the day when training programs will be regularized. Some universities are attempting to find alternates to this external press by designing internships which bring the student more intimately into the collegial partnership. A primary aim in these moves is to improve the status of the prospective teacher and to reduce the distance he feels between where he is and where he wants to be. Many authorities believe that one of the first steps in this direction must be to increase the stipend paid to teaching assistants and to involve them more directly in those decisions which affect their identification with and progress in the educational world.

Conscious of the growing complexities in the challenges met by college teachers, and in reaction to charges that they have failed to give adequate support or status to those who teach, several professional groups have organized national commissions on college teaching. Such commissions attempt to promote information on effective teaching practices and offer support and encouragement to those who wish to devote themselves to the development of programs of teaching preparation. For example, the Commission on Undergraduate Teaching in the Biological Sciences and the Commission on Teaching College Physics recently held conference workshops in which concerned faculty members and graduate teaching assistants discussed the problems and promises in the current teaching preparation practices at major universities. Operating as working groups, and using a research base on which to plan, the conferees produced many promising ideas and programs on which planning for teaching preparation might be predicated. The graduate students who attended these conferences made it patently clear in their comments and reports that graduate students will put pressure on universities until they accept their obligation to students and to society to improve the quality of the teaching preparation that the Ph.D. program offers.

Outside pressures toward this same end are in the offing, or are already being exerted, by federal agencies and private foundations which have been supporting fellows or providing scholarships for Ph.D. hopefuls. Spokesmen for these agencies say that institutions that design programs which include preparation for teaching, as well as for research, will be favored.

Changes in
Graduate Education

13

On every level the educational world is in ferment. Stages in this eruption range from attempts to generate explosive reforms to programs characterized by a quiet effervescence. At the lower levels, the movement is well-developed, but at higher levels it is more or less inchoate. Educational planners who look to the horizon for a portent of things to come find new rearrangements of knowledge, new curriculum patterns, new methods of organization for learning, new interrelationships between disciplines, and new ethnic studies programs. However, the bulk of this activity occurs at lower levels. Practically none goes on at the graduate level. It is here that time is running out for planners.

The transcendental changes in the world of ideas render traditional methods of programming graduate education inadequate and unsuited for present, much less for future, needs. If McLuhan's thesis is correct that individuals perceive the preceding environment to be the present, planning at best represents a lag. Faculty members who plan graduate curriculum especially appear to be afflicted with retrogressive vision. Many who severely criticized the requirements and practices in their own Ph.D. programs as outmoded or unrealistic seem strangely incapable of suggesting modifications or of designing imaginative new patterns when they are in charge of planning graduate study. Berelson's observation that "more than in any other profession . . . present practices are perpetuated precisely because the judges of the product are themselves the producers" suggests that a closed system is in operation.

A comparison of the problems identified at the turn of the century by West and James and in the thirties and forties by Lowell and others with those identified in the sixties by Berelson, Carmichael, and our own studies at Berkeley reveals striking similarities. The major difference is in the fact that the problems of graduate schools today are compounded by the added problems of intensity, size, and numbers. Such a comparison also reveals the apparent inertia of the graduate school toward change. Ironically, the very institution charged with major responsibility for opening new systems or expanding known ones does not always present itself as a viable model.

Although most graduate departments have responded additively to changes in the scope and nature of knowledge in their fields, only a limited number of institutions have responded with real innovation. A comprehensive review of the literature on graduate and professional education leads to the conclusion that there have been practically no new ideas in the basic format of graduate study during the past three or four decades. If change by deletion occurs, it generally does so by default or as an unplanned consequence—for example, a professor resigns, retires, or dies and "his" course is dropped from the program.

It is rare that a university submits to surgery on a whole program. Although one chairman in this study reported that two degree programs had recently been eliminated on the recommendation of his faculty, he added that the programs had "actually been dead for years because no students had registered for them." And while every chairman could point to recent changes within his department, practically all of these were identified as specific to certain courses rather than to the program as a whole. Only one reported that the department had undergone a system-wide review within the past three years.

If the degree and direction of their change is a reliable measure of institutional vigor, many graduate institutions are in deep trouble as far as their vitality or intellectual health is concerned. In too many cases, the basic pattern for graduate study appears to have been set in concrete. And, in the case of many newly created graduate programs, Riesman's analogy applies. New institutions in the academic procession strain to model themselves on those already established instead of developing distinctive or unique qualities of their own. The urge "to be like Harvard or Berkeley" may pose serious restraints on an institution born in an age of educational revolution.

There is a growing interest in the idea that the university needs restructuring as a center for learning. Heyns (1967), Millett (1968), Katz (1966), and others point to the fact that today's student wants to be involved more directly with his environment. They suggest that if the education process were organized so as to give him more responsibility for his own learning, this desire could be met. One of the probable reasons for the malaise or disinterest among students is the fact that educational institutions are organized so tightly around teaching that learning becomes for the student a passive experience. Rogers (1964) and others call for a reversal in the traditional teacher-learner roles. They suggest a reorganization in the instruction process to make the student an active seeker of the knowledge he needs to solve a problem which he and his instructor have identified. In the process, learning becomes personalized, dynamic, and cooperative because at some points the learner becomes the teacher and the teacher becomes the learner. Such a reversal of roles would require a radical restructuring of the methods of instruction that are currently in use in the university.

If we assume that the end-means concept has relevance for educational planning, the graduate faculty can be criticized for its failure to explain its academic goals and the means whereby it proposes to achieve them. Student complaints about the discreteness, repetitiveness, imbalance, lack of coherence, and absence of central focus in their programs document the general problem. Their criticism generally highlights the poor quality of articulation between course ends and means and departmental ends and means, but ultimately it reveals the fact that faculty members hold divergent and sometimes conflicting goals, or no coherent goals that can be related to departmental or institutional purpose, much less to student goals. Faculty members are inclined to respond to this allegation by arguing that an educational roadblock is erected when ends are purposefully designed and means are neatly structured.

In a pluralistic culture, or a fast-changing technology such as ours, the task of reconciling the divergent goals of individuals, professional disciplines, and society is monumental. When the university attempts to accommodate itself to the needs of disparate publics, it exposes itself to the risk of appeasing one group and alienating others, and, in terms of its own well-being, it may find that with each accommodation, its clarity of purpose grows dimmer. In the absence of clear-cut goals—particularly in an era of rapid transitions—a university department may be caught, in the words of one of Auden's poems, "lecturing on navigation while the ship is going down."

On the assumption that departmental goals are articulated through the curriculum, faculty members in the twelve fields were asked to state the aims of the Ph.D. program in their department as they perceived them. Among the respondents, 41 per cent saw the goals in their departments as the development of teacher-researchers, 25 per cent as the development of researchers, and 16 per cent as the "production of scholars for the field." Additionally, 3 per cent saw their departments as the producers of teachers, 5 per cent as the developers of "the educated person," and 5 per cent ascribed to the department the pragmatic goal of helping the student to "pass examinations" or "to meet the university requirements." Approximately 3 per cent responded in cynical terms, such as "to develop grantsmen or operators." Slightly more than one per cent said that their departments had no clear-cut goals.

Although the lecture method has often and assiduously been denounced as an ineffectual means of transmitting knowledge, it continues to be the most frequently utilized teaching method in the university. Supporters of it point to the fact that there is no conclusive evidence to show that the lecture is any less effective than most other methods. Much of the criticism directed against teaching by the students in this study pertains to the quality and content of the lecture or to the style of the lecturer rather than to the method per se. The charge that a dependence upon the lecture method tends to depersonalize the interaction between faculty and students and limit their opportunities for discussion has prompted some institutions to use junior faculty members, teaching assistants, or senior students as leaders of small groups in which the lecture topics given by a senior professor are reviewed and analyzed.

Some colleges and universities have developed a tradition for great lecturers which they strive to continue. However, in the electronic age in which, according to McLuhan, "the medium is the message," the lecture as a teaching tool has lost much of its appeal. In response to the press for change, some chairmen reported that their departments were attempting to revive other methods or create new ones. On each of the campuses in the study some portion of the faculty engaged in supervising independent study, tutorials, undergraduate or graduate seminars, small group dialogues and discussions, workshops, student-faculty colloquiums, intergroup conferences, retreats, films and film-making, field study, or community-centered interdisciplinary studies. Some chairmen reported that in response to the available research—which shows that students who vary on such characteristics as intelligence, cognitive style, sex, independence, flexibility, responsibility, motivation, authoritarianism, or anxiety respond differently to different kinds of teaching methods or behavior—some faculty members have modified their approach to teaching. Many have moved in the direction of less formality.

The lack of data on the effectiveness of various teaching methods on learning inclines most instructors to question the often expressed assumption that the ideal educational situation is one in which the student receives the personal attention of his instructor. Some respondents suggested that a more realistic goal would be to attempt to educate each student to the best of his and his institution's capacity. This implies a responsibility on the part of the institution to offer a variety of instructional choices and a commensurate responsibility on the part of the student to select the learning methods he finds conducive to this development.

The mere logistics of trying to match and mesh the instructional methods that are best suited to the personalities of the student and professor, and are appropriate to their particular fields of study, loom as formidable barriers to graduate program committees. With rare exceptions, restraints are imposed on planning by the orientation or commitments of the existing personnel, so that planners must lean upon the principle of accommodation rather than upon the more attractive concept of achieving compatibility between teaching style and the learner's needs.

At the graduate level the seminar is the popular medium for teaching and learning because it focuses on the process and products of research. It is generally assumed that the ideal seminar consists of a small group of students and faculty members who have an interest and some background in the topics studied. In practice, however, in some institutions in the study, seminars range in size from four or five participants to several hundred and may include students who vary widely in their preparation, interest, and understanding. The components which doctoral students selected as vital to the success of a seminar included the professor's competence in the subject and his ability as a discussion leader; the intrinsic interest in the subject matter; and the caliber of the students' readiness and participation. The importance of these and other factors are shown in Table 30.

Some students in all fields reported that their seminars were uneven in quality and often lacking in stimulation. Specific criticisms included charges that sessions were often structured and conducted like lecture courses; were built additively rather than dialectically; were threatening to the shy or less verbal student; were highly specific and narrowly focused; or were sometimes presented with such erudition that the student felt intimidated or was reluctant to ask questions or participate. In a few isolated cases, a student cited a particular seminar for the inspiration it had given to his own research interest or focus. Some students commented on the value they derived from informal encounters with seminar speakers during the coffee hours which preceded or followed their formal talks. Others noted that they had gained insight into "how researchers think" by observing a variety of seminar speakers.

One of the major drawbacks in planning a variable ap-

Table 30

FACTORS IMPORTANT TO THE SUCCESS OF SEMINARS,
DOCTORAL STUDENTS' PERCEPTION
(in percentages, N = 3013)

	Highly important	*Moderately important*	*Not important*
Organized around unified topic	46	37	17
Students were challenged to participate	16	24	59
Professor's competence as discussion leader	61	23	16
Professor's command of the subject	85	13	2
Diversity of students' research interests	12	33	57
Diversity of students' approaches to the topic	22	36	41
Similarity of students' research interests	6	24	70
Similarity of students' approaches to topic	4	20	76
High academic caliber of student participants	46	39	15
Students were responsible for preparation	45	30	25
Students were responsible for structure	15	29	56
Quality of students' oral contribution	48	32	20
Intrinsic interest of subject matter	77	20	3
Limited size of seminar	37	32	30

proach to teaching is the tightness of the academic time schedule. The practice of dividing knowledge into fifty minute segments (known as Carnegie units) created the condition which fostered the lecture method and appears to be one of the main obstacles to educational experimentation and change. In the interest of maintaining order in academic housekeeping, knowledge is compressed and teaching methods are adapted to accommodate tidy administrative units that are standardized for expeditious purposes. Recently a few institutions in the sample reasserted the primacy of academic priorities over administrative convenience. By offering a diversity of scheduling patterns, teachers and students in these institutions were given the option to select a schedule that appeared best suited to their needs and interests. Reports on these innovations indicate that students tend to be better motivated toward learning and achieve better under a flexible time schedule, while the faculty report that with more direct control over the distribution of their teaching schedule, they can use more variety in their methods and respond adaptively and individually to the needs of their students.

In any given discipline the mounting body of available knowledge is formidable—both for the teacher and for the learner. The notion that in a doctoral program one can contact—much less master—all of it is unrealistic, but as the quantity of knowledge mounts the need for careful and systematic curriculum planning grows daily more acute. Millett (1968) warns that academic planning must be undertaken on the basis of clearly defined objectives and be guided by the theory that learning is a developmental process which involves the personality needs of the individual as well as the special needs of society for well-educated citizens. Department chairmen observed that unless the curriculum is carefully planned and coordinated around the essential knowledge in the disciplines, students will become fragmented scholars whose learning lacks an integrative quality.

To an appreciable extent, the special interests and skills of the graduate faculty determine the nature and content of the research emphasis and dictate the order in the instructional schedules of the department. For this reason, Ph.D. programs are more or less built around the available professors, and seminars and research groups tend to become identified with particular persons. In large departments, in which the faculty represent breadth as well as depth of interest, such specificity presents few problems. On the other hand, in small departments the lack of faculty depth narrowly limits the curriculum. This can have advantages as well as disadvantages. For example, in one institution in this study the curriculum in physics is, for practical reasons, limited to the study of its theoretical aspects. In another institution, the biochemistry faculty shares a common interest in a particular branch of biochemical research and will accept as doctoral students only those applicants who show an interest in that specific area of the discipline.

It is probably accurate to say that most faculty members are disinterested in curriculum planning on a departmental or campus-wide basis, and that faculty members in general have little aptitude for it. Because their preparation for participation in academic development has been narrowly circumscribed, specialists feel uncomfortable making judgments about curriculum reform. Their natural tendency is to react conservatively with respect to innovations —especially when those innovations are proposed by those whom they do not personally know. Department chairmen reported that they frequently had difficulty in finding faculty members who were willing to work on curriculum committees or on program reform. Some reported that although the department had a curriculum committee its members rarely met except to give "rubber-stamp approval" to proposals for new courses. Committee debates tended to be reserved for proposals which involve "required" courses.

In general, deans and department chairmen expressed the need for finding new channels of cooperation with respect to the development of basic academic reforms. Some expressed the need for coping mechanisms which could give integrative vision to the contributions of related fields. Others suggested that the corollary between the fragmentation of basic disciplines and the current discontinuities in social goals and values, points unerringly to the need for systematic curriculum reform. In most departments the discussion revolves around those who would make Ph.D. programs more comprehensive and those who hold out for sharp specialization within a limited choice of program options.

As a rule, graduate schools have been slow to initiate reform in their academic programs. The process through which fundamental curriculum changes are made at the Ph.D. level is almost always circuitous. It requires many detours, meets many roadblocks, and is subject to long delays. The current frustrations among advocates of Black Studies programs typifies the problems which a university faces when it wishes to innovate. One department chairman cited the literary observation that on the road to progress, for every man who wishes to introduce something new, thirty stand in his way to block his intent. While presumably, faculty blocks are motivated by an interest in preserving the quality and integrity of the university, the approval process is often so frustratingly cumbersome as to discourage efforts to introduce necessary change.

In general, in the universities in this sample, an idea for curriculum change may arise at any level within the institution—including the student level. The proposal for change is usually presented to the department chairman, who then refers the item to the curriculum committee or to the executive committee. In the absence of these committees, the chairman may appoint an ad hoc committee to review the request. If the proposal meets with committee approval, that information is reported to the chairman with a recommendation for faculty consideration. The chairman then places the item on the agenda of the faculty meeting. At this point several things might happen to the recommendation. It might be debated and modified. It might be referred to a subcommittee for further study. It might be, but rarely is, adopted by the faculty after a first hearing. If the faculty eventually approves the change the chairman is so advised. In most cases, he has discretionary power to veto a recommendation, but the chairmen who were interviewed for this study said that they would be reluctant to veto a faculty vote unless they had evidence of a sharp division in the faculty. When faced with a dilemma some department chairmen observed that they would base their decision on the quality of the personalities who supported or opposed the proposed change.

If a change does not involve budgetary matters or other units on campus, it can usually be put into operation without further approval. If it involves internal budgetary rearrangements these, too, can generally be accomplished without going to higher authority. On the other hand, if the proposal is for a new academic program, or requires additional subvention, the matter must then go to the academic dean who will bring it before the entire faculty for its approval. If approved at this point, the recommendation is forwarded through channels leading through the graduate dean, the academic senate, the budget officer, the vice-president for academic affairs, the vice-president for research, the president, the board of regents and, in the case of public universities, it may be transmitted to a state coordinating council for higher education. In each of these offices, the request is screened for specific details before being moved to the next higher channel. The process may take months. In the case of new degree programs it is not unusual for it to take years.

Departments use various techniques or subterfuges for avoiding this long, man-hour consuming process. A common technique is to introduce change by adding it to a program that has already been approved. In this way the department becomes self-authenticating and retains control within itself.

In terms of curriculum changes within the next five years, academic deans thought that these would come through reform rather than through major reorganization or innovation. Although most of them envisioned a redefinition of the traditional requirements such as courses, credits, grades, residency, and examinations, most of the deans thought that the major changes would occur in areas that represent the bulwark of traditionalism, specifically the humanities and to some extent the social sciences.

Some deans expect that faculty members will sharpen their concepts of purpose and modify the curriculum in favor of fewer course requirements, more independent study, and more face-to-face encounters with students. They believe that the faculty will do less teaching—particularly less lecturing, and that their role will be redefined to that of a facilitator or expediter of learning. Reductions in the time required in the preparation of lectures should increase their capacity as scholars and put them in closer contact with students. Deans expect that in some fields traditional teaching methods will be replaced or supplemented by learning technologies and research will be greatly expedited by information retrieval systems, data banks, and shared computer services.

Each of the deans voiced misgivings and apprehension about the imponderables ahead for graduate education. One, who represented one of the largest universities in the sample, was especially concerned about the impact of the profound and traumatic changes in our social system on the university. He noted that in the years immediately ahead "there will be changes accompanying changes at the interface of the university and society . . . the full impact of which few people realize." He observed further that congressional attitudes are becoming increasingly critical of the objectives, relevance, and quality of the research that has been supported by public funds. The impotence of universities in offering assistance toward reducing the distrust and disunity that are abroad in the land has made skeptics of those who, up to now, have been supportive of university activities. In the judgment of this dean, there is need for intensive soul-searching on the part of the faculty with respect to these questions.

For the most part academic deans expressed cautious optimism regarding the growth and development of their graduate programs. Depending to some extent on the outcome of the Vietnam conflict, they anticipate a gradual increase in enrollments for the years immediately ahead and a leveling off in the mid-seventies. Budget restrictions have caused some departments to be more selective in their admissions so as to husband valuable resources for those who are committed to full-time study. In several cases the Masters degree has been eliminated as an economy measure or as a means of discouraging those who have short-range goals which can be accommodated in other institutions.

Academic deans foresee more students entering graduate schools immediately following the baccalaureate or even before its completion. They expect that this might accentuate the problems of student morale by requiring that individuals face the rigors of the graduate discipline at the heights of their personal need to be independent. Some deans anticipated that more and more graduate students will be on fellowship support for approximately four years and that stipends will be standardized at a level that will remove the competitiveness. They expect that a net result of this will be to scatter graduate students more broadly and to involve them in more diverse educational programs. None of those interviewed was sanguine about the financial pressures that lie ahead.

A few academic administrators anticipate substantial changes in the nature of the Ph.D. research requirement. Some expect to see wider variation in the form of the dissertation and a broader interpretation of its purpose. By removing the requirement for originality in the research project, they believe that the number of

A.B.D.'s may be substantially reduced. On the other hand, deans expect to see a rise in the number of post-doctoral students during the next few years.

Some deans anticipate that programs of graduate study will be differentiated within some departments so as to provide professional experience in addition to research experience. They foresee increased activity with respect to providing supervised teaching experience, but most deans think this problem will continue to grow unless structural changes are made in the degree programs. Almost all agreed that some doctoral students need preparation for college teaching, but none was optimistic about the prospects of their institution providing this opportunity for all who sought it. Four deans expect that a new degree for college teaching will be forthcoming and two predicted that a post-doctoral year will be required for those who wish a university appointment. During his post-doctorate period they expect that the Fellow would receive teaching as well as research experience. While the deans foresaw the need for an increased concern about preparing good staff members for small liberal arts colleges, not all were convinced that major universities should play a role in this education.

When department chairmen were asked to comment on the changes they foresaw in their disciplines within the next five or ten years they almost invariably reflected first on the speed with which the structure of their discipline was changing and then said that they would have difficulty in predicting, even for the next five years, what form it would eventually take. The amorphous states of sociology, biochemistry, and physiology make it impossible, according to their administrative heads, to define present boundaries precisely, and no one expected that those boundaries would stabilize in the immediate future. Economists said that their field of study had swung full circle back to econometrics "where it began in 1820." Chemists were in fairly general agreement that their discipline was changing so rapidly that it was becoming increasingly necessary to give doctoral students broad training lest some might be prepared for specialties that were no longer viable when they graduated.

The biological sciences appeared to be in the most dynamic state of flux. Department chairmen in these fields observed that unprecedented discoveries in molecular biology, genetics, and physical chemistry will make it necessary in the future for these disciplines to resist atomization. While some foresee great differentiation and specialization others see a return to a generalized approach. In either event, practically all those interviewed in the biological sciences expect that the lines between their fields and other disciplines will become increasingly fuzzier as the former move from test-tube experimentation toward research on the whole organism. As an example of this apparent trend, one department chairman reported that in a course on cell biology that is now offered jointly by six departments, the nature of the discussions now indicates a need for an emphasis on the philosophy of science; hence next year a professor from philosophy will be added to the group.

Some department chairmen in biochemistry reported that they expect to see an increased dependence upon technology and the physical sciences for the development of the instrumentation which the bioscientist will require. They expect that the high cost of instruments, such as the machines needed in X-ray crystallography, will lead to the development of multidisciplinary laboratories and other shared services. Contingent upon the availability of financial underwriting, many of those interviewed anticipate that through the use of automated hook-ups researchers will be able to obtain direct feedback as they attempt in their laboratories to probe highly complicated processes or life systems.

In preparation for these new methods and techniques, department chairmen essentially agreed that students will require more math, some competence in computer science or electronics, and a background in one or more areas of the physical sciences. This added preparation will extend the time needed for the degree or make a post-doctoral experience almost a requirement for university placement. There appeared to be general agreement among the department chairmen in the biological sciences that a new breed, the biogeneticist, will emerge within the next decade to bridge the gap between biochemistry and genetics. Others see an emphasis on neurological biochemistry and possibly a dwindling of interest in biochemistry as an isolated field. Still others observe that a valuable tension is developing between scientists in the biosciences and scholars in other fields who have an interest in human ecology.

There seems to be little doubt that as a result of their dramatic discoveries and inventions the biological sciences have displaced the physical sciences as the "glamour fields" and are currently riding the crest of the academic wave. Some chairmen view this as a mixed blessing. As they observe the pressures which visibility, sprawling growth, and spiraling affluence exert, some administrators said that they have reservations about the price of "popularity."

Department chairmen in physiology were unanimous in their opinion that that field would undergo sweeping changes during the next decade. However, they did not agree on the direction those changes would assume. Some contended that the classical study of physiology would continue and be expanded. Others believed that the emphasis in the future would be on applied, clinical, and environmental physiology. Some affirmed that physiology is integrative—in the sense that it involves systems which must be studied in relation to each other—thus, aided by man's new knowledge of molecular biology and the genetic structure, the field will move inevitably toward increasing cohesiveness. The computer and other advanced technological instruments are already playing an important role in expediting this unification. Several chairmen speculated that the advances of the next decade will exceed the achievements of physiologists over the past one thousand years because they now have the basic knowledge and tools needed for research on systems. Their aim is to make physiology "programmable."

On the other hand, some department chairmen believe that physiology is already badly split (especially with respect to its home) and is destined for even greater divisiveness as it relates to and subdivides with physics, chemistry, biochemistry, engineering, and the space sciences. As a result of new tie-ins with these and other fields, some chairmen anticipate that all biological fields will undergo new rearrangements within the next five years. Some expect to see physiology splitting away from its medical school housing and moving in the direction of interdisciplinary graduate study. Several observed that with the availability of new microscopic scanning techniques and the knowledge unlocked by the discovery of DNA, enormous horizons for research on human behavior have been opened. They speculated that future students in physiology will move from the study of organs—such as the brain—to the study of the physiological base of their particular functions—such as memory.

Some observers expect that within the next decade electronic physiology will develop appreciably, instrumentation will become more complex and sensitive, and the sociological and philosophical aspects of physiological research and experimentation will become an important part of the graduate student's education. In preparation for these developments, department chairmen believe that students will need a strong background in chemistry, mathematics, physics, and biology, and a basic knowledge of electronic circuitry and of the genetic control of transfer mechanisms. A few believe that some background in social science will also be recommended.

Physiologists are apparently now coming to grips with the need to strike a balance between free-wheeling research and that which responds to the needs of society. To this end, department chairmen expect to see more mission-oriented research undertaken in the future and they expect to see the development of men in their field who can bridge a two-contact world. These may take the form of "specialists in general," or some current associations may be reversed—for example, biochemistry may become the functional field of chemical biology. As in the natural sciences, physiology appears to have received a boost because it undertook research for certain federal missions. According to one chairman, space research has revitalized interest in environmental physiology which "dates back to 1880 when a balloon ascent overshot its mark." The recent success achieved in landing men on the moon will probably produce astronomical growth in this aspect of physiology in the decades ahead. Department chairmen believe that physiology will reach a crest of popularity during that period.

Characteristically perhaps, department chairmen in psychology looked mainly at the changing motivations and behavior of their graduate students when they were asked to speculate on the changes that might lie ahead in their field. They noted that both the interests held and the pressures exerted by students seem to point to a shift away from research as a career goal toward professional or clinical service. Hence a majority of the interviewees believed that clinical psychology will expand considerably in the years immediately ahead. In the words of one chairman: "Although we have a small, totally alien group who are primarily interested in getting ahead themselves, most of our students today want to be helpers. They want to cure people . . . they have a deep commitment to personal involvement."

The problem of selection and recruitment appears to be critical for psychology's future. To a large extent this is currently directed and controlled in some institutions by efforts to match the students' declared interests in the field with the interests held by the faculty in the particular institution. Since, in several cases, these interests are narrowly specialized or particularized, some departments are finding it difficult to cover all the bases to which current research in psychology beckons. Some departments expect to face internal strain within the next few years as they attempt to rebuild their faculties along a broader base. Pressure to do so has come from students and from some faculty members whose interests branch out from psychology per se into physiological, comparative, or ethnological psychology. Departments which lack a competent staff in these areas face hard decisions. They may have to limit their programs within controlled specialties.

In terms of directional changes, department chairmen reported that they foresee three distinct tracks which the future graduate student might pursue: general psychology, which will equip the candidate for a professional or clinical career; experimental psychology, which will involve the student in quantitative or programmed aspects of the field; and physiological psychology, which will put the student in direct contact with physiology, biochemistry, and related fields. Although some expect a slight increase of interest in industrial psychology and a waning of interest in social psychology, almost all agree (some with reluctance) that the major thrust for the immediate future will be on clinical psychology. The curriculum implications suggested by these trends include: a broader substantive base; more training for technical competence; increased requirements in quantitative skills such as mathematics, statistics, and computer usage; and education and experience in the art of dissemination in order to improve the impact which the field might have on social needs.

Judging by the opinion of department chairmen, the humanities appear to be poised for a new thrust forward. Some believe that the force of that thrust may be powerful enough to reinstate the humanities once again in the center of the academic limelight. To some extent the resurgence of interest in the humane fields may be due to the development of the National Academy for the Humanities, which supports their scholarly efforts. However, it may also be traceable to a renewed interest in the study of man as man, rather than as an abstraction, and to the students' rejection of those fields which do not relate directly to man.

Not all those interviewed were hopeful that the humanities will provide man with the knowledge he needs to become the "regenerative consumer of knowledge" described by Fuller (1964). One department chairman voiced this apprehension when he said:

> The humanities are in a bad way. For all the gains we have made and all the financial advantages accruing to us from our scientific brethren . . . (their largess is spread around) the study of languages and literature is apologetic. It strikes grand poses; it offers rare and even mystical resolutions to the questions raised by any inquiring mind; and many inquiring young minds come to us for expressions of the truth we must have found in the texts we expose and profess to understand. But since the major texts—the masterpieces of the past half century and more—have concerned themselves with the debasement of man, the corruption of civilization, with the necessity for public expression of most private feelings and with a vast contempt for the world as it is in its greediness, business, even its humanity, our students who listen to us are themselves spokesmen for a distrust of mankind, a contempt for ordinary thought and action and a revulsion against contemporary civilization for which we, their teachers, are responsible. For all the militancy and social activism of our graduate students I see the marks of a withdrawal, a grand rejection of the world and a cultural malaise leading to the modish abstention so noticeable in our time.

Arrowsmith's (1967) warning that academic institutions should have a conscience about the chaos that unmediated or misused knowledge creates was expressed in the hoped-for changes which department chairmen foresaw happening in their fields. For example, department chairmen in philosophy reported a diminution of interest in analytical philosophy corresponding to a decreased interest among students for science and mathematics to which analytical philosophy is related. By the same token, they note an increased interest in existentialism and phenomenology which, through literature and psychology, relate directly to man as being and becoming. As a result of this shift in emphasis, chairmen in philosophy departments expect that the future in that field will include a streamlining along generalist lines; a decrease of interest in "fad" philosophies; greater interdisciplinary involvement, particularly with the social sciences, law, art, and music; special emphasis on the philosophy of language, of science, and of aesthetics; and the possibility that the Ph.D. student in philosophy will be required to have four or five years of experience before admittance to the degree program.

Several chairmen expressed concern about the increased numbers who seek the Ph.D. in relation to the placement realities. Three interviewees commented that the proposed speed-up in the degree process, which will reduce the program from six to eight years down to four, may cause a glut on the market. They note that the market has begun to level off in top universities and that departments may have to reevaluate their programs in terms of placement needs in undergraduate colleges. Since, ordinarily, these do not require a strong research background or commitment, Ph.D. programs in philosophy may have to redirect their attention to emphasize teaching preparation.

Department chairmen in English unanimously agreed that in the future their discipline will show a decided increase in interdisciplinary activity. The pacemaker of this trend is the new student who comes to the Ph.D. program with a background and interest in politics, fine arts, sociology, psychology, and music in addition to a basic foundation in literature. Some chairmen foresee a greater use of the literature in these fields to study the impact of their style, form, and substance on American and English literature. Thus, the some extent, administrators expect that the future direction of English departments will be determined, if not dominated, by other disciplines. Some department chairmen suggested that to prepare for the new interdisciplinary emphasis, the reorganization of departments along new dimensional lines might be needed.

This arrangement could expedite the interaction and prevent the administrative bottlenecks that would occur if five or six departments attempted to consolidate their ideas and services.

In terms of changes in specialties, some department chairmen predicted a continuing effort on the part of traditionalists to stem the drift toward contemporary literature and new stylistic models. Others expressed the belief that the field had gone as far down the road as it can go in the production of "technical critics." Among the changes noted by department chairmen were the decline of interest in critical analysis, in linguistics, and in survey fields, and an increased interest in comparative literature, contemporary literature, and in a "generalist" rather than a "century" approach.

Although they noted that a small number of professors and their students were using the tools and techniques of computer science, department chairmen in English tend to believe that, except for information storage and retrieval, few professors will rely on automated techniques and services for their research. They do not rule out the use of these tools by students, however. Among other changes anticipated by English department chairmen were: a screening out of the technically oriented; fewer part-time students; three full years of continuous residence (in lieu of a fixed number of credit hours); fewer continuous year-long seminars; personalized evaluation and self-criticism in place of grades; a supervised teaching experience for all; a pluralistic admissions policy; and, if increased financial support can be found, a reduction in the time required to complete the Ph.D.

Ideological differences about the education of future scholars in French were manifested among the department chairmen who were interviewed on this question. Some firmly believe that all students will be expected to spend some time abroad, others hold that Ph.D. students in increasing numbers will spend time in a language research institute. At least one chairman felt that the distinction would be made on the basis of the student's pedagogical potential—that is, those who exhibit weakenesses as prospective teachers would be advised to do research!

Some chairmen reported that the emphasis in French has changed from historical and biographical interests to an interest in literary criticism modeled on the approach used in English. However, they also expect to see future growth in the combination of French with linguistics, cultural anthropology, sociology, history, or other cultural fields of study. In one institution the French program recently was separated from other romance languages. The department chairman in this institution expects to see greater specialization as a result of the shift. At least two department chairmen believed that the course requirements in French would increase and that more emphasis would be placed on professional pedagological practice, and on the methodology of language teaching. Because of the wide diversity in the language base which Ph.D. students bring to their graduate programs, some chairmen foresee the need for honors seminars, or for special groupings which would accommodate those who have advanced competence. Three chairmen were of the opinion that the recruitment of Ph.D. prospects must become international but that "differences in the philosophical approach to study would first have to be ironed out."

Chairmen in departments of economics were in unanimous agreement that future economists would need broad preparation in math, statistics, and the use of computer tools and methods. Most of the chairmen anticipate a linear extrapolation of what is apparently already occurring with respect to quantitative emphasis, but they are somewhat divided on whether the Ph.D. program will devote more attention than it currently does to applied economics. In the judgment of a few respondents the principal purpose of the academic program will be to lay a strong foundation in economic theory and on methods that will prepare the future economist to tackle a variety of problems. Others seem convinced that given the present need for interdisciplinary economists, the field will become more applied or problem-oriented.

In at least two institutions department chairmen expect to see more subfields or interdisciplinary fields emerging out of their present structure. These include regional and urban economics, managerial economics, and international economics. Others see the emergence of programs in mathematical economics and closer ties between economics and the fields of health, education, and social welfare. One chairman commented that the department's involvement in training Peace Corps personnel had convinced some members of the faculty of the need for an examination of economic problems which would involve the development of human resources. Others foresee a continual shift in interest from macro- to micro-economics. One, who referred to himself as a "young fuddy-duddy traditionalist," was concerned lest the emphasis on developing economists who also act as "social philosophers" might result in a gradual erosion of the standards of scholarship.

Faculties in history were described by their department chairmen as generally conservative and slow to adopt change, but current movements in that field indicate that that description does not apply to many younger historians. Two factors may account for the disparity. First, young historians and many graduate students show a greater interest in the dynamics of history (as gained through insight obtained in contacts with other areas of the social sciences) than in historical theories. Second, having acquired knowledge of the computer as a research tool, they believe that scholarship in history is capable of a more effective scope or coverage than it currently enjoys.

The pressure to place more emphasis on the social uses of history will, in the opinion of department heads, promote greater interaction between historians, psychologists, sociologists, and anthropologists and lead to dissertation research which will reflect that association. Some chairmen expect to see a greater emphasis on professionalization and on education for teaching. This may result in greater specialization along geographically based lines or in "pre" and "post" historical eras. For example, one chairman noted: "We get increasing calls for specialists. No one expects a man to teach European History if he was trained in American History. Formerly everyone taught surveys."

Department chairmen expect to see several changes in Ph.D. requirements. These will broaden the available options for research; eliminate or reduce the foreign language requirement unless it is needed for the dissertation; introduce new interdisciplinary seminars; speed up and streamline the degree process; and reduce the attrition among doctoral students. They expect the last goal to be accomplished by better selection and financing and by requiring full-time study for at least three years. Some expect the M.A. to be eliminated or to become a terminal degree. Almost all expect to see greater efforts made to provide teaching preparation or teaching experience during the doctorate. And they anticipate that almost all students will be expected to spend time in the Library of Congress, or abroad, if his specialty requires "knowledge of acquaintance" with other parts of the world.

The field whose department chairmen appeared to have the greatest problem envisioning the changes in its immediate future is sociology. According to the statement of one chairman (and the inference of others): "Chaos is ahead in the next five years." Sociology is under pressure to systematize its knowledge and conceptualize its methodology before it can chart its direction. Several chairmen expressed their conviction that no progress will be made in sociology until the nature of the discipline is agreed upon and some theory is developed. According to these sources, the absence of a coherent focus and an inherent content has produced departments in which four or five schools of sociology exist within the same department with little, if any, understanding or communication among them. Currently, according to one chairman, the field is a diffuse, overlapping conglomerate which is "thrashing out to cover the sociology of everything."

The computer and other technologies for handling quantitative data are looked upon by sociologists as the analog to the physicists' cyclotron. Department chairmen were unanimous in their agreement that future graduate students will need a strong background in computer usage and in statistical methods as sociology becomes more narrowly specialized around quantitative data. Some suggested that as sociology continues to develop its own journals and specialized literature, it may gain a basic paradigm around which graduate education might be designed. Others believe that the eclectic approach will continue to lead sociologists into "fashionable areas" such as comparative studies or ethno-methodological approaches. One department head expressed frustration about his efforts to lead a department "that does not know where it wants to go."

Because the quantitative aspects of sociological research are in conflict with the students' desire to be directly involved with social problems, department chairmen report that they are facing a crisis in their inability to provide adequate research assistantship training. To a large extent the computer has freed the student from his role as a "statistical clerk." The need now is for the development of models around which a number of training devices might be available along some basic designs, rather than happenstance experiences. Some hope that this need will be answered through the organization of interdisciplinary research seminars or through small groups of three or four students working on a major research project together. This may mean that admissions will be limited to more manageable numbers. The problem of training for research appears to be one of the most sensitive aspects of student morale and dissatisfaction in this field. According to department chairmen, criticism of the research in their field has caused sociology students to organize in order to place strong pressure on the department for academic reform. At the professional level the Radical Sociologist Student Union verbalized these demands at the 1969 Conference of the American Sociological Association.

Department administrators in chemistry expect to see a growing reliance upon instruments and a sophisticated dependence upon technicians. They envision more cross-discipline grouping in the experimental areas of chemistry but are not optimistic about the administrative and departmental holdouts in certain areas which wish to retain their identity as purists.

The increased narrowness of some aspects of chemistry has brought about in the departments a need for various specialized skills. Some chairmen noted that not enough planning has been done to determine the nature of this need or to organize the campus resources and personnel who can respond to it. Currently a tie-in with engineering serves present needs, but some chairmen said that alliance becomes increasingly uneasy as engineers become more interested in research on their own.

Chemists of the future will, according to some department chairmen in this field, need a broad general training. Some expect to provide breadth by forming interdisciplinary relationships with appropriate fields, whereas others expect that the generalization will occur by having the graduate work in several subdivisions within chemistry. At least two of the chairmen saw an opposite trend, an emphasis on "more and more specialization." One of the small institutions in the sample expects to broaden its base by joining a consortium in which the strengths of several institutions would be used reciprocally. The faculty see this as one response to the increased cost of the instrumentation required in the education of chemists.

The primary concern among department chairmen in chemistry was the growing competition for top-quality students. Even though applications may increase, they expect that competition for good students (and faculty) to stiffen as more and more institutions become competitive through scholarship offerings. Small institutions, and those less favorably located geographically, report that competition will become increasingly acute. These concerns probably reflect the fact that 15 per cent of the first-year males in 600 graduate departments in chemistry and physics had entered service or been ordered to induction prior to June 1968, and many others dropped out to seek jobs which provide occupational deferments.

Department chairmen in mathematics were in agreement that revolutionary changes in that field have so strengthened the high school and undergraduate curriculum that students enter graduate school today "knowing mathematics which some of their professors do not know." They reported that graduate programs now start from a much higher base than those offered a decade ago and that students today do not have to spend time learning certain math processes because instruments are available to perform them. They foresee an increased development in applied math and in functional analysis and increased pressures on the department to develop mathematics courses which will serve the needs of other disciplines. However, chairmen anticipate that a primary interest in abstract math will continue to occupy the time of their research faculties.

Although they believe that a substantial part of the mathematicians will remain in the mainstream of the discipline, the chairmen expect that some will strike out to develop new areas. In some cases, these ventures will represent interdisiciplinary alignments, as in the case of complex variable theories which have become the bedrock of some areas in physics research. In other cases, the department chairmen envision changes that are ephemeral outgrowths of "fashion." Believing that what happens in related fields will have an important impact on mathematics, and vice versa, some were of the opinion that the division within mathematics per se will be less sharp than it is currently. As a result, department chairmen expect requirements for admission to courses to be less restrictive. They agreed that while the field will continue to have great growth, the direction of that growth cannot be plotted with any degree of accuracy. The computer has apparently contributed to some scattering of interests among mathematicians. In some institutions its technology has brought some faculty members into contact with men in other fields who are attempting to develop their research on mathematical models. In other instances the "pure math people" have withdrawn either academically, psychologically, or physically from the "computer people."

The changes that department chairmen predicted for graduate education in mathematics over the immediate future include: a more selective admission at the Ph.D. level; increased efforts to identify math potential at the undergraduate level and to encourage early admission or advanced placement; tailormade Ph.D. programs in lieu of basic requirements for all; general broadening in the graduate students' contacts with other fields or with other areas within mathematics; a reduction in the time required for the Ph.D.; an appreciable increase in the number of post-doctorates who will devote their efforts toward "pure mathematics"; and increased efforts to offer supervised preparation for college teaching in mathematics.

Department chairmen in physics expect that the years ahead will show a continued movement toward greater sophistication at an earlier time in the student's career. Although they acknowledge that some who reach high levels of sophistication early may have sacrificed broad training in favor of factual learning, most department chairmen believe that future students will be their own academic pacemakers. To this end, they anticipate that Ph.D. programs in physics will place less emphasis on formal course requirements and more emphasis on the development of a well-rounded and balanced professional background. On the premise that it will become increasingly difficult to train theorists, some department chairmen view the trend toward a broader academic background with mixed feelings. Conversely, some noted that by combining an interest in physics with an interest in biology, social science, philosophy or religion many top physicists have broken out of the conventional narrowness of their training and made physics relevant to life. They expect to see this influence apparent in the degree program. Some departments may offer two tracks, one for researchers and another for undergraduate teachers.

Partly in response to the diversity in the levels of knowledge achieved by students before they enter graduate school, some department heads expect that assessment examinations will replace the routine course requirements. The results of these examinations would provide the base on which academic advising would be predicated. According to them, because of improved teaching at the high school and undergraduate levels bright students will be encouraged to take graduate work while still in the undergraduate program. "Book learning will be streamlined" or become an independent activity and students will "plunge into" research as soon as they are admitted to graduate standing.

Almost all of those interviewed said that they expect to see a shortening of the time required for the degree process. However, they qualified this observation by saying that future research physicists will almost be forced to take an additional two-year post-doctoral training. One observed that most physicists are self-educated in the sense that they learn physics at the professional level by teaching it or doing it. For this reason he saw the need for a post-doctoral experience during which the individual was given an opportunity to relate to graduate students in both a teaching and a research capacity.

In terms of their preparation for graduate study in physics, department chairmen expressed the belief that applicants will be expected to have a strong background in mathematics, in quantum mechanics, and in programming or computer usage. Some chairmen believe that the fundamental tools, techniques, and materials in physics will soon require repackaging. For example, in place of actually building their own research instruments students will be expected to understand their purpose and function but the instruments themselves will be built by engineers. Some expect that computer science may replace the foreign language requirement as a research tool and programmed experiments may replace manual operation and evaluation.

Although some chairmen expressed a cautious optimism

about the wisdom of requiring all students to acquire the same basic background before they are advanced to the dissertation stage, the majority indicated that differentiation in education and experience may begin at the moment of entrance for future physics graduates. In the opinion of two chairmen, research in physics has become so competitive and the academic programs in the top schools are so nearly similar that some departments may soon break out of their normal patterns and opt for greater diversification. A few departments are planning for this move by appointing professors whose research interests are different from those of the existing staff. Some chairmen said that they are deliberately recruiting mavericks who will introduce more radical changes in career styles.

Commenting on the pressures exerted on the university for equality of educational experience, one chairman speculated that while the purists may die holding out for standards, physics departments will probably respond by taking more doctoral students and then adding a two-year post-doctoral requirement for those who aspire to positions in prestigious institutions or in theoretical physics. With respect to other changes, some chairmen saw the elimination of the oral examination, a shortened period during which the student will be expected to demonstrate his abilities, an increased competition for good graduate students, a "pricing out" of some institutions because of the competition and the increased costs of graduate support, and an increase in interdisciplinary programming.

Recommendations
and Commentary

14

In formulating recommendations based on this survey, certain basic characteristics of a modern university should be acknowledged. First, it should be recognized that one of the primary objectives of a university is research and that its status and the security of its faculty are dependent upon its productivity. Failure to acknowledge the extent to which the research productivity of universities has contributed to the quality of life in America would be invidious. The great strides made by its researchers have all but eradicated some of the diseases and environmental problems that were widespread less than fifty years ago. Findings of university researchers have improved housing, transportation, and water supplies; produced labor-saving devices that removed the incredible burdens which men in less fortunate countries still carry on their backs; improved the quality of daily existence through the discovery of vitamins; improved the general standard of living for large numbers of people and freed men from superstitions and other irrational forces which constrained them. From the quest for civil rights for all to the development of space science, the university has played a vital role in the life and times of the nation. In conjunction with these activities it served an indispensable function for society, namely, the education and preparation of its future scholars and leaders. That it has left much undone, that some of its priorities are difficult to defend, and that it has sometimes appeared to be more involved in the pursuit than in the use of knowledge must also be acknowledged.

Second, it should be recognized that under present arrangements the university and its professors, like the church and its clergy, must often beg for or otherwise solicit the funds or other resources needed to perform the work which their mission entails. Given the nature and scope of that mission, it is probably realistic to expect that the bulk of its research support will continue to come from external sources. The extent to which the solicitation of that support makes inroads on the time and energy of the staff and exposes them and their institutions to internal and external social and political pressures is considerable. Dependence on sponsored research grants and contracts or on philanthropic donations must be counted as an attrition factor in academic life and operation. The effect of this practice on the academic mendicant must also be acknowledged. Some faculty members have virtually become "grantsmen," adept at attracting grants and contracts. Many have become "academic technicians" who exert awesome power and influence in the university yet rarely teach or concern themselves with the administration or governance of their institutions. Still others behave as academic entrepreneurs for whom the university appears to represent little more than a prestigious mailing address.

Third, it should be assumed that a university ought not to be expected to perform tasks that are incompatible with its nature as a humane educational institution or to perform tasks that can be accomplished better by some other institution. Fourth, it should be assumed that faculty members ought not to be expected to take responsibility for guiding or directing passive, dependent students who lack commitment to clearly perceived goals which they strive to achieve for themselves. Fifth, it should be assumed that at the

Ph.D. level students will look upon the university as an organization whose services they use to help them to arrive at a particular goal. Having made an investment in the organization the investor will feel free to criticize it but will not be unduly disturbed or deterred from his course if the institution is sometimes unable to respond with maximum efficiency.

Finally, it should be assumed that the various graduate disciplines have effective selection processes which reasonably assure that the interests and intellectual capacities of the students who are admitted are compatible with the interest and intellectual capacities of the faculty. If these assumptions are tenable, the investigator considers the following recomomendations to be appropriate.

It is imperative in this "age of discontinuity" that universities reexamine their goals and set their priorities. In their efforts to be accommodating, universities in America appear to have obscured their roles and exposed themselves to the danger of being reduced to diploma factories or service centers. If they are to reverse this trend and survive the criticism which currently engulfs them, they must, in a spirit of candor and openness, reexamine their mission, explicate their goals, and strengthen their defenses against the intrusion of forces which would distort their nature. If they are to maintain their integrity as institutions devoted to the pursuit of truth, they must reestablish themselves as autonomous universities and prove themselves capable of self-government, self-criticism, and self-renewal or reform.

To this end, the investigator supports the recommendation of the American Association for Higher Education which was adopted as a resolution in its national conference on March 5, 1969, in Chicago, Illinois:

> Each college and university, through wide discussion and with clarity and precision, must determine its particular mission. If, in the language of the day, it wishes to do its thing, it must define what its thing really is. It must consider the outcomes it proposes to achieve in terms of teaching and learning, scholarship and research, and public and community service. Since no institution can be all things to all men, each higher education institution must order its priorities. . . . Furthermore, it must inform its many pub-

lics of its limitations as well as its scope and that some characteristics are essential to its existence. For example, a college or university emphasizes reason and the rational approach to establishing priorities and to resolving disagreements. . . . Each college and university must determine or redefine its goals in the context of today's social and political ferment. It should also—more than ever before—significantly involve all portions of the collegiate community in the reexamination process. Each must carefully analyze its whole system of internal governance . . . and include in this examination students, faculty, and administrators. The balance of power among the latter will vary with the problems under consideration. In a given area of responsibility, the balance of power should reflect the relative expertise of each segment of the collegiate community.

If universities have a conscience about the chaos in our times, they should use their good offices not merely to criticize society but to assist society in its self-renewal and reform. As much as, if not more than, other men, scholars should be concerned about the social consequences of their research and teaching. If they limit their interest and comprehension to the ever-fragmenting area of their specialties, they reduce their ability to observe the effect of their activities on mankind or on the human spirit. The role of the critic is too easy. As thought informs action so action can inform thought. Universities, as the respositories of thought, should through self-determinattion decide how they can best serve as regenerative agents for society and advance and nourish the rich cultural and social diversity of the peoples of the world. As advocated by the 1970 conference of the American Academy of the Advancement of Science, scientists and scholars should, at this moment in history, rededicate themselves to enriching the society which enriches them.

Universities should clearly define the general principle or rationale on which they accept and perform sponsored research. Probably no issue serves more dramatically to illustrate the need for a reappraisal of the university's function than does the charge that universities have allowed themselves to become the pawns of the so-called military-industrial complex. Dissident students and others have insistently reasoned that the university cannot, on moral grounds, participate in research that leads to the implementation of war without simultaneously participating in the legitimization of war as an instrument for the resolution of conflict. Their disapproval is directed particularly toward those whose work results in the development of offensive instrumentation, but it is not appreciably less critical of those who work on defensive agents or systems. These critics believe that if the university must accommodate itself to the problems of war and peace, it should do so by an intense preoccupation with the latter. They are no less critical of the universities involvement with business, industry, or agriculture on projects that lack positive consequences for man.

Given a system of research support which makes the university dependent upon the largess of outside agencies, criticism of this nature probably can be allayed, but short of drastically limiting its research activity or organizing separate research institutions, it can probably never be eliminated. In the interest of reassuring those who have a deep concern about the integrity of their educational institutions and to inform their critics, universities should reveal the policies on which they accept financial support from outside agencies. Unless they are willing to pay a terrible price—especially in the loss of confidence among the university youth—universities must reflect deeply on their responsibilities as humane educational institutions. Having done so, they must make their positions explicit and be willing to defend them on morally defensible as well as educational grounds.

Essentially, university resources, programs, and policies should be organized so as to create an environment which focuses more on learning than on teaching. There is an imperative need for a variety of innovative educational and social inventions in higher education which will assure more effective use of faculty skills and excite the intellectual interests of students. The malaise which the students exhibit and the anger which they express about their educational programs probably can not be resolved simply by shoring up old structures. Bolder, more imaginative innovations are needed at the doctoral level if education is to be a pacesetter toward self-renewal and growth. The nature of the students' complaints about their educational experiences underscores the fact that universities are, by and large, organized to place teaching—rather than learning—in the forefront of their activities. That is to say, professors spend their time developing course bibliographies, outlines, and topics, arranging course materials, and gathering pertinent information to present to students, who, by the nature of this process, become passive recipients in a one-sided intellectual exercise. Because they have little part in planning the ends and means of intellectual exploration, students charge that they rarely have the opportunity to be totally involved in the educational process or to reflect on the antecedents and consequences of the knowledge they acquire. If the organizational structure placed the learner at the center of the campus world, teachers would be viewed as facilitative components or co-partners in learning and students would be directly involved in their developmental progress.

In this arrangement a partial role reversal would occur. Teachers would serve as resource persons and expeditors, and students would be viewed as independent and responsible seekers of the particular knowledge they need. Both would be held responsible for organizing, synthesizing, integrating, and relating knowledge in such meaningful ways as to discover new information and new concepts. The model of the teacher as a lifelong learner would be projected and both the student and the teacher would be involved constructively in the evaluation process. On the assumption that in the learning process individuals may sometimes have to be wrong on the way to becoming right (or accurate), the evaluation process should place major emphasis on the developmental aspects of learning.

Although the paramount interest of the graduate department is the production of specialists for the discipline, it should not permit the academic program or the process to become dehumanized in the interest of developing the discipline. The responses of doctoral students in this study revealed their concern about certain imbalances in their educational preparation. In particular, they voiced a need for emphasis in those areas of learning which develop the expressive and appreciative life as well as in those which produce and advance the life of the specialist. In commenting on their educational experiences students frequently described them as "dehumanized in the interest of scientism." This criticism was pervasive throughout the twelve disciplines in the study. Even as the students in the sciences expressed a wish to have ideas in their disciplines modified by, or related to, the observations of poets and philosophers, students of the latter registered their disappointment in finding that the poets and philosophers in the university had become scientific and technical.

In view of the doctoral student's need to achieve identity as a scholar and yet maintain a personal identity, the various elements of the Ph.D. program should be designed to promote his need for affective as well as cognitive learning. Above all, the educational process should not stunt his growth toward greater regard for humanity or increased cultural awareness. Ideally, the educational environment at the graduate level should radiate a charisma that is matched by the desires of faculty and students to become not merely learned, but learned persons. It should offer a variety of life styles which reflect with integrity interrelationships that promote the civilized dialogue. To the fullest extent possible, students should be viewed as junior colleagues rather than as marginal entities. The emphasis in the academic program should be on education, not on training. It should recognize the individual's need for gaining knowledge outside of his discipline and refrain from placing obstacles or sanctions against those with diverse or divided interests.

Academic reform at the graduate level should include changes in the organization of instructional units and in the introduction of more diversified methods of transmitting knowledge. The practice of subdividing the content of a discipline into discrete segments called courses and then subdividing the content of courses into thirty or forty class presentations over a period of fifteen weeks appears to have lost its utility for graduate education, if not for most aspects of higher education. Although this standard practice may have been valid fifty years ago when knowledge grew at a slow pace, the information explosion has made the course approach to graduate teaching untenable. Likewise, at this level, the semester or quarter approach to teaching has become increasingly difficult to defend. Year-long seminars which focus on a broad topic, such as ecology, prove more useful and amenable to the kinds of learning situations required for broad exploration, depth analysis, comprehensive integration, and synthesis. The contentment of students in the physical and biological sciences implies that laboratory situations involve the student physically and intellectually in the learning process and give him a sense of personal responsibility. Analogs should be sought by instructors in the humanities and social sciences.

While a few institutions have experimented with calendar changes in the interest of making better use of their faculties and resources, this is an economic risk difficult for universities to calculate in the face of current "stop out" trends. Few institutions can afford to take that risk. They seek reform in other directions. Many believe that the course structure is the place to start. Given the specificity and breadth of knowledge available today, almost any course that relies on a single professor's ideas is bound to be abortive. For this reason more and more institutions use the team teaching approach which was first utilized by professional schools. They also make increasingly heavy use of off-campus professional or semi-professional persons who are knowledgeable about the topics under discussion. These persons complement or supplement the professor's expertise and give the students opportunities to assess different perspectives. In many cases the use of practitioners can serve as a response to the student's plea for relevance in his program.

Curriculum revision, reform, or innovation should be systematic, involve the careful deliberation of the best minds, and be pursued under conditions which remove the constraints imposed by time schedules, fatigue or other interfering commitments. At the moment in history when graduate education faces its greatest challenge and moves into an era of great uncertainty and complexity, it is in grave danger of diminishing the clarity of its objectives because the pressures of modern university life leave the faculty little time or energy for systematic long-range academic planning. The nature of the changes that are destined to occur in graduate education are of such fundamental importance and so comprehensive in scope that they do not lend themselves to sporadic or piecemeal planning. Demands for new fields of study and for the reorganization or recombination of existing programs are accelerating. If responses are hurriedly assembled, the problems of the university may be compounded. On the other hand, decisions cannot be put off without great risk. If universities fail to make a continual analysis of their academic needs, they may react but they probably will not renew. The need for adequate time for planning and for implementing innovation and reforms in graduate education has reached a critical point.

Universities should give immediate and high priority to securing contingency funds which would allow key members of each faculty to give full time for several months to curriculum planning. Students, administrators, and other faculty members should be involved on a part-time basis or consulted as their skills and interests dictate. It is of crucial importance that when the basic pattern of reform has been initiated, a standing curriculum committee assist in the implementation of the change and institutionalize continual review and planning. What has been described as the "accelerating acceleration of history" requires a dynamic, not a dormant, academic review process and a faculty that acts effectively as an agent of change.

The administrative barriers to the use and integration of full-time researchers, creative artists, performers, and knowledgeable externs who can contribute relevantly to the academic program should be removed to the fullest extent possible. A large pool of unused talent and teaching potential can be found among the full-time research staff in any major institution. Because these persons are organized into separate administrative units, their usefulness to the institution's teaching program is often overlooked. For example, department chairmen reported that one can find psychologists working in five or six different units on their campuses who have no communication with one another and are therefore often completely unaware of the contributions they can make to each other's work or to the instructional program. Each person's socialization is to his own unit. Although some institutions in the sample do give courtesy appointments which make it "administratively correct" to invite "outsiders" to participate in the curriculum, such participation is generally on a sometime basis and is not an integrated part of the unit's educational program.

The loss of this talent to the teaching role is considerable. It is suggested that the full-time research staff should be used to provide a service to the teaching faculty in the form of a continual professional colloquy or seminar in which instructors and students are informed about research findings and researchers have opportunities to subject their methods to critical review. Such a seminar would provide opportunities for Ph.D. students to observe the way various kinds of scholars think and interact with others. In the spirit of the "free university," creative persons—whose presence can enrich the cultural or intellectual environment while they find a temporary haven in which to develop their special talents—should have open access to institutions of higher education. Graduate students should be encouraged to seek informal conferences with such visitors or to arrange informal colloquiums or performances that would be mutually beneficial. Such experiences are particularly important for students in the humanities, whose contacts with artists and scholars should be personalized or more humanized.

The size of many universities militates against collegiality and communication. To extend the scholarly dialogue and reduce the distance between faculty member and student, informal learning space should be made accessible. It has been observed that man's technology has transformed man's work into a huge process of collaboration. The magnitude of the tasks performed by the university practically mandates its dependence upon complex systems and subsystems the very structure of which makes the institution subservient to a wide variety of individuals whose input skills keep the system operating. Impelled by self-interests, some subsystems tend to develop their individual images and to define their special roles. As their numbers grow, both gaps and log-jams occur in the information process. Control of the system becomes, finally, a matter of controlling communication. At most major universities contending groups now vie for that control. In some cases, graduate student organizations are found among the contenders.

As the number of disassociated or second-class citizens of the academic city grows, the divisive wedge widens and the prospect for political action grows apace. In too many instances graduate students swell the ranks of political militants. It is imperative that universities plan seriously and work diligently for the development of attitudes, social conditions, and collaborative devices which promote informal relations, reduce distances, and provide opportunities for personal encounters with persons who care about one another or hold similar interests.

At the level of faculty-student interaction, the sociological-humanistic model is more appropriate than the economic-adminis-trative model. To promote and encourage personal encounters, each department should provide informal space where faculty and students can meet briefly for conversation. In addition, each department should review its space utilization and decide whether some area could not be used as a gathering place where formal and informal university news can be posted, students can interact with their peers, and all would feel free to participate in the intellectual discourse of their disciplines.

Few students are strangers to Spartan simplicity, hence their meeting places need not be elaborate. Basically, they should be quarters where individuals might find brief respite from the rigors and loneliness of doctoral study among other congenial human beings. In particular they should offer opportunities for the social integration of foreign students and for all others who seek these amenities. The alternative would be to keep the system and subsystems simple and relatively small. However, to reduce the size or stem the growth of top-ranked institutions in a period of insistent demand for more access to higher education could court disaster for the national purpose. Ways must be found to manage large units to convey the impression that collegial cooperation and cordiality are important values within the system.

Disciplines should give serious thought to the possible advantages in reorganizing under a structure that is more comprehensive or more conducive to the development of scholarship in their field than is the departmental pattern. The departmental structure appears to have become dysfunctional for scholarly progress. Socially and politically it tends to inhibit the flow of communication and encourages the formation of enclaves or separate interest groups. Large or powerful departments often dominate the outcome of decisions and overshadow smaller and less visible units. In terms of the Ph.D. requirements, some departments limit the horizon of the student by requiring him to take all of his work within its confines. In too many cases it operates as a collective bargaining agency rather than as an administrative vehicle for negotiating the road to scholarship.

Academic organizational forms have not kept up with the dynamic changes that have occurred in the structure of knowledge.

New organizational patterns must be devised to accommodate the changes induced by the new fields of study that are rapidly forming —ethnic studies, ecology, urban studies, space sciences. Careful consideration should be given to the development of a Division of Interdisciplinary Studies which, in lieu of more sweeping reorganization, would provide an administrative mechanism for facilitating the development of these fast-growing bodies of knowledge. Cornell's organization around graduate fields suggests a viable model for removing academic fences and exposing students and scholars to a broader range of experiences and ideas. At Berkeley and Stanford the formation of "Ph.D. research groups" serves a comparable function, although in both institutions departments approve the composition of the "group" and retain control.

If established institutions are too "fixed" to allow change, newly forming institutions should avoid their mistakes by borrowing and adapting from models that were designed with the next era in mind—for example, Santa Cruz, the Claremont Graduate School, or Irvine, which are planned on alternate organizational forms that build on the interdepartmental, divisional, or interinstitutional approach to scholarship. "Cluster disciplines," within or between institutions, might be organized to serve the same functional role served by cluster colleges.

In planning Ph.D. programs, careful consideration should be given to the inclusion of education that prepares the graduates for a career that will be spent in the electronic or space age and in the early decades of the twenty-first century. Those who plan education for the twenty-first century are obliged to make intelligent guesses about the nature of the problems that will confront future generations. Their task is complicated by the obscure shape and direction of that future. Thus, unlike scholars in Chesterton's time, who could "live on the intellect of a former age," Drucker finds present needs so markedly different from those of the past that today's planners can borrow nothing from yesterday's; and in their commentaries on obsolescence, McLuhan, Brzezenski, and other observers predict that science and technology will so radically transform society by the end of the century that present social forms will have almost completely disappeared and totally new ones will have formed.

Despite the imponderables in the future, evidence is convincingly accumulating to indicate that such complex issues as population control, environmental quality, automation, migration, international relations, and the problem of human survival will engage the minds and energies of scholars far into the foreseeable future. Many of those scholars are currently students in graduate schools. If they are to be adequately prepared to cope with these global problems they will require education and experience beyond the narrow limits of their specialties or the limited confines of their campuses. In particular, they will need exposure to the new systems of information processing, retrieval, and dissemination and to computer technology, which in geometric increments is increasing the amount of research in every discipline, altering methods of instruction, and realigning relationships within the worldwide academic community.

The expanding boundaries of the modern university and the extensive communication network which unites institutions of higher education portend the development of new institutional forms and new ways of academic programming—such as the urban grant university (Kerr 1967), the world university (Taylor 1969), or the newly formed educational syndicates which have begun to program certain basic curricula. Many of the designers and implementers of these new organizations are now in graduate school. Their education there should provide them with knowledge of fact, if not of knowledge of acquaintance, with the electronic media and the teaching-learning technologies which will be important adjuncts in the new institutions.

To broaden the scope of its scholarshsip and to promote concern for the interconnectedness of knowledge, faculty members and graduate students should have easy access to communication with, or to study in, other disciplines. The goals and values of the new generation of scholars illuminates the need for reforms leading away from the narrow specialization commonly found in doctoral programs or departmental offerings. As a result of curriculum revisions and upgraded teaching at lower levels, many students now enter graduate school with a breadth of interests and with analytical skills that are useful in the study of problems which conjoin disciplines. Departmental requirements or constraints are often so strong as to inhibit the development of these interests or discourage the student's growth in interdisciplinary methods of analysis. To avoid this, each specialty should attempt to advance the development of interdisciplinary relationships by providing joint seminars, research projects, colloquia, independent field study, and other mechanisms which would enlarge the scope of possible insight into knowledge that is both basic to a specialty and tangential to other fields.

At the Ph.D. level, programs of study should be individualized to the particular needs of the student, and the student, as an investor, should be responsibly involved in its design. At the time of his entrance into graduate school the student should be encouraged to articulate his goals. With the advice of a faculty member he should plan a course of study and develop a tentative plan for implementing it. Throughout his program he should be encouraged to utilize responsibly those resources of the university that will advance his development. In seeking these he should not expect the faculty to act as his surrogate, but in the interest of learning through self-involvement he should seek his own sources. This does not release or excuse the faculty from its role as a facilitator or expediter.

A persistent complaint among doctoral students concerns the amount of independence they find in planning and pursuing the degree process. Some think they do not have enough. A smaller number think they have too much. The problem of finding an appropriate balance is complicated by two simple facts: some students do not know realistically how much independence or dependence they need, and some faculty members do not know how much to give. The probability is that each responds to the other in terms of behaviors learned as the result of exposure to a particular educational system. The wide diversity in those systems presents problems when the frame of reference or expectations of one is the obverse of the other.

Most of the psychological stress and educational disillusionment resulting from too little independence seems to occur during the first year of graduate study, when many students are locked into a rigid pattern of required courses and examinations. Stresses associated with too much independence are commonly found at the dissertation stage when students are often largely "on their own." More often, the stress seems to spring from faculty indifference or from the tendency of some faculty members to treat graduate students as though they were "parts of the problem" instead of potential sources of the answer. Faculty advisers and sponsors should attempt to make realistic assessments of their students' need for independence or for assistance (especially through the normal stress stages in the Ph.D. process) and respond to that need accordingly.

It seems fairly clear that while many students overstate the amount of effort required of them in the degree process, their anxiety over the process is real. In the interest of reducing that strain, faculty advisers should periodically review the progress or needs of their students. While the latter should demonstrate a commitment to scholarlship by their willingness to accept its reasonable rigors, the faculty should not expect a beginner's commitment to be fully focused, polished, or "total."

The orientation and advising of doctoral students should be systematically thorough and offered on both a formal and informal basis. In general, doctoral students want a higher level of interaction than they currently experience. They want to become a part of the intellectual community rather than remain on the fringes or have a mere bowing acquaintance with scholars. To foster more effective integration into the life of the university, each department, in cooperation with its graduate student organization or its advanced candidates, should offer a program of general orientation for new doctoral students. This orientation should include the distribution of a handbook describing the interests of the department and other information of import to doctoral students. In addition, an informally structured orientation meeting or meetings to introduce the faculty to new students, and to explain the offerings, resources, facilities, and policies of the department, should be held early in the semester, at a time convenient to the majority of students and in a place where faculty and students can meet and converse informally. Specific orientation should be given by an adviser and should be individually tailored to the student's needs. Students should be encouraged to seek at least a tentative sponsor shortly after (if not before) the completion of their first full semester in the doctoral program, and the method through which an adviser is normally obtained should be clearly explained to students on admission.

The structure of Ph.D. programs should liberate the student from a preoccupation with grades, credits, course examinations, and similar constraints which replicate his undergraduate role and experiences. In the organization and administration of graduate study, operational criteria that are based on the logic of administrative efficiency have sometimes strained the logic of the learning process in the mature person. Because graduate education deals with knowledge in its dynamic state—and with the particularized needs of individuals—standardized and conventional fixation on such details as grades, credits, deadlines, examinations, and registration requirements can take the edge of excitement from the graduate experience and, in some cases, corrupt its meaning. Students soon grow tense and dispirited when they find that graduate school represents a continuation of the same restraints and pressures they encountered at the undergraduate level. For those who must mold themselves into a procrustean bed if they wish to survive, the touted freedom of university study is illusory.

In his report to the steering committee on the study of education at Stanford, Mancall (1969) painted the following dismal picture of the Ph.D. student:

> Having worked toward the degree by taking a requisite number of units, fulfilling specified requirements, achieving a certain grade average, passing qualifying examinations, and writing an often crushingly boring dissertation that passes as an "original contribution to knowledge," the graduate student, his imagination probably restricted and dulled, his mind perhaps withered and exhausted, his soul jaded, dreamless and unwondering, his enthusiasm gone with his youth, is suddenly transformed by the magic of a degree into an educator charged with the responsibility of imparting to those who come after him the excitement of learning and a sense of the high adventure in ideas. Often he leads them no further than into the intricacies of the footnote.

While significant numbers of the students in this study do not fit Mancall's description, too many, by their own admission, have begun to take on some of the characteristics he describes.

The need for new educational strategies which would enable Ph.D. students to determine their own conditions for learning is cogent. Variable options or alternate programs should be made available to meet the needs and retain the interest of the mature graduate. Those who select options should do so with the understanding that they must be willing to accept the consequences of their decisions. The goal toward increased self-determination should be accompanied by increased ability in self-evaluation. Unless there are contrary indicators, the learning environment should impose a minimum of structural restraints on the doctoral student. If the trend toward narrowing the graduate students' academic encounters to formal course work is to be counteracted, serious thought must be given to the search for new patterns of curriculum design or new program models. The newly forming fields of knowledge and changes in the structure of existing disciplines warrant the breaking away from stereotyped patterns of academic programming at this advanced level.

Opportunities for fortuitous learning experiences should be made available to Ph.D. students who demonstrate their ability to think and work innovatively. For those who can find a rational level and combination of environmental factors in which they can be productive, waivers of standardized academic requirements should be permitted. If admission to graduate education is viewed as a contract in which each side is responsible for maximizing its goals, the 1916 challenge of Andrew West to his Princeton faculty seems legitimate and appropriate for consideration by planners of graduate education today: "Why shouldn't the graduate student be free? Why should there be any fixed number of courses he must take? Why should he not study what he likes? Is there not enough knowledge in any important subject to exhaust a lifetime of the most ardent intellectual effort? The prescient among observers today add: "Why should the graduate student not be free from the confines of the campus? Why should he not use the total environment as his learning laboratory? Why should not the graduate school be viewed as a place for the creative use of freedom in the exploration of the nature of first principles or the development and testing of hypothesis?" These are questions to which the graduate school must address itself if it is to provide the personnel needed in leadership or decision-making roles in the decades ahead.

Ph.D. students should be given a wide degree of freedom in their choice of a thesis topic. Although it should continue to serve as the capstone in the doctoral program, the substance, form, and length of the dissertation should represent a wider range of scholarly styles and methods than are currently acceptable. This recommendation is predicated not only on the fact that the nature of the problems in most disciplines lends itself to variable approaches but also on the fact that most students today want to be intimately involved in solving problems that have meaning for today.

There is general agreement among faculties in higher education that the current generation of students is better prepared academically and more sophisticated and aware than any previous generation. Collectively it represents a reservoir of intelligence, resourcefulness, and commitment that is of vital import to future society. Individually, its members have demonstrated that commitment through service in the Peace Corps, Vista, and hundreds of similar voluntary activities. Their knowledge of man's struggle to achieve a place in society has been sharpened by experience of the sights and sounds of that struggle, which enables them to be direct observers of the character and strategies of contending forces. As they note the imbalances in those forces, many students move from passivity to action. The recent history of student movements bears testimony to the role they played and the influence they have had in shaping the prevailing social and political tides. To dismiss them as though they were callow youth is to ignore the fact that, unlike others, this generation has had a ringside seat for practically every major event that has occurred during their lifetime.

Although their knowledge of history may be short, it does not lack in vividness. The vividness and transcience of events which they observed during the past two or three decades prompts them to suspect that an institution which offers a ready-made educational program is not only irrelevant or obsolete but would prevent them from developing self-reliance or earning personal freedom. As graduate students they are not inclined to accept with grateful docility the paths laid down by those who arbitrarily make the rules of the road. Having had a taste of realism with respect to the problems of society, they have little patience with rituals or traditions which delay or prevent the solution of those problems. This is evident in their growing insistence that the substance of the Ph.D. dissertation is more important than its prescribed form. Their requests for less esoteric detail seem reasonable and are supported by the heavy layers of criticism the dissertation has received during recent years.

The concept of academic freedom and responsibility should be extended to students as well as to the faculty.   There is evidence in the data for this study that some of today's graduate students represent the vanguard of a new breed of scholars. Some are veterans of the various protest movements which began to rock universities in the mid-sixties. Their awakened political consciousness has given them the courage to take risks and if necessary to place themselves in opposition to the establishment. In their press for self-determination some have had the courage to confront the awesome weight of guild disapproval and to test the limits of academic and personal freedom which their democratic institutions purport to support and protect. That they have posed serious questions for the academy is evident in the fact that some faculty members are reexamining their own positions and questioning their values. As they observe their students mount campaigns against the spoilation of the land, air, and water for purely economic returns—and without regard for the ecological consequences—they begin to understand the admonition, "when things are in the saddle they ride mankind." Faculty members who were at first reluctant to accept students as competent judges are beginning to support their right to advocate, to participate in curriculum planning and academic governance, or if necessary to protest.

Interest in the university as an instrument for structuring or restructuring society runs high in periods of great social stress or political realignment. Because the issues on which it is asked to make judgment rarely lend themselves to single answers—or because answers might be construed as supportive of a particular position or ideology—the university rarely feels that it can take a corporate position on social or political issues. On the other hand, professors may—and often do—speak out on matters that fall within the area of their expertise.

Commensurate with their right to academic freedom and responsibility, doctoral students should have the same prerogatives as the faculty. Whatever arrangements it can make to protect these rights and to encourage their use should be made by the university. At the same time, the educational process should demonstrate through its policies and programs the clear distinction between the authority represented by accumulated wisdom, technical skill, and spiritual insights, and the authoritarianism representing power "over" rather than power "with" individuals and events.

Universities should do all in their power to protect the academic interests of graduate students who are eligible for military service, are drafted, or drop out of school to enlist in that service. The satisfactions which normally accrue from the systematic process of acquiring knowledge are obfuscated for today's student by the sword of Damocles which hangs over his head. No matter how appealing he might find the pursuit of ideas to be, his overriding preoccupation with the thought that he must participate in (or has participated in) war disconcerts him from focusing on his goals and dulls the luster of the life of study. Many of the students in this survey were inclined to question the wisdom of exposing themselves to double jeopardy for the better part of their youthful years by adding the discipline of graduate study to the discipline of military duty or vice versa. Unfortunately, there is considerable presumptive evidence that many resolved their dilemma by giving up graduate study.

Universities should attempt to recruit back into the university without penalty those students who complete military service. Wherever necessary and feasible they should provide special help to the returning veteran and permit his lateral entry into the program. Although they should not be used as an adjunct of the military, universities should study the needs of the country for alternate forms of emergency service and suggest criteria which are based on the interests, skills, and qualifications necessary for such service. They should lend their good offices primarily to the welfare of the students so long as those interests are not contrary to those of the general welfare.

The purpose and responsibilities of the research assistantship should be clearly defined. If it is intended as instructional for the student, it should provide experiences that are developmental. If it represents activities or employment primarily in the interest of faculty research, this should be clearly understood. In either case, care should be exercised to protect the academic plans, timetable, and goals of the student.   The traditional master-apprentice relationship in which the latter acts as "a hewer of wood and drawer of water" for the former is an unacceptable model on which to build the research assistantship. It is rejected on psychological and existential theories that a life devoted largely to consumption by others (as some assistantships require) tends to lead to limited or distorted self-development, dulls the functional pleasure derived from meaningful independent effort, and sets the stage for the frustration which can result when aspirations are unfulfilled. The collegial model, in which parity is based on intellectual competence and effort, is more appropriate for the relationship between the Ph.D. student assistant and his mentor.

Teaching should be reinstated as a primary purpose and responsibility of the university.   Since 1940, when the federal government and other off-campus agencies began to engage the research skills of university professors on a campus-wide scale, emphasis on teaching as a primary purpose of the university has declined. At that point, universities virtually changed from being the teachers of teachers to become the teachers of researchers. While the transformation is visible in the physical changes that have occurred on the campus, it is nowhere more evident than in the status and awards it gives to research, and in the attitudes and messages it conveys in the Ph.D. program which incline students away from an interest in teaching.

A compelling issue in the preparation of college and university teachers—and one which involves both their self-perception and their socialization into the life of the academic person—is the failure of the graduate school to give status to teaching or to teach for teaching. The probability is that so long as research remains at the apex of the reward system, and the research scholar is ensconced alone on the scholarly pedestal, the prospective academic man will aspire to climb aboard his pedestal via the research route. Not until the teacher-scholar gains status commensurate to that of the research-scholar will the seduction of the faculty into research diminish and the status and preparation of college teachers receive attention. This is a fact of university life which finds expression in the mythology of the "publish or perish" ultimatum.

The candor of many doctoral students in openly pressing

for better teaching, and for education which would prepare them to be effective teachers themselves, appears to spring from their desire to respond to the undergraduates to whom they relate as teaching assistants. Generally they are closely attuned to the rhetoric of the young which, through its music, art, theater, and ideology expresses disenchantment with the establishment and its educational process. Their activities as both student and teacher place teaching assistants in a mediating role.

Mounting internal pressures from graduate and undergraduate students and external pressures from the public and from teaching unions should alert the university to the need for a redress in the imabalances in the researcher-teacher status. If universities do not move quickly and positively to relieve these pressures, all segments of education and society will suffer. So long as research "productivity" (often without regard to quality) remains the main criterion for appointments and promotion, teaching will perforce be a secondary activity. The consequences of this will be pervasive throughout the educational system and subsystems.

In lieu of the token and tentative support that is given to teacher education, strong leadership is needed in the higher education profession to promote the search for criteria which can be used to measure and reward effective teaching. The leadership should not be dissuaded from the task by the fact that teaching effectiveness or quality varies along many dimensions and is not consistently measurable. This fact has not deterred the development of criteria for measuring research, which is often equally ambiguous. Until such criteria can be defined, teaching should be measured on those characteristics which are assumed to produce effective teachers.

To restore the status of teaching, universities should reserve the honorific title Professor for those who teach. They should also experiment with new designations for the faculty or reestablish titles that were once in use. The increased numbers of joint appointments suggest that academic titles should identify the instructor with an academic division, such as Professor of the Humanities, instead of with a narrow specialty, such as Professor of History. The title Professor-at-Large or University Professor might be bestowed on those who are truly initerdisciplinary scholars. When junior members of the faculty are given joint appointments they should be assigned to departments on an uneven ratio or percentage of time. The department which holds the larger percentage of his appointment should be considered his home and voting address. The chairman of that department should be responsible for initiating his promotion and otherwise promoting his welfare.

In response to the criticism leveled against college and university teaching, and in view of the radical changes in teaching strategies and technology, the graduate school should reaffirm its responsibility as the teacher of teachers by offering carefully designed programs of teacher preparation for doctoral students who plan to enter academic careers. As a result of concerted attacks on the quality of undergraduate teaching, and in response to the requests of their doctoral students some institutions are now seriously trying to prepare Ph.D.'s for college teaching. In some instances all doctoral students are required to have some teaching experience. Considering the fact that 50 per cent of the Ph.D.'s do not enter the academic field, this is probably unwise. It seems more realistic to make this experience available for those who anticipate careers in higher education and excuse those who elect other careers.

In some institutions the lack of adequate support for the teaching function—especially at the undergraduate level where large enrollments are common—has caused some departments to violate the institution's integrity. By claiming to provide programs for prospective college teachers when, in reality, they provide limited, on-the-job experiences that are often unspecified, unsupervised, and unevaluated in terms of their impact on the educational goals of the prospective teacher or the undergraduate, these institutions open a Pandora's box which releases problems that are cumulative in their effects.

As openly and vigorously as they seek support for their research activities, institutions which profess to prepare students for academic careers should seek support for teaching. This involves the enlistment of influential and respected persons on the campus whose interest in and support for a teaching program will give it status and attract others who can contribute positively to it. It also involves enough financial subvention to allow the institution to staff the program with those who have the competence and time to devote to the development of imaginative, flexible model programs of teacher training.

Colleges and universities that are too hard-pressed in terms of their staff shortages and financial limitations to hire adequate numbers of experienced teachers should make a frank admission that the graduate assistant serves an important institutional need. In return for his services they should offer the graduate a well-planned, supervised orientation to college teaching. Such a program should give the novice enough instruction and guidance to enable him to plan and conduct an undergraduate class in the area of his subject-matter competence. Both the instruction and practice should apply to real, rather than to contrived, teaching problems and situations. The total program should be evolutionary in nature. That is to say, it should provide sequentially for the student's developmental needs and include in it provisions for a systematic, continuous self-evaluation.

If the department is large, it should probably designate one of its faculty members to organize a system for the selection, assignment, and supervision of teaching assistants. This person might establish a pool of individuals from which to choose needed assistants. He might also interview each applicant in order to evaluate his interest in teaching and his general reaction toward working with undergraduate students. Only those who express an interest in teaching should be appointed to a teaching assistantship. The teaching assistant should be advised at the time of his selection that his continuance is contingent upon satisfactory performance. A handbook or some similar information form describing the functions and duties of a teaching assistant should be available for teaching assistants. Topics in it should be discussed at a series of orientation meetings for new assistants. Irrespective of its type, any program for the preparation of college teachers should represent a thoughtfully planned and carefully coordinated program and strong administrative leadership. It cannot be left to those who are already heavily burdened with teaching responsibilities nor to those whose primary interest and competence is in research.

In order to smooth the entrance of the neophyte into the academic life and to initiate him into this professional status, it is strongly recommended that each department foster a climate of professional respect for its teaching assistants. This would include such amenities as adequate physical facilities for both their teaching duties and their own studies; a careful review of the work assigned to them, so as to assure its appropriateness and to avoid assigning duties that are too heavy or too menial; and student-faculty discussions of standards, workable ways of handling students' requests, and other matters of professional concern.

As an alternative or option to the teaching assistantship, an internship in college teaching is recommended. If this experience is carefully coordinated, the internship might have more value for both parties if it is secured in a college off-campus. Mutual exchange arrangements might be made between the university and the off-campus college whereby an instructor whose classes are conducted by a Ph.D. candidate might teach undergraduate courses in the university and also audit courses which would update or expand his knowledge of his field.

The increased accessibility of junior colleges suggests that these institutions could provide a broader base for beginning teaching than does the university setting. Possibly graduate experience could alternate between both. The wide diversity in their student populations and in their organization would give the beginning teacher greater opportunities to respond to the full range of student needs and differences. It seems important to emphasize here that the intern or teaching assistant's actions and attitudes should receive critical comment and supervision if teaching is to be a developmental experience for him. Lacking these he may merely reinforce the poor practices he has observed or acquired.

On the basis of their survey, researchers at the Michigan Center for Learning and Teaching suggest that an optimal model of teacher preparation should start out with considerable structure and direction and proceed in three functional stages. In stage one, the student would familiarize himself with the content, methodology, and structure of the course he will teach, obtain practice in the preparation of resource materials, construct and score examinations, and observe the teaching style of one or two experienced professors. Under supervision, the assistant or intern might prepare and present three or four class sessions that are videotaped as presented so that in a subsequent conference with his faculty supervisor, he might analyze his own style as it influences the dynamics in his classroom.

In stage two, the assistant would be given a general outline of a course he will teach to a class of his own. He would be held responsible for planning the sessions, selecting the methods of presentation and evaluating his students. This stage would be accompanied by regular supervision and consultation or by a workshop focusing on test instruments, group dynamics, and the new learning and teaching technologies.

In stage three, the intern-assistant would have complete responsibility for all phases of an entire course and participate to a limited extent in departmental affairs, including attendance at faculty meetings and service on faculty committees. In addition, at this stage the intern-assistant might assume a supervisory role for entering students. If he does this, his teaching load should be reduced and he should understand that the guidance aspect of this supervisory role is part of *his* training as a prospective college teacher. Doctoral students who are responsible for teaching undergraduate courses in the university, or serve as interns in an off-campus institution, should hold the title of Instructor instead of the pejorative title "teaching assistant" or "practice teacher." Above all, in implementing the academic program, the university and its faculty should demonstrate in their policies and practices that excellence in teaching is as much a value as excellence in research.

Informed by the need for approximately 200,000 undergraduate teachers in the next five years and by the pressures for reform in their basic preparation, graduate schools should give serious consideration to the need for a new degree for college teaching such as the Doctor of Arts or the doctorate in a substantive field. The use of a single degree program to certify the preparation of researchers, teachers, leaders in government, business, industry, and many other careers has been criticized for decades as unrealistic. More recently the branching of disciplines, the nature and scope of the research enterprise, and the changing life styles of educated persons have accentuated the need for more varied approaches to scholarship. Most of the criticisms of the Ph.D. centers on the charge that the program emphasizes research preparation and neglects preparation for teaching.

The argument against the heavy emphasis on research is that the majority of the Ph.D. holders who teach at the undergraduate or junior college level are overprepared for activities they do not perform (research and publications) and unprepared for those they are obliged to perform (teaching, student advising, curriculum planning, evaluation, and test preparation). This affects not only the quality of teaching at this level but creates problems of teaching morale. The flight from teaching is symptomatic of these facts. Universities should recognize their obligation to teach systematically and responsibly for college teaching. As recommended by Spurr, Dunham, and others, they should experiment with new degree programs, such as the Doctor of Arts offered at the Carnegie-Mellon Institute and at the University of Washington or the Ph.D. in Math-Science and Education at the University of California, Berkeley, which are setting the pace toward teaching improvement. The major intent in these programs is to produce synthesizers and disseminators of research, not researchers per se.

If a program to prepare college teachers is ever to emerge as a viable and respected degree, it must have strong and aggressive administrative leadership, effective representative support from the teaching faculty, and a political place and power within the university structure. Above all, the degree must be shielded from the second-class label which some would pin on a teaching degree. If none are willing to speak for teaching, or if those who speak are defeated by the wall of silence which confronts them, patchwork efforts at reform will continue to be applied in place of new and different doctoral programs that educate integrated teachers, not just specialized scholars. If major universities fail to act in the face of the needs for improving the preparation of college teachers, the probability is that the response will come from lesser institutions.

Any plan for reform in the preparation of college teachers must resist the temptation to transfer the responsibility to "teach for teaching" over to the schools of education. While students would undoubtedly profit by some study in the psychology of learning, the sociology of educational institutions, tests and measurements, and a seminar on the problems in college teaching which are now available in most universities, to avoid over-professionalization, the student's academic department should assume major responsibility for providing the environment and experiences in which the principles of teaching are applied directly to his field. The admission requirements and the academic performance of those who elect the teaching doctorate should demand the same high level and rigor of scholarship expected of Ph.D. students in the same substantive field. Universities should mount a vigorous campaign to improve the quality of teaching by converting the concept of tenure in teaching to a concept of security in academic employment.

Universities should improve their articulation with undergraduate institutions, especially with regard to their curriculum changes. Recent studies show that curriculum changes and experimental rearrangements of programs have been more dramatic and far-reaching in many undergraduate institutions than in the undergraduate programs of universities. The result is that students who enter the university as graduates of dynamic or experimental programs are often disillusioned with what appears as a regressive level of content or instruction in the first year of graduate study. Students who experienced tutorials, honors programs, independent study, and other methods which fostered greater freedom, responsibility, and scope are let down by the undifferentiated requirements for all first-year students. Individual departments should make a special effort to keep abreast of the curriculum offerings in the undergraduate institutions from which they attract their students and upgrade their first-year programs accordingly.

A seminar on the American college and university should be available and recommended for all Ph.D. students who plan to enter academic careers. A University Seminar should be available for new faculty members or as an in-service activity for all interested faculty members. There is more than presumptive evidence to support the theory that the inadequacy of the university in addressing itself to the problems it faces arises, to a large extent, from the fact that leadership does not reside with the administration. The day-to-day problems of universities are so vast, compelling, and complex that those in administrative positions have little time to guide or direct the institution toward long-range academic goals. Almost by default, decisions are based on pragmatic or expedient planning and the vacuum in leadership is filled by a policy of drift.

According to Millett (1969), before 1964 the administration of American universities was the administration of expansion. Since 1964 it has become the administration of conflict. The sources of that conflict have been many, including students, faculties, trustees, legislatures, and the general public. Added to these encounters are the daily tasks of responding to budgetary reversals while facing inflationary financial trends, increased demands for new programs or services, and spiraling enrollments. Of all institutions in modern society the multiversity is probably the most complex. Its administration should be in the hands of those who have had preparation for academic leadership. Its academic program should be designed by those who understand the importance and intricacies of academic planning and programming.

A major task and responsibility of the faculty is academic planning and reform. However, the evidence is all too clear that most faculty members lack interest, creativity, and leadership in this role. Their apparent neglect or insecurity may arise from a lack of knowledge of the dynamics of an institution in which change is a constant and in which major change in one part often evokes the need for reorganization, new synthesis, or reintegration in others to insure unity in degree programming. Universities should offer themselves as objects of study to their faculty members and students. This might be done through occasional workshops, conferences, public forums, or position papers in which information about the problems and plans of the university are shared. They should also offer administrative internships to promising members of the faculty who demonstrate an interest and commitment to academic leadership. This could be either an in-house internship or experience in another university of similar size and character. In either event, efforts should be made to interest department chairmen and other administrators in making a professional commitment to academic leadership. The division of higher education might be invited to conduct a yearly workshop or seminar for newly appointed chairmen, directors, or division heads.

The rapid turnover in personnel at top levels sometimes results in other individuals being catapulted into management positions with little or no orientation. One who moves into middle administration from the department is often transformed from its culture to the culture of administration in twenty-four hours, or in the time it takes him to walk from one office to the other.

Although the deans in this study had high praise for the academic competence of their faculties, some expressed disappointment in finding that most professors leave beleaguered administrators in lonely isolation when confrontations occur. For some, the collegiality which attracted them to the academic life is suddenly and mysteriously curtailed when they accept an administrative appointment. Because the reward system for administrators rarely compensates for this loss, many become disenchanted and soon ask to be returned to their professorial rank. A better understanding of their role by the faculty, and professional education for administrative responsibility, might ameliorate some of the problems which create the "separateness" between faculty and administrators.

To equalize educational opportunities and to prevent the loss of talented individuals, the federal government should assume major responsibility for the establishment of fellowships that are open to applicants of demonstrated ability. It should likewise refrain from taxing philanthropic educational foundations whose record indicates an interest in the general welfare and in the special welfare of the educational development of those of diverse class, race, and creed.   Data at the Center for Research and Development in Higher Education document the fact that for the majority of Ph.D. students the decision to devote three or four of their mature years to prepare for a life of scholarship is largely contingent upon their ability to finance such an investment. Many highly qualified individuals are deterred by the difficulties this poses. Others who make the initial investment find it necessary to limp along on a part-time basis only to drop out at the dissertation stage, if not before. Some persevere by mortgaging their futures. Still others survive on fairly adequate support.

Society cannot afford the consequences of the 45 per cent dropout rate in the Ph.D. program. To forestall this waste the recommendations of the Carnegie Commission on Higher Education should serve to guide federal agencies as well as private foundations in the allocation of their educational funds. As the Commission suggests, certain universities should be funded, on the basis of spe-

cific program proposals, to undertake the task of identifying poten-
tially able students—especially in those population groups that need
opportunities to participate more fully in the nation's life—and in
recruiting them for graduate work. It further recommends that to
expand opportunities and institutional choices, fellowships and contingent loan programs be made available to students. Loans should
be open to all to the level of their yearly educational and subsistence
costs officially recognized by the institution in which they are enrolled.

     *The availability of adequate numbers of competent faculty
members and qualified students and of sufficient financial support
for graduate education is so tenuous and competitive that at least
for the foreseeable future it seems prudent to recommend that doctoral study be conducted mainly by institutions that are already
approved for this responsibility.* The ability to maintain quality in
graduate education in the face of greatly increased costs and the
shortage of well-qualified faculty members suggests that universities
should strive for excellence in a limited number of fields rather than
scatter their resources or duplicate programs that are already well
covered by a sufficient number of other universities. The press for
"instant universities"—which aim for comprehensiveness at the end
of a ten-year plan—poses serious concern to those who are interested in preserving the quality and integrity of universities. In some
cases their thrust has seriously impaired the quality of institutions
whose faculties they have raided. The hasty development of new
graduate programs not only threatens the quality of education at
this level but may cause serious imbalances in the supply and demand for Ph.D.'s in certain fields.

     The economics of graduate education dictates the need for a
better utilization of existing facilities rather than the accumulation
of resources that cannot be adequately staffed or financed for operation. To this end, graduate schools or departments should consider
the organization and development of consortiums, cluster university
programming, reciprocal instructional experiences, and, on a cooperative basis, the use of facilities that might be available in other
types of institutions or agencies. The possibility of coordinating or
consolidating such details as admission to a top-ranked university
might automatically bestow the privilege of using the facilities or of

taking course work in the institutions in the same rank without separately applying. Or, once a person has been admitted to graduate
school his admittance might be made valid "for lifelong learning"
without the need for formal readmittance. The use of the Social
Security numbers of students as a nationwide record of those who
have been admitted to graduate study might be developed to obvi-
ate the need for extensive bookkeeping on transfers.

 *The organization and administration of graduate education
should be under the leadership of a Vice-President for Graduate
Studies and a Council of Academic Deans with shared authority,
responsibility, and budgetary control over graduate education.* In
most cases the title of graduate Dean is a misnomer. Because he does
not have the budgetary authority and control, which any strategic
academic leadership role requires, he lacks the necessary "clout" to
spark academic change or reform. The administration of so viable
a segment of the university should not be subject to tenuous or tentative supervision or to such doubtful authority as the power of persuasion. If the graduate office were directly related on an administrative basis with that of academic deans, better articulation and
coordination of overall academic programming should result.

 *A National Policy Board on Graduate Education should
be organized by the Associated Research Councils, the Council of
Graduate Schools, and the American Council on Education.* The
need for a Graduate Board whose purpose would be to research and
promote actions that would improve the quality of graduate education, review manpower needs, and provide ready access to information for planning new programs or for determining costs of graduate
study seems indicated by the issues reviewed in this study. Essentially, a proposal for such a board was included in the *Report on
the Conference on Predoctoral Education in the United States,*
which was sponsored in August of 1969 by the Office of Scientific
Personnel of the National Research Council.

 *Professional associations should spell out the extent to which
their professional norms permit organizational responsiveness to important social issues or to problems which could benefit by the expertise of their membership.* Professional associations have been
under heavy criticism for dragging their feet with respect to the
important issues in social change. Dissidents within and critics out-

side of these organizations have accused them of serving primarily as interest organizations which maximize benefits taken from the public sector without contributing substantively to it in return.

Unless they wish to be reduced to merely status-conferring, self-interest organizations (or to the role of bargaining agencies), professional associations should take immediate steps to initiate dialogue between those within their organization who hold diverse viewpoints on such issues as the role of the organization in society as an association of professional experts; its roles in improving the academic preparation of members; the imbalances and strains between younger and senior members of the organization with regard to the relationship between the major precepts of the discipline; and the support or acquiescence the association gives to questionable research activities or programs. These associations should also play an active role in the orientation of doctoral students into the aims and ideals of the profession.

Bibliography

Academic Senate, University of California. *Education at Berkeley: Report of the Select Committee on Education.* Berkeley, Calif., 1966.

ADELMAN, H. (ed.). *The University Game.* Toronto: Anansi, 1968.

ALCIATORE, R. T., AND ECKERT, R. *Minnesota Ph.D.'s Evaluate Their Training.* Minneapolis: University of Minnesota Press, 1968.

American Council on Education, Problems and Policies Committee. *The Price of Excellence: A Report to Decision-Makers in American Higher Education.* Washington, D.C.: American Council on Education, 1960.

ANDREWS, F. "Tax Bill Impact Foundations; Colleges Say Proposed Changes in Law Threaten Them." *Wall Street Journal,* September 12, 1969.

ARROWSMITH, W. "The Future of Teaching." In *Issues and Problems in Higher Education.* Washington, D.C.: American Council on Education, 1966(a).

ARROWSMITH, W. "The Shame of Our Graduate Schools," *Harpers,* 1966, *232*(1390), 51–59(b).

ARROWSMITH, W. "A Conscience about Chaos." Paper delivered at opening convocation of York College of The City University of New York, September 1967.

ASHBY, E. *Technology and the Academics.* London: Macmillan, 1958.

ASHBY, E. *Universities under Siege.* Johannesburg: University of Witwatersrand, 1962.

ASHBY, E. "Machines, Understanding and Learning: Reflections on Technology," *Graduate Journal,* 1967, *12*(2), 359–373.

Association of Graduate Schools in the Association of American Universities. *Journal of Proceedings,* 1962–65, p. 140.

ASTIN, A. W. *The College Environment.* Washington, D.C.: American Council on Education, 1968.

AXELROD, J. (ed.). *Graduate Study for Future College Teachers.* Washington, D.C.: American Council on Education, 1959.

AYDELOTTE, F. *Breaking the Academic Lockstep.* New York: Harper, 1944.

BABBIGE, H. T., JR., AND ROSEZWEIG, R. M. *The Federal Interest in Higher Education.* New York: McGraw-Hill, 1962.

BAIRD, L. L. "Role Stress in Graduate Students." Unpublished doctoral dissertation, U.C.L.A., 1966.

BAIRD, L. L. "A Study of the Role Relations of Graduate Students," *Journal of Educational Psychology,* 1969, *60*(1), 15–21.

BARZUN, J. *Graduate Study at Columbia.* New York: Columbia University Press, 1958.

BARZUN, J. *The American University.* New York: Harper & Row, 1968.

BENEDICT, D. L. Conversation concerning the new Oregon Graduate Center, Portland, Ohio, 1967.

BERELSON, B. *Graduate Education in the United States.* New York: McGraw-Hill, 1960.

BERNARD, J. *Academic Women.* University Park, Pa.: Pennsylvania State University Press, 1964.

BISSELL, C. T. *The Strength of the University.* Toronto: University of Toronto Press, 1968.

BJERRUM, C. A. Forecast of Computer Developments and Applications, 1968–2000, *Futures,* 1969, *1*(1), 331–338.

BOULDING, K. *The Meaning of the 20th Century—The Great Transition.* New York: Harper & Row, 1964.

BOULDING, K. "The University as an Economic and Social Unit." In W. J. Minter and I. M. Thompson (eds.), *Colleges and Universities As Agents of Social Change.* Western Interstate Commission for Higher Education and Center for Research and Development in Higher Education: University of California, Berkeley, 1968.

BRESLER, J. B. "Teaching Effectiveness and Government Awards," *Science,* 1968, *160,* 164–167.

BREWSTER, K. "The Strategy of a University," *Ventures,* 1966, *VI*(1), 6–10.

BRZEZENSKI, Z. "The American Transition," *The New Republic,* December 23, 1967, *157*(26).

BRZEZENSKI, Z. "Toward the Technetronic Society," *Current,* 1968, *92,* 33–38.

BURKHARDT, F. H. "The Changing Role of the Professor." In L. E. Dennis and J. F. Kauffman (eds.), *The College and the Student.* Washington, D.C.: American Council on Education, 1966.

BUSWELL, G. T., MCCONNELL, T. R., HEISS, A. M., AND KNOELL, D. M. "Training for Educational Research," 1966. Cooperative Research Project No. 51074, University of California, Berkeley: The Center for Research and Development in Higher Education.

BYSE, C., AND JOUGHIN, L. *Tenure in American higher education: Plans, practices and the law.* Cornell Studies in Civil Liberties, New York: Cornell University Press, 1959.

CAMPBELL, D. T. "Ethnocentrism of Disciplines and the Fish-scale Model of Omniscience." In M. Sherif (ed.), *Problems of Interdisciplinary Relationships in the Social Sciences.* Chicago: Aldine, 1969.

CAPLOW, T., AND MCGEE, R. J. *The Academic Market Place.* New York: Basic Books, 1959.

CARMICHAEL, O. C. *Graduate Education: A Critique and a Program.* New York: Harper & Row, 1961.

CARMICHAEL, O. C. "Improving the Quality of Graduate Education for Prospective College Teachers," *Journal of Teacher Education,* special issue: The Preparation of College Teachers, September 1962, *XIII*(3), 253–257.

Carnegie Commission on Higher Education. *Quality and Equality: New Level of Federal Responsibility for Higher Education.* Hightstown, New Jersey: McGraw-Hill Book Company, 1968.

Carnegie Foundation for the Advancement of Teaching. "The University at the Service of Society." In *Annual Report.* New York: The Foundation, 1967.

CARPER, J. W., AND BECKER, S. "Adjustment to Conflicting Expectations in the Development of Identification with an Occupation," *Social Forces,* 1957, *36,* 51–56.

CARTTER, A. M. "A new look at the supply of college teachers," *The Educational Record,* 1965, *46*(3), 267–277.

CARTTER, A. M. *An Assessment of Quality in Graduate Education.* Washington, D.C.: American Council on Education, 1966(a).

CARTTER, A. M. "The Supply and Demand for College Teachers," *Journal of Human Resources,* Summer 1966, 22–38(b).

CARTTER, A. M. "Discussion of the Berelson Heresy." In *Doctoral Programs in Small Liberal Arts Colleges*. Symposium at Bowdoin College, Brunswick, Maine, April 1967.

CARTTER, A. M. "The Aftereffects of Putting a Blind Eye to the Telescope." Paper read at American Association for Higher Education Annual Conference, Chicago, Illinois, March 2–4, 1970.

Center for the Study of Democratic Institutions. *The University in America*. Santa Barbara, California: The Center, 1966.

CLARK, B. R. "Faculty Cultures." In *The Study of Campus Cultures*. Proceedings of conference sponsored by Western Interstate Commission for higher education and Center for Research and Development in Higher Education, Berkeley, California, 1963.

CLARK, B. R. "Faculty Organization and Authority." In *The Study of Academic Administration*. Proceedings of a conference sponsored by Western Interstate Commission for Higher Education and The Center for the Study of Higher Education, Berkeley, California, 1963(b).

CLARK, B. R. "The New University." Paper read at Annual Meeting of the Society for the Study of Social Problems, San Francisco, August 1967.

COBURN, J. "Defense Research: Pressure on Social Sciences," *Science*, May 30, 1969, *164*(3883), pp. 1037–1041.

Committee of Fifteen. *The Graduate School Today and Tomorrow: Reflections for the Profession's Consideration*. New York: Fund for the Advancement of Education, 1955.

Commission on College Physics. "Graduate Student Revolution Kit." Commission on College Physics *Newsletter*, March 1970, No. 21.

COOPER, R. M. "The College Teaching Crisis," *Journal of Higher Education*, 1964, *XXXV*, 6–11.

CRAIG, C. M. *Graduate Education*. New York: Center for Applied Research in Education, Inc., 1965.

CUNINGGIM, M. "The Integrity of the University." Paper read at the symposium on Societal Influences and University Integrity, University of California, Berkeley, January 1968.

DAVIS, J. A. *Great Aspirations*. Chicago: Aldine, 1964.

DEARING, G. B., AND LEDERER, G. P. Trends and developments in graduate education. In E. H. Hopkins (ed.), *New Dimensions in Higher Education*, No. 26. Durham, North Carolina: Duke University and the U.S. Office of Education, April 1967.

DEVANE, W. C. *Higher Education in Twentieth-Century America*. Cambridge: Harvard University Press, 1965.

DIAMOND, M. C. "Women in Modern Science," *Journal of the American Women's Association*, 1963, *18*(11), 891–896.

DIEKHOFF, J. S. *Tomorrow's Professors: A Report of the College Faculty Internship Program*. New York: The Fund for the Advancement of Education, 1960.

DRUCKER, P. *Age of Discontinuity*. New York: Harper & Row, 1968.

DUBERMAN, M. An Experiment in Education. *Daedalus*, Winter 1958, p. 340.

DUBIN, R., AND BEISSE, F. "The Assistant: Academic Subaltern," *Administrative Science Quarterly*, 1966–67, *11*, 521–547.

DUNHAM, A. *Colleges of the Forgotten Americas*. New York: McGraw-Hill, 1969.

DUNHAM, R. E., WRIGHT, P. S., AND CHANDLER, M. O. *Teaching Faculty in Universities and Four-year Colleges, Spring 1963*. U.S. Office of Education Report OE-53022-63. Washington, D.C.: U.S. Department of Health, Education, and Welfare, 1966.

EASTON, D. Presidential address, Annual Political Science Conference, New York. *Chronicle of Higher Education*, September 15, 1969.

ECKERT, R. E. *A University Looks at Its Program*. Minneapolis: University of Minnesota Press, 1954.

ECKERT, R. E., AND STECKLEIN, J. E. *Job Motivations and Satisfactions of College Teachers: A Study of Faculty Members in Minnesota Colleges*. Washington, D.C.: U.S. Government Printing Office, 1961.

ECKERT, R. E., AND NEALE, D. C. "Teachers and Teaching," *Review of Educational Research*, 1965, *35*(4), 304–317.

EDGAR, R. W. "The Moral Professor in the Immoral University." American Association of University Professors *Bulletin*, 1964, *50*(4), 323–326.

EELS, W. C., AND HOLLIS, E. V. *Teaching Faculty in Universities and Four-year Colleges, Spring 1963*. OE-53022-63. Washington, D.C.: National Center for Educational Statistics, 1966.

ELDER, J. P. *A Criticism of the Graduate School of Arts and Sciences at Harvard University and Radcliffe College*. Cambridge: Harvard University Press, 1958.

ENGEL, M. "Thesis and Antithesis: Reflections on the Education of Researchers in Psychology," *American Psychologist*, 1966, *21*(8), 781–787.

EURICH, A. C., KENNEY, L. B., AND TICKTON, S. G. *The Expansion of Graduate Education During the Period 1966 to 1980*. Studies in the Future of Higher Education, Report No. 2. New York: The Academy for Educational Development, April 1969.

Faculty of Arts and Sciences, Harvard University. Report of the Committee on the Future of the Graduate School. March 1969.

FASSETT, F. G. (ed.). *Development of Doctoral Programs by the Small Liberal Arts College.* Proceedings of a symposium presented at Bowdoin College, Brunswick, Maine, April 21–22, 1967.

FLEXNER, A. *Medical Education: A Comparative Study.* New York: The Macmillan Company, 1925.

FLEXNER, A. *Universities: American, English, and German.* New York: Oxford University Press, 1930.

FREEDMAN, M. *Chaos in our Colleges.* New York: David McKay Co., Inc., 1963.

FRIEDENBERG, E. Z., AND ROTH, J. *Self Perception in the University: A Study of Successful and Unsuccessful Graduate Students.* Chicago: University of Chicago Press, 1962.

FULLER, B. *Education Automation: Freeing the Scholar to Return to His Studies.* Carbondale, Ill.: Southern Illinois University Press, 1964.

GALBRAITH, J. K. *The Affluent Society.* Boston: Houghton Mifflin, 1958.

GALBRAITH, J. K. *The New Industrial State.* Boston: Houghton Mifflin, 1967.

GARDNER, J. W. *Self Renewal: The Individual and the Innovative Society.* New York: Harper & Row, 1963.

GARDNER, J. W. *Agenda for the Colleges and Universities: Higher Education in the Innovative Society.* New York: Academy for Educational Development, paper No. 1, 1965.

GARDNER, J. W. "The flight from teaching." In Fifty-ninth *Annual Report,* The Carnegie Foundation for the Advancement of Teaching, 1963–64. Republished in O. Milton and E. J. Shoben, Jr. (eds.), *Learning and the Professors.* Athens, Ohio: Ohio University Press, 1968a.

GARDNER, J. W. "Uncritical Lovers and Unloving Critics." Commencement address, Cornell University, New York, June 1, 1968b.

GIDEONSE, H. D. "The purpose of higher education: A re-examination." In L. E. Dennis and J. F. Kauffman (eds.), *The College and the Student.* Washington, D.C.: American Council on Education, 1966.

GOLDBERG, M. H. "The New College Teacher and His Professional

Self-image," *The Educational Forum,* 1965, *XXIX*(4), 451–459.

GOODMAN, P. *The Community of Scholars.* New York: Random House, Inc., 1962.

GOTTLIEB, D. "Processes of Socialization in American Graduate Schools." Unpublished doctoral dissertation, University of Chicago, 1960.

GOTTLIEB, D. "American Graduate Students: Some Characteristics of Aspiring Teachers and Researchers," *Journal of Educational Psychology,* 1961, *52*(5), 236–240.

GOULDNER, A. W. "Cosmopolitans and Locals: Toward an Analysis of Latent Social Roles, I," *Administrative Science Quarterly,* 1957, *2,* 281–306(a).

GOULDNER, A. W. "Cosmopolitans and Locals: Toward an Analysis of Latent Social Roles, II," *Administrative Science Quarterly,* 1957, *3,* 444–480(b).

GRAHAM, G. "Turmoil in the Graduate Schools," *New York Times Magazine,* April 7, 1968.

GRAHAM, R. H., AND HANSEN, W. L. "The Foreign Language Imbroglio in Graduate Education." Workshop on Human Resources, Working paper No. 4, University of Wisconsin, August 1968.

GROPPER, G. L., AND FITZPATRICK, R. *Who goes to Graduate School?* Pittsburgh, Pa.: American Institute for Research, 1959.

GUSTAD, J. W. "What are the Respective Responsibilities of the Graduate School and the Employing College for Developing Attributes and Competencies of the College Teacher?" In *Current Issues in Higher Education.* Washington, D.C.: Association for Higher Education, 1963.

HALL, D. "Graduate Education as Personal Choice and Identity Development: Some Observations at Yale, New Haven, Connecticut, 1968." Mimeographed.

HALL, W. C. "Predoctoral Education in the United States: Current Parameters and the Data Base." Paper read at the Conference on Predoctoral Education, National Research Council, National Academy of Sciences, National Academy of Engineers. Woods Hole, Massachusetts, August 24–29, 1969.

HANSEN, W. L., AND GRAHAM, R. H. Footnotes and Foreign Language Requirements. Workshop on Human Resources. Working paper No. 7, University of Wisconsin, August 1968.

HARE, K. *On University Freedom.* Toronto: University of Toronto Press, 1968.

HATCH, W. "What Standards do we Raise?" *New Dimensions in Higher Education*. Washington, D.C.: U.S. Department of Health, Education, and Welfare, 1964.

HEARD, A. *The Lost Years in Graduate Education*. Atlanta, Ga.: Southern Regional Education Board, 1963.

HEFFERLIN, J. B. *Dynamics of Academic Reform*. San Francisco: Jossey-Bass, 1969.

HEISS, A. M. "Berkeley Doctoral Students Appraise Their Academic Programs," *The Educational Record,* Winter 1967, 30–44.

HEISS, A. M. "Graduate Education Today: An Instrument for Change?" *Journal of Higher Education,* January 1968, *34*(1).

HEISS, A. M., DAVIS, AND VOCI, F. *Graduate and Professional education: An annotated bibliography*. Center for Research and Development in Higher Education: University of California, Berkeley, 1966.

HEIST, P. A. "Intellect and Commitment: The Faces of Discontent." In O. A. Knorr and W. J. Minter (eds.), *Order and Freedom on the Campus*. Western Interstate Commission for Higher Education and Center for Research and Development in Higher Education, Berkeley, 1965.

HEIST, P. A. *The Creative College Student: An Unmet Challenge*. San Francisco: Jossey-Bass, 1968.

HEIST, P. A., AND WILLIAMS, P. A. *Manual for the Omnibus Personality Inventory*. New York: The Psychological Corporation, 1962.

HELMHOLTZ, H. *Popular Lectures on Scientific Subjects*. London: Longmans, 1893, p. 29.

HENDERSON, A. D. "The aims of University Faculties in Liberal and Professional Education in the United States," *Report on the Conference on Education and Student Life in the United States*. Ann Arbor: The University of Michigan, 1956.

HENDERSON, A. D. *Policies and Practices in Higher Education*. New York: Harper & Bros., 1960.

HENDERSON, A. D. (ed.). *Higher Education in Tomorrow's World*. Ann Arbor, Mich.: The University of Michigan, 1968.

HECHINGER, F. "Student Targets: Professors are Next," *Change,* 1969, (107), 34–35.

HEYNS, R. W. "The Nature of the University." Paper read at the American Council on Education Annual Meeting, New Orleans, Louisiana, 1966.

HEYNS, R. W. "The Graduate Student: Teacher, Research Assistant, or Scholar?" *The Graduate Journal,* 1967, *XII*(2), 310.

HEYNS, R. W. "The University as an Instrument of Social Action." In W. J. Minter and I. M. Thompson (eds.), *Colleges and Universities as Agents of Social Change*. Center for Research and Development in Higher Education, Berkeley, and Western Interstate Commission for Higher Education, November 1968, 25–40.

HOFSTADTER, R., AND METZKER, W. *The Development of Academic Freedom in the United States*. New York: Columbia University Press, 1955.

HOLLIS, E. V. *Toward Improving the Ph.D.* Washington, D.C.: American Council on Education, 1945.

HOROWITZ, M. "Research in Professional Education," *New Dimensions in Higher Education*, No. 22, U.S. Department of Health, Education, and Welfare, 1967.

HOWE, H., II. "Higher Education's Strange Paradox." Paper read before the 54th Annual Meeting of the American Association of University Professors, Washington, D.C., April 26, 1968.

HUGHES, R. "Graduate Education: A report of a Committee of the American Council on Education," *The Educational Record*, April 1934, 192–234.

HUNT, E. M. "An Ed.D. for College Teachers," *The Journal of Teacher Education*, special issue on The Preparation of College Teachers, 1962, *XIII*(3), 279–283.

HUNTER, J. S. "The Academic and Financial Status of Graduate Students, Spring 1965." Washington, D.C.: U.S. Government Printing Office, 1967.

HUTCHINS, R. M. *Education for Freedom*. New York: Grove Press, 1936.

HUTCHINS, R. M. *The Higher Learning in America*. New Haven, Conn.: Yale University Press, 1936.

HUTCHISON, W. R. "Yes, John, there are teachers on the faculty," *The Graduate Journal*, 1967, *VII*(2), 347.

JAMES, W. "The Ph.D. Octopus." In *Memories and Studies*. New York: Longmans, Green and Company, 1911.

JASPERS, K. *The Idea of the University*. Boston: Beacon Press, 1959.

JENCKS, C., AND RIESMAN, D. *The Academic Revolution*. Garden City, New York: Doubleday and Company, Inc., 1968.

JEROME, J. "The American Academy 1970," *Change*, 1969, *1*(5), 10.

JOHNSON, E. "The Tightening Tension." In *Proceedings of the Institute on Higher Education*. Berkeley, California: Center for Re-

search and Development in Higher Education and Western Interstate Commission for Higher Education, July 1968.

JOHNSON, R. C. "Reflections on the Ph.D.," *College English,* 1965,
26(4), 304–306.

JONES, H. M. *Education and World Tragedy.* Cambridge, Mass.: Harvard University Press, 1946, p. 64.

JONES, H. M. *One Great Society: Humane Learning in the United
States.* New York: Harcourt, Brace & Co., 1959.

KATZ, M. B. "From Theory to Survey in Graduate Schools of Education," *Journal of Higher Education,* June 1966, 325–334.

KELLY, A. J. (ed.). *The Quest for Relevance: Effective College Teaching.* American Association for Higher Education, March 1969,
IV.

KENISTON, H. J. *Graduate Study and Research in the Arts and Sciences at the University of Pennsylvania.* Philadelphia, Pa.: University of Pennsylvania Press, 1959.

KERR, C. *The Uses of the University.* Cambridge: Harvard University
Press, 1963.

KERR, C. "Education in the United States: Past Accomplishments and
Present Problems." Paper read at International Conference on
the World Crisis in Education, Williamsburg, Virginia, October
1967.

KERR, C. *New Challenges to the College and University.* Reprint, Carnegie Commission on Higher Education, 1969(a).

KERR, C. The Pluralistic University in the Pluralistic Society. Reprint,
The Great Ideas Today. Encyclopedia Britannica, Inc., 1969(b).

KIDD, C. *American Universities and Federal Research.* Cambridge:
Harvard University Press, 1959.

KLOTSCHE, J. M. *The Urban University and the Future Structure of
Our Cities.* New York: Harper & Row, 1966.

KNAPP, P. B. "The Role of the Library in College Teaching," *Liberal
Education,* 1960, *XLVI*(3), 388–394.

KNOELL, D. *Training for Educational Research.* Berkeley, California:
Center for Research and Development in Higher Education,
1966.

KNOELL, D., AND MEDSKER, L. M. *Articulation between Two-year and
Four-year Colleges.* Berkeley, California: Center for the Study
of Higher Education, 1964.

KOEN, F., AND ERICKSEN, S. C. "An Analysis of Specific Features Which
Characterize the More Successful Programs for the Recruitment

and Training of College Teachers." Final Report, January 1967, Project #482, U.S. Office of Education.

KOENKER, R. H. "A Proposed Statement on the Specialist Degree." Paper read at the National Committee on Intermediate Degrees and the Graduate Studies Committee of the American Association of State Colleges and Universities, April 1968.

KREPS, J. M. "Sex and the scholarly girl." American Association of University Professors *Bulletin,* March 1965, *51*(1), 30–33.

LEE, G. (chairman). *The University of the Air.* Report presented to Parliament, February 1966. London: Her Majesty's Stationery Office, reprinted 1968.

LERNER, M. "Death at an Early Age: Report from the Graduate School," *The New Journal,* 1967, *1*(2), 3–5.

LICHTMAN, R. "The Ideological Function of Universities," *International Socialist Journal,* 1967, *24.*

LICHTMAN, R. "The University: Mask for Privilege?" Santa Barbara: *The Center Magazine,* Center for the Study of Democratic Institutions, January 1968.

LIKERT, R., AND HAYES, S. (eds.). *Some Applications of Behavioral Research.* UNESCO, 1957.

LILGE, F. *The Abuse of Learning.* New York: Macmillan Co., 1948.

LINDQUIST, C. B. *Staffing the Nation's Colleges and Universities.* Washington, D.C.: U.S. Office of Education, 1957.

LOWELL, A. L. *et al. The History and Traditions of Harvard College.* Cambridge, Mass.: Harvard Crimson, 1928.

MC CONNELL, T. R. "Academic leadership." Address to the Institute for College Presidents held by the Institute for College and University Administrators, Cambridge, Massachusetts, June 17, 1959.

MC CONNELL, T. R. "Colleges and universities as agents of social change: An Introduction." In W. J. Minter and I. M. Thompson (eds.), *Colleges and Universities As Agents of Social Change.* Western Interstate Commission for Higher Education and the Center for Research and Development in Higher Education, Berkeley, California, November 1968, 1–12.

MC CONNELL, T. R. "Faculty Interests in Value Change and Power Conflict." In W. J. Minter and P. Synder (eds.). *Value Change and Power Conflict in Higher Education.* Center for Research and Development in Higher Education, Berkeley, and Western Interstate Commission for Higher Education, October 1969(a).

MC CONNELL, T. R. "The individual and the organized university." Paper read at the seminar on Organization and Administration, University of Toledo, October 30, 1969(b). Mimeographed.

MC CONNELL, T. R., AND HEIST, P. A. "The diverse college student population." In N. Sanford (ed.), *The American College*. New York: John Wiley and Sons, Inc., 1962.

MC GRATH, E. *Are Liberal Arts Colleges Becoming Professional Schools?* New York: Teachers College, Columbia University, 1958.

MC GRATH, E. *The Graduate School and the Decline of the Liberal Education*. New York: Teachers College, Columbia University, 1959.

MC GRATH, E., HOLSTEIN, E. J., AND WORBURG, A. *The Quantity and Quality of College Teachers*. New York: Institute for the Study of Higher Education, Teachers College, Columbia University, 1961.

MC KEACHIE, W. J. "The Instructor Faces Automation." In H. A. Estrin and D. M. Goode (eds.), *College and University Teaching*. Dubuque, Iowa: William C. Brown Co., 1964.

MC KEACHIE, W. J. "Significant student and faculty characteristics relevant to personalizing higher education." In *The Individual and the System*. Western Interstate Commission for Higher Education and The Center for Research and Development in Higher Education, November 1967.

MADDEN, H. *On the Origin of Universities and Academic Degrees*. London: Taylor Publishing Co., 1935.

MANCALL, M. *"The study of education at Stanford: Graduate Education."* Stanford, Calif.: Stanford University Press, 1969.

MASLOW, A. H. "Neurosis as a failure of personal growth," *Humanities*, 1967.

MAUL, R. C. (ed.). *Teachers' Supply and Demand in Universities, Colleges, and Junior Colleges*. Washington, D.C.: National Education Association, Biennial Report, 1953.

MAYER, F. *Creative Universities*. New York: College and University Press, 1961.

MAYHEW, L. B. (ed.). *Higher Education in the Revolutionary Decades*. Berkeley, Calif.: McCutchan Publishing Corporation, 1967.

MERTON, R. "The Matthew Effect in Science," *Science*, 1968, *156*, 56–63.

MEYERSON, M. *Higher Education and National Affairs*. American Council on Education, September 12, 1969.

MILLER, J. P. "The Teaching Assistantship: Chore or Challenge?" *Ventures,* 1964, *IV*.

MILLER, J. P. "The Graduate School in the University Community," *Ventures,* 1965, *V*(1).

MILLER, J. P. "The Master of Philosophy: A New Degree is Born," *Ventures,* 1966, *VI*(1), 1–4(a).

MILLER, J. P. "A Report on Graduate Education at Yale," *Ventures,* 1966, *VI*(2)(b).

MILLER, J. P. "Under the Tower: A Report on Graduate Education," *Ventures,* Fall 1966, *VI*(2), 1–5(c).

MILLER, J. P. "Reorganization of the teaching assistantship: An interim report," *Ventures,* 1967, *VII*(1), 1–9.

MILLETT, J. D. "Graduate Education: A Reappraisal," *The Journal of Teacher Education,* special issue on The Preparation of College Teachers, 1962, *XIII*(3), 258–261.

MILLETT, J. D. *Reconstruction of the University.* University of Cincinnati: The Institute for Research and Training in Higher Education, 1968.

MILLETT, J. D. "Value Patterns and Power Conflict in American Higher Education," in W. J. Minter and P. Synder (eds.), *Value Change and Power Conflict in Higher Education.* Center for Research and Development in Higher Education, Berkeley, and Western Interstate Commission for Higher Education, October 1969.

MITCHELL, J. "The Curious World of University Tenure," *Compact,* 1968, *2*(4).

MOCK, K. R., AND YONGE, G. *Students' Intellectual Attitudes, Aptitudes, and Persistence at the University of California.* Berkeley: Center for Research and Development in Higher Education, 1969.

MORRIS, W. H. (ed.). *Effective College Teaching: The Quest for Relevance.* American Council on Education, 1970.

National Education Association, Research Division. *Teacher Supply and Demand in Universities, Colleges, and Junior Colleges, 1963–64 and 1964–65.* Washington, D.C.: Research Report 1965-R4, 1965.

National Research Council, Office of Scientific Personnel. *Report on the Conference on Predoctoral Education in the United States.* Woods Hole, Massachusetts, August 24–27, 1969.

National Science Board. *Graduate Education: Parameters for Public Policy.* Washington, D.C.: U.S. Government Printing Office, 1969.

NESS, F., AND JAMES, B. *Graduate Study in the Liberal Arts College.* Washington, D.C.: Commission on Professional and Graduate Study, Association of American Colleges, 1962.

NEWCOMB, T. M., KOENIG, K. E., FLACKS, R., AND WARWICK, D. P. *Persistence and change: Bennington College and its Students' Years.* New York: John Wiley & Sons, Inc., 1967.

NEWMAN, J. H., CARDINAL. *The Idea of a University.* New York: Longmans, Green and Co., 1947.

NICHOLS, R. T. "Administering Graduate Schools." In E. Walters (ed.), *Graduate Education.* Washington, D.C.: American Council on Education, 1965.

NICHOLS, R. T. "A Reconsideration of the Ph.D." *The Graduate Journal,* 1967, *12*(2), 325–335.

NOWLIS, V., *et al. The Graduate Student as Teacher.* Washington, D.C.: American Council on Education, Education Monograph, 1968.

ORLANS, H. *The Effects of Federal Programs on Higher Education: A Study of 36 Universities and Colleges.* Washington, D.C.: The Brookings Institution, 1962.

ORTEGA Y GASSET, J. *Man and Crisis.* New York: W. W. Norton Co., 1962.

PARSONS, T., AND PLATT, G. "Considerations on the American Academic System," *Minerva,* Ilford House, London, Summer 1968, *VI*(4).

PERKINS, J. *The University in Transition.* Princeton: Princeton University Press, 1966.

POLANYI, M. *Personal Knowledge.* Chicago: University of Chicago Press, 1958.

Proceedings of the University of California All University Conference. *The Research Function of the University.* Riverside, Calif.: April 1960. University of California Press, Berkeley.

PUTMAN, F. W. "Toward a Public Policy for Graduate Education in the Sciences," *Science, 163,* 1969, 1147.

REIF, F. "Science Education for Nonscience Students: Interdisciplinary Effort at Berkeley," *Science,* 1969, *164,* 1032–37.

RIESMAN, D. *Constraint and Variety in American Education.* New York: Doubleday & Co., 1958.

ROBBINS, L. *The University in the Modern World.* London: Macmillan Publishing Co., 1966.

ROGERS, C. R. *Graduate Education in Psychology: A Passionate State-*

ment. La Jolla, California: Western Institute of Behavioral Science, 1964.

ROGERS, C. R. "The Facilitation of Significant Learning." In L. Siegel (ed.), *Instruction: Some Contemporary Viewpoints.* San Francisco: Chandler Publishing Co., 1967.

ROGERS, J. *Staffing American Colleges and Universities.* Washington, D.C.: U.S. Office of Education, 1963.

ROSENHAUPT, H. *Graduate Students: Experiences at Columbia University, 1940–56.* New York: Columbia University Press, 1956.

ROSS, S., AND HARMON, J. "Educational facilities and financial assistance for graduate students in psychology 1964–65," *American Psychology,* December 1963, *18*(12), 814–841.

ROSSMAN, J. E., AND BENTLEY, J. C. *Factors Which Led College Seniors to Choose College Teaching as a Career.* OE-5-10-419, 1966 Project No. 5-8238, U.S. Department of Health, Education, and Welfare.

RUSSELL, J. D. "Faculty Satisfaction and Dissatisfaction," *Journal of Experimental Education,* December 1962, *31*(2), 135–139.

SAMPSON, E. E. "A modern Sisyphus Goes to College." Paper read at the annual meeting of the American Psychological Association, San Francisco, California, 1968.

SANFORD, N. (ed.). *The American College: A Psychological and Sociological Interpretation of Higher Learning.* New York: Wiley, 1962.

SAWYER, R. A. "The Graduate Student and the University Research Program," *The Graduate Journal,* 1954, *7*(2), 317.

SCHELLING, F. W., JR. *On University Studies.* Columbus, Ohio: Ohio State University Press, 1966.

SCOTT, E. Statistical data for academic women at Berkeley. Unpublished, mimeographed. University of California, Berkeley, 1969.

SCULLY, M. G. "Teaching-oriented Doctorate Needed Today, Study Says," *The Chronicle of Higher Education,* 1970, *IV*(16).

SEIGEL, L. "The Contributions and Implications of Recent Research Related to Improving Teaching and Learning." In M. Ohmer and J. Shobern (eds.), *Learning and the Professor.* Athens, Ohio: Ohio University Press, 1968.

SHARP, L. M. "Graduate Study and its Relation to careers: The Experience of a Recent Cohort of College Graduates," *Human Resources,* 1966, *1,* 41–58.

SIMON, H. "A Computer for Everyman," *The American Scholar,* 1966, *XXXV,* 264.

SIMON, K., AND FULLAM, M. G. *Projections of Educational Statistics to 1975–76*. OE-10030-66. Washington, D.C.: U.S. Office of Education, 1966.

SIZER, T. R. "Education in the Ghetto: The Case for a Free Market," *Saturday Review*, January 11, 1969.

SMITH, B. O. *Teachers for the Real World*. Washington, D.C.: American Association of Colleges for Teacher Education, 1969.

SNOW, C. P. *Science and Government*. Cambridge: Harvard University Press, 1961.

SNOW, C. P. *The Two Cultures: And a Second Look*. Cambridge University Press, 1959.

SNYDER, P. O. *Graduate and Professional Opportunities for Minority Students in the West*. Boulder, Colorado: Western Interstate Commission for Higher Education, August 1969.

SPURR, S. H. *Degree structures in American higher education*. New York: McGraw-Hill (1970).

Stanford University. *Graduate education*. Report to the University Steering Committee of the Study of Education at Stanford, *VII*, 1968–1969.

STECKLEIN, J. E., AND ECKERT, R. E. *An Exploratory Study of Factors Influencing the Choice of College Teaching as a Career*. Minneapolis: University of Minnesota Press, 1958.

STINNETT, T. M. *Teachers in Politics: The Larger Role*. Washington, D.C.: National Education Association, The Citizen Committee, 1968.

TAVE, S. "A Word on Behalf of the Ph.D.," *The Journal of Teacher Education*, special issue on The Preparation of College Teachers, 1962, *XIII*(3), 444–447.

TAYLOR, H. *Students Without Teachers: The Crisis in the University*. New York: McGraw-Hill, 1969.

TAYLOR, H. *The World as Teacher*. New York: Doubleday, 1969.

THEOPHILUS, D. R., JR. "Professorial Attitudes Toward Their Work Environment at the University of Michigan." Unpublished doctoral dissertation, University of Michigan, 1957.

TRENT, J. W. *Catholics in College: Religious Commitment and the Intellectual Life*. Chicago: University of Chicago Press, 1967.

TRENT, J. W., AND MEDSKER, L. L. *Beyond High School: A Psychosociological Study of 10,000 High School Graduates*. San Francisco: Jossey-Bass, 1968.

TROW, M. "Reflections on the Recruitment to College Teaching." Paper read at the Conference on College Teaching Supply,

Demand, and Recruitment, New England Board of Higher Education, Boston, November 1959.

TROW, M. "Undergraduate Teaching at Large State Universities," *The Educational Record*, Summer 1966, 303–319.

TUCKER, A. *Factors Related to Attrition Among Doctoral Students.* Cooperative Research Project No. 1146, U.S. Office of Education, Michigan State University, 1964.

United States Office of Education. *Projection of Educational Statistics to 1974–75.* Washington, D.C.: Government Printing Office, 1965.

United States Office of Education. *Projections of Educational Statistics, 1966,* OE-10030-66. Washington, D.C.: U.S. Department of Health, Education, and Welfare.

United States Office of Education. *Final Report of Conference on Higher Education,* Tenth annual college and university self-study institute, 1968, OE-6-10-106, Project No. 5-0248-3-6. Washington, D.C.: U.S. Department of Health, Education and Welfare.

VEBLEN, T. *The Higher Learning in America.* New York: Hill and Wang, 1965.

VESEY, L. R. *The Emergence of the American University.* Chicago: University of Chicago Press, 1965.

WALTERS, E. *Graduate Education Today.* Washington, D.C.: American Council on Education, 1965.

WATTS, W., LYNCH, S., AND WHITTAKER, D. "Alienation and Activism in Today's College-age Youth: Socialization Patterns and Current Family Relationships," *Journal of Counseling Psychology,* 1969, *16*(1), 1–7.

WEINBERG, A. M. "The Two Faces of Science," *Journal of Chemical Education,* 1968, *45,* p. 74.

WEITZ, H., BALLANTYNE, R., AND COLVER, R. "Foreign Language Fluency: The Ornamentation of a Scholar," *Journal of Higher Education,* 1963, *34,* 443–449.

WEST, A. Discussion comments on Mr. Hall's paper "How Can the University be so Organized as to Stimulate More Work for the Advancement of Science?" *Proceedings of the Sevententh Annual Conference of the Association of American Universities,* Clark College, November 10–11, 1916, p. 52.

WEST, A. *Present College Questions.* New York: D. Appleton and Co., 1903.

WEST, A. *The Graduate College of Princeton*. Princeton: Princeton University Press, 1913.

WHALEY, W. G. "An Editorial: The Graduate Dean," *Journal of Proceedings and Addresses of the Association of Graduate Schools in the Association of American Universities*. Seattle, Washington, October 26–27, 1965, 4–10.

WHALEY, W. G. "In Place of Slogans," *Graduate Journal*, Spring 1967, 7(2), 281–299.

WILSON, A. "Wisdom is Better than Strength," *The Educational Record*, January 1960, 41(1), 25–28.

WILSON, ROBERT C., AND GAFF, JERRY. "Student voice—faculty response," *The Research Reporter, IV*(2) 1–4.

WISE, W. M. "Who teaches the teachers?" *Current Issues and Problems in Higher Education*, 1966, 86–98.

WOLFF, R. P. "The Ideal of the University," *Change*, 1969, 1(5), 48.

WOLFLE, D. *Teachers for Tomorrow*. Report of the Commission on Human Resources. New York: Ford Foundation, 1955.

Index